ESSENTIALS OF SUPPLY CHAIN MANAGEMENT

Strategy, Planning and Operations

ESSENTIALS OF SUPPLY CHAIN MANAGEMENT

Strategy, Planning and Operations

Mohammed Majeed
Abdul Rasheed Alolo Alhassan Akeji
Seidu Alhassan
S. Sekar
Editors

APPLE ACADEMIC PRESS

First edition published 2025

Apple Academic Press Inc.
1265 Goldenrod Circle, NE,
Palm Bay, FL 32905 USA

760 Laurentian Drive, Unit 19,
Burlington, ON L7N 0A4, CANADA

CRC Press
2385 NW Executive Center Drive,
Suite 320, Boca Raton FL 33431

4 Park Square, Milton Park,
Abingdon, Oxon, OX14 4RN UK

Library and Archives Canada Cataloguing in Publication

CIP data on file with Canada Library and Archives

Library of Congress Cataloging-in-Publication Data

CIP data on file with US Library of Congress

ISBN: 978-1-77491-880-7 (hbk)
ISBN: 978-1-77491-881-4 (pbk)
ISBN: 978-1-00361-984-0 (ebk)

About the Editors

Dr. Mohammed Majeed, DBA, PhD (Dr^2)

Mohammed Majeed, PhD, DBA, is a distinguished academic and researcher currently serving as a Senior Lecturer at Tamale Technical University, Ghana, where he holds the position of Head of the Department of Logistics and Procurement Management. With an impressive academic background, Dr. Majeed has earned two doctoral degrees—a Doctor of Business Administration (DBA) and a Doctor of Philosophy (PhD) in Marketing, earning him the title "Dr^2."

Dr. Majeed is also known for his strong presence in the publishing world, collaborating with eminent academic publishers and contributing articles featured in renowned academic publications from Emerald, Wiley, Taylor & Francis, Springer, Cogent, Routledge, and Apple Academic Press. His research interests span several vital areas in contemporary marketing and business, such as value co-creation, digital marketing, green and sustainable practices, branding, and consumer behavior.

In addition to his role at Tamale Technical University, Dr. Majeed lectures at prominent institutions across Ghana, including the University for Development Studies (UDS), Kwame Nkrumah University of Science and Technology (KNUST), and the University of Cape Coast (UCC). His prolific contributions to academic literature include six published books, with ten more in production with leading publishers such as Springer, Apple Academic Press, and Bentham Science. Furthermore, Dr. Majeed has authored over 40 book chapters, solidifying his influence as a scholar and thought leader in his field.

Furthermore, his experience as a department head in Logistics, Procurement, and Marketing has enriched his academic perspective, bridging theoretical insights with real-world applications.

Abdul Rasheed Alolo Alhassan Akeji, PhD

Abdul Rasheed Alolo Alhassan Akeji, PhD, is an Associate Professor in the School of Business attached to the Department of Logistics and Procurement

Management at the Tamale Technical University (TaTU), Ghana. His research interests include governance of inter-organizational relationships in business ecosystems, open innovation and ecosystems, application of game theory in business, why organizations govern certain transactions and how these shape organizational performance, methodological issues in strategic management, application of big data analytics on firm performance, supply chain management, blockchain operational capabilities on firm performance, application of IoT in business, etc. He received his doctorate degree in Management Science and Engineering from Jiangsu University, People's Republic of China. His MSc in Logistics and Supply Chain Management and MBA in Strategic Management and Consulting were awarded by Kwame Nkrumah University of Science and Technology (KNUST), Ghana; his MA in HRD and MSc in Organizational Development were earned from the University of Cape Coast and the College for Community and Organisational Development (CCOD) (UDS), Ghana, respectively.

Seidu Alhassan, MPhil

Seidu Alhassan, MPhil, is a Lecturer at Tamale Technical University, Tamale, Ghana. His current research interests include social media marketing, branding, political marketing, hospitality and tourism, and service marketing. Mr. Alhassan has published in reputable journals from Emerald. He holds an MPhil in Marketing, MBA in Management, a Bachelor of Technology in Management, and HND in Accounting.

S. Sekar, PhD

S. Sekar, PhD, is currently working as a Guest Lecturer in the Department of Commerce (CA) at the Government Arts College (Autonomous), Tamil Nadu, India, where he has 12 years of teaching experience. His area of interest is marketing, human resources, and finance. He has published more than 15 research articles in various Scopus, Web of Science, and UGC Care listed journals. He has participated and presented more at than 50 national and international level conferences. He has published more than 15 national and international patent publications, including edited book chapters, and was appointed as an editorial board member of several peer-reviewed journals.

Contents

Contributors .... *ix*

Preface .... *xi*

1. **The Impact of Logistics Outsourcing on Performance of Retail Outlets: A Case of Retailers in Tamale 1**
   Mustapha Abdul-Aziz, Abdul Ganiw Hussein, and Adam Osman Oscar

2. **Make-or-Buy Decision Strategy in Critical Procurement and Supply Chain Management with Break-Even Analysis: A Comprehensive Review 29**
   Shalom Akhai

3. **The Role of Industry 4.0 Software Tools in Creating Sustainable Supply Chain Management in Emerging Markets 43**
   Ketan Rathor

4. **The Effect of Supply Chain Integration on Financial Performance: A Case Study of Hospitals in Northern Region 63**
   Mohammed Majeed, Abaah Akansake Joseph, and Jonas Yomboi

5. **A Study of the Relationship among Supply Chain Performance Management Factors and Organizational Performance of Manufacturing Industries 91**
   K. Bhavana Raj, S. Sreenivasa Murthy, Divyeshkumar Jitendrakumar Gandhi, and Sunil Adhav

6. **The Influence of Transportation System on Manufacturing Firm's Performance in Ghana: A Case Study of Ghana Nuts Company Limited in Techiman 113**
   Mohammed Majeed, David Inusah Offei, and Sumaila Seidu Salaam

7. **A Study of the Factors that Affect the Performance of the Supply Chain with Reference to SME in Chennai City 145**
   R. Pradeep Kumar Patnaik, K. Soundarapandiyan, Vishalkumar Jagdishchandra Mali, and T. Rajamanickam

8. A Study on Food Supply Chain Management, System Implementation, and Future Research 165
S. V. Pradeepa, Purvi Dipen Derashri, Arup Roy Chowdhury, and Mano Ashish Tripathi

9. Components of SC Management in the Hospitality Sector 185
Mustapha Abdul-Aziz

10. Overview of Logistics Functions 205
Mukul Pandey

11. The Green SCM Practices and Its Impact on Indian Business Environment 213
Mridul Dharwal, Veena Prasad, K. D. V. Prasad, Sathi Jyothirmaye Reddy, and Kirti Agarwal

12. Demand Planning in Supply Chain Management Process 231
Abdul Ganiw Hussein

Index 247

Contributors

Mustapha Abdul-Aziz
Department of Logistics and Procurement Management, Tamale Technical University, Tamale, Ghana

Sunil Adhav
Faculty of Management (PG), School of Management (PG), Dr. Vishwanath Karad MIT World Peace University, Pune, India

Kriti Agarwal
ITERC College, Institutional Duhai Road, Delhi, India

Shalom Akhai
Department of Mechanical Engineering, Chandigarh Engineering College, Jhanjeri, Mohali, Punjab, India

Arup Roy Chowdhury
School of HRM, XIM University, Bhubaneswar, Odisha, India

Purvi Dipen Derashri
Faculty of Management Studies, Parul Institute of Management and Research, Parul University, Vadodara, Gujarat, India

Mridul Dharwal
School of Business Studies, Sharda University, Greater Noida, India

Divyeshkumar Jitendrakumar Gandhi
Naran Lala School of Industrial Management & Computer Science, Navsari, India

Abdul Ganiw Hussein
Department of Logistics and Procurement Management, Tamale Technical University, Tamale, Ghana

Abaah Akansake Joseph
Tamale Technical University, Tamale, Ghana

Mohammed Majeed
Marketing Department, Tamale Technical University, Tamale, Ghana

Vishalkumar Jagdishchandra Mali
Department of Commerce (CA), Naran Lala School of Industrial Management &Computer Science, Navasari, India

S. Sreenivasa Murthy
Institute of Public Enterprise (IPE), Hyderabad, Telangana, India

David Inusah Offei
Procurement Directorate, Tamale Technical University, Tamale, Ghana

Adam Osman Oscar
Department of logistics and Procurement Management, Tamale Technical University, Tamale, Ghana

Mukul Pandey
Arka Jain University, Jharkhand, India

R. Pradeep Kumar Patnaik
K L Business School, Koneru Lakshmaiah Education Foundation, Vaddeswarm, India

S. V. Pradeepa
School of Management, Ajeenkya D Y Patil University, Lohegaon, Pune, India

K. D. V. Prasad
Symbiosis Institute of Business Management, Hyderabad, India
Symbiosis International (Deemed University), Pune, India

Veena Prasad
NKES College of Arts Commerce and Science, Mumbai, Maharashtra, India

K. Bhavana Raj
Department of Management Studies, Institute of Public Enterprise, Hyderabad, India

T. Rajamanickam
PG Department Commerce, Naran Lala School of Industrial Management &Computer Science, Navasari, India

Ketan Rathor
Senior Project Manager, GyanSys Inc., Carmel, IN, USA

Sathi Jyothirmaye Reddy
Faculty of Management Studies, Marwadi University, Morbi Highway Road, Rajkot, Gujarat, India

Sumaila Seidu Salaam
Automotive Engineering Department, Tamale Technical University, Tamale, Ghana

K. Soundarapandiyan
Department of Commerce, BS Abdur Rahman Crescent Institute of Science and Technology, Vandalur, Chennai, India

Mano Ashish Tripathi
Department of Humanities and Social Sciences, Motilal Nehru National Institute of Technology, Prayagraj, Uttar Pradesh, India

Jonas Yomboi
University for Developing Studies, Tamale, Ghana

Preface

The management of supply chain is the pillar of all firms. Yet, there can be no successful supply chain without the efficient execution of procurement activities. The uncertain ongoing discussions and research on purchasing/procurement and supply chain researchers and managers across many industries from around the world resulted in this proposal to edit this book *Essentials of Supply Chain Management: Strategy, Planning, and Operations.*

This book is made up of chapters and contributions in areas that are very important to supply chain management (SCM)/procurement, including logistics planning, logistics sourcing/outsourcing, inventory management, logistics function, transportation function, warehousing, return of goods, demand planning, and customer service.

Readers will learn the basics of purchasing as it pertains to the supply chain and other business processes and systems such as marketing, logistics, and operations.

Each chapter is structured to give readers an introduction to SCM and procurement, the definition of key terms, and explanations of how SCM and procurement affect different types of businesses and markets. The book also provides actual evidence supporting the importance of certain technologies, methods, and requirements for efficient and effective implementation in workplaces and businesses.

This book is groundbreaking because it brings together elements of technology, logistics, procurement, supply chain, and transportation that have only recently been the subject of scholarly investigation. This book offers a fresh perspective on SCM ideas by synthesizing academic research with practical examples and industry insights. To give the seasoned researcher and the industry practitioner a thorough grounding in its principles and to illustrate SCM as an approach for enhancing industries' management success, the research of leading international academics has been drawn together with the experience of some of the industry's foremost SCM practitioners.

CHAPTER 1

The Impact of Logistics Outsourcing on Performance of Retail Outlets: A Case of Retailers in Tamale

MUSTAPHA ABDUL-AZIZ, ABDUL GANIW HUSSEIN, and ADAM OSMAN OSCAR

Department of Logistics and Procurement Management, Tamale Technical University, Tamale, Ghana

ABSTRACT

The aim of this research is to examine how logistics outsourcing impacts the performance of businesses, focusing on retail companies situated in Tamale, Ghana. The study also aimed to explore different aspects of logistics outsourcing that are utilized in the supply chain operations of Tamale's retailers. Employing a quantitative approach, the study involved a sample of 50 retail establishments in the Northern region of Ghana, specifically in Tamale. Data analysis was carried out using SPSS-AMOS for this investigation. All four predictors were found to have a notably positive influence on the retail businesses in Tamale, Ghana. This validates the four hypotheses put forth in this study. As a result, this framework is expected to comprehensively gauge the variables in question. The data provided upheld the validity of H1, H2, H3, and H4, revealing a noteworthy and favorable correlation between supplier relations, stock administration, technological integration, order handling, and the effectiveness of retailers. To summarize, it was deduced that businesses in Tamale typically excel in managing inventory, although there remains space for ongoing enhancements.

Essentials of Supply Chain Management: Strategy, Planning and Operations.
Mohammed Majeed, Abdul-Rasheed Akeji Alhassan Alolo, Seidu Alhassan, and S. Sekar (Eds.)

1.1 INTRODUCTION

1.1.1 BACKGROUND OF THE STUDY

In the last quarter century, the practice of outsourcing has emerged as a prominent supply chain strategy that has garnered global attention (Akbari and Hopkins, 2016). The significance of supply chain management (SCM) had a substantial increase among practitioners throughout the mid-1990s (Konig and Spinler, 2016). As a result, there has been a substantial uptick in research and academic focus on supply chain management and outsourcing in recent years. The phrase "supply chains" refers to the interconnected set of activities that culminate in the delivery of a product or service to the end user (Christopher, 2016). SCM refers to the systematic coordination and oversight of managerial operations and activities, as highlighted by Varsei et al. (2014).

Logistics may be defined as the intricate coordination of a complex endeavor that encompasses a substantial number of people, facilities, or resources (Mangan and Lalwani, 2016). Commonly referred to as logistics, this refers to the systematic development, execution, and oversight of protocols aimed at ensuring the optimal and productive movement and retention of commodities and services (including data) from their initial location to their final destination. The source of this expression can be dated to the latter portion of the 1800s, particularly in a military setting, where the frequent necessity of moving both personnel and equipment became apparent. The aforementioned phenomenon has significantly influenced the extent and consequences of logistics in the ensuing years. According to Papadopoulou (2001), logistical tactics and systems were primarily used by the military throughout the 1950s and 1960s.

As a result of rising customer demands and fiercer competition in expanding markets, many companies and organizations have turned to outsource their noncore business activities as a supply chain strategy. Today's vast and intricate supply networks have made supply chain management more crucial than ever before to the success of businesses (Christopher, 2016; Konig and Spinler, 2016). Logistics is also being outsourced to third-party vendors as businesses focus on their core capabilities (Konig and Spinler, 2016; Marasco, 2008). As a result, external vendors have the power to significantly affect SCM efficiency (Christopher, 2016). Shippers' use of logistics outsourcing, also known as third-party logistics (3PL), increased by 5% in 2016 according to the results of a study performed that year. As a consequence, the percentage of people using these services rose from 68 to 73%.

The research examined three retail establishments located in the city of Tamale. The aforementioned outlets include Forsmuel Retail Centre, Quality First Ltd. Company, and Nasant Ventures. The selection is predicated upon the observation that these retail malls are the largest in the city of Tamale. I refrained from using Melcom due to the fact that its headquarters is located in Accra. Based on my first observation, it seems that Accra is the designated location for obtaining the necessary data. As a result of limited financial resources, my attention was directed only toward those residing in Tamale.

1.1.2 PROBLEM STATEMENT

Research states as a problem statement that the supply chain (SC) and its management have significant relevance within the retail business. The data presented also indicates a growing inclination toward the outsourcing of logistics operations and activities, such as transportation and storage, in the region of Tamale. Although many organizations have the capability to directly undertake manufacturing and service-providing operations, a significant number still choose to hire a 3PL company to handle all of this for you (Bailey, 2016). The practice of outsourcing logistics offers notable time and cost savings compared to the alternative of domestically acquiring supplies in-house. By using the services of third-party logistics (3PL) providers, enterprises may circumvent the need of making investments in warehouse infrastructure, technological resources, transportation systems, and human resources for the purpose of conducting internal logistics operations. The business is able to keep up with industry developments and trends thanks to the utilization of 3PL providers.

Numerous studies have been undertaken to determine whether or not logistics outsourcing is related to a company's overall performance. Gikonyo (2016) performed research to determine how common it is for manufacturing companies to outsource their logistical operations. The impact that outsourcing order storage, packing, and transportation logistics has on the efficiency of the logistics industry as a whole in Kenya was investigated. The effects of outsourcing on the efficiency of the shipping industry's operations were studied by Makabira and Waiganjo (2014). The study's major goal was to investigate how outsourcing has affected productivity in Kenya's shipping industry. The study was carried out in two distinct periods. Masiko (2013) conducted a research that examined logistics outsourcing in the context of key industrial firms in Nairobi. The study primarily aimed to compare the strategies and performance of these enterprises in relation to logistics outsourcing.

The study findings indicate that the adoption of logistics outsourcing practices by major manufacturing firms led to notable improvements in productivity, organizational efficiency, profitability, ongoing enhancement, and quality.

The assertion made in the conclusion is that there is a scarcity of accessible evidence about the impact of outsourced logistics services or activities on the performance of retailers. Since there is a lack of research into this area, the authors of this study set out to fill it by developing fresh ideas on the elements that affect businesses' knowledge systems, vendor connections, purchase handling, and stock control. The study also aimed to determine whether or not there was a correlation between logistic outsourcing and the actions and results of supply chain management. As such, this study's major goal is to shed light on the impact logistics outsourcing has on organizational performance, particularly as it pertains to businesses operating in the retail sector in Tamale, Ghana. The findings of this study may have implications for businesses in the retail sector of Ghana's economy that are looking to improve their efficiency.

1.2 RESEARCH OBJECTIVES

1.2.1 MAIN RESEARCH OBJECTIVE

The major objective of this research is to analyze the effects of logistics outsourcing on the productivity of retail businesses in Tamale, Ghana. The stated problem is what this investigation is attempting to address.

1.2.2 SPECIFIC RESEARCH OBJECTIVES

To effectively execute the stated aim with the intention of resolving the identified issue, a set of secondary objectives was formulated.

1. To find out the influence of technology on retail performance in Tamale, Ghana.
2. To determine the influence of supplier relationships on retail performance in Tamale, Ghana.
3. To examine the influence of order processing on retail performance in Tamale, Ghana.
4. To examine the influence of inventory management on retail performance in Tamale, Ghana.

1.3 LITERATURE REVIEW

1.3.1 GHANAIAN RETAIL INDUSTRY

The retail industry in Ghana has seen a significant transformation as a result of several causes, such as the global expansion of retail trends, the increasing prevalence of both online and offline consumer buying behavior, and the need for merchants to provide seamless shopping experiences (Genov, 2018). The industry in question has had significant growth and rapid development due to the increasing customer knowledge and the need for enhanced brand offerings (Firmus Advisory, 2019). The market has seen the entry of international firms such as Game, Shoprite, Citydia, and other comparable enterprises, driven by the changing preferences of customers. Consequently, in a rapidly expanding sector, it is vital to comprehend the market and its consumer preferences.

The prevalence of open-air markets remains substantial in Ghana's retail sector, despite a general trend toward formal retail locations and e-commerce, which may be attributed to the growing accessibility of the internet. The advent of the internet in Ghana in 1995 has had a significant impact on several facets of Ghanaian society, including the economy, social interactions, and commercial activities (Firmus Advisory, 2019). A significant proportion of small retail enterprises engage in marketing and selling their goods and services using social media platforms, including Facebook, Instagram, and WhatsApp. Retailers that have successfully kept pace with the evolving trends in the retail business, together with current and prospective investors, have effectively addressed customer demands and established a sense of trust among them (Genov, 2018).

The advent of mobile shopping apps, like DHL Africa, has provided customers in Ghana with unrestricted access to a wide range of items from many global sources. These applications empower customers to choose not only the most affordable options but also those that give the most satisfactory shopping experience (Genov, 2018). Based on the findings of our survey, it is evident that a majority of customers, namely, 58%, exhibit a greater inclination toward patronizing firms that provide them items customized to their own requirements. The alteration in payment methods will yield advantages for both online and offline shops, although it will also provide them with novel challenges. Although a significant portion of customers still use cash as their preferred payment method during purchasing activities, there is a growing inclination among them to explore other payment options such as mobile and card payments (Genov, 2018). In the realm of payment, several firms have chosen to use mobile money as a means of facilitating transactions, and others have chosen to adhere to conventional payment methods. Based on the findings of a study conducted by Firmus Advisory in 2019, it was determined that a majority of millennials, namely, 63%, exhibit a preference for flexible payment options throughout their shopping experiences.

1.3.2 LOGISTICS OUTSOURCING

The significance of supply chain management (SCM) has seen substantial growth in both academic study and practical application with the advent of globalization in the 1980s. According to Konig and Spinler (2016), the supply chain exhibited an increased level of resilience, complexity, and costliness over time. According to Christopher (2016), a contemporary rivalry is often characterized as a confrontation between supply chains rather than individual businesses. The realization of the potential of good supply chain management (SCM) to significantly enhance global competitiveness has led senior management of organizations to acknowledge its importance (Coyle et al., 2016). The sector in the realm of logistics administration (LM) encompasses the movement of products or substances, alongside the delivery of assistance and distribution of data, from providers to end consumers. The research outcomes of Chopra and Meindl (2015), Christopher (2016), Coyle et al. (2016), and Govindan et al. (2015) each provide evidence for this. The practice of outsourcing logistics has gained popularity among organizations as they increasingly prioritize focusing on their core capabilities and entrusting their logistical operations to third-party service providers (Aziz et al., 2020).

According to Lou et al. (2020), the majority of markets have undergone globalization. Consequently, the skillful management of logistics has emerged as a crucial tool utilized by global supply networks (Mentzer et al., 2001). Logistics encompasses the systematic control of the procurement, transportation, and warehousing of commodities, assets, components, and stockpiles, with the goal of optimizing profitability through efficient order fulfillment (Christopher, 2016). Reverse logistics, also known as reverse supply chain management, entails the structured handling of the movement of products and materials from the consumption point back to their original source or point of origin (Jaaron and Backhouse, 2016; Roger and Tibben-Lembke, 2001; Turrisi et al., 2013). Attaining a comprehensive grasp of the influence of logistics on profit margins holds utmost significance.

One of the significant issues in the field of service supply chain management, as highlighted by Choi et al. (2016), pertains to the prominence of service outsourcing. The authors provide a concise overview of the existing body of research on service outsourcing. Tang and Veelenturf (2019) conducted an experimental investigation to examine the structural correlations between prospective hazards and the failure of an outsourcing contract. The conventional business model focuses on the transportation and distribution of tangible goods in various manifestations. The involvement of the customer in the service process is now significant, and the assessment of service quality has great significance in relation to market demand (Wang et al., 2019). The practice of outsourcing has become a widespread phenomenon within the service sector, serving as an effective strategy for enhancing service quality. The existing collection of studies regarding the concepts of single-sourcing and multisourcing can be sorted into two clear categories: single sources and multiple sources. This section centers on examining the outsourcing of services within a supply chain that involves a lone client and a solitary service giver. The research carried out by Zhang et al. in 2019 explores two notable instances of outsourcing: customer service centers and order completion. The scholars analyze the impacts of uneven information about demand on the two parties involved and come to the deduction that dual-pricing strategies can effectively ensure comprehensive information. When a coordinating logistics service provider delegated a logistical task to two rival functional logistics suppliers, Liu et al. (2018) investigated the distinct issues of fairness faced by logistics service providers in this fiercely competitive market. An entity responsible for manufacturing under contract, an original equipment manufacturer, and a seller constitute the points within this illustration of an outsourced supply chain

1.3.3 DIMENSIONS OF LOGISTICS OUTSOURCING

1.3.3.1 SUPPLIER RELATIONSHIPS

Initially, there was a perception that including and integrating consumers, suppliers, and other infrastructure investors in a company's expansion and promotion efforts was a worthwhile endeavor. In relation to this subject, Bailey (2016) proposed a widely acknowledged definition of relationship marketing, which encompasses all marketing endeavors aimed at cultivating, overseeing, and sustaining prosperous relationships among marketing counterparts, such as suppliers and buyers. According to Gikonyo (2016), relationship marketing may be described as a business approach that aims to reorient customers and suppliers in a mutually beneficial manner. The provided definition of relationship marketing is really commendable. These endeavors foster a sense of collaboration and cooperation, leading to the development of relationships that exhibit synergy, trustworthiness, and mutual benefits.

Bailey (2016) highlighted the enduring and beneficial characteristics of these relational exchanges. However, there has been a recent shift in focus toward the reciprocal nature of these enduring and beneficial interactions, as shown in the recent article by Bailey (2016). The subject matter under consideration pertains to the comparative gains derived from those associations, as presented by Kothari (2014). Expanding upon the theoretical framework known as the "service-dominant logic of marketing" or the more encompassing "broader service logic," Bailey (2016) underscored the significance of services as an intermediary element in the facilitation of reciprocal value generation between buyers and suppliers. In this context, genuine value is not solely derived from transactions but rather from the active involvement and integration of partners in one another's operational procedures (Bailey, 2016). This is better aligned with the notion of relationship marketing since it is often used interchangeably with the concept of a buyer–supplier network.

1.3.3.2 INFORMATION TECHNOLOGY (IT)

The integration of many areas of logistics performance is greatly facilitated by the experience and industry knowledge offered by third-party logistics (3PL) providers, in addition to their provision of IT services and physical assets. The use of third-party logistics (3PL) providers equips shippers with the necessary expertise and technological proficiencies to effectively integrate logistics operations with other functional areas, hence enhancing the overall value-creation process and ensuring the delivery of high-quality logistics services. The move from an economy of scale to an economy of skills is a convincing reason for outsourcing logistics according to Mentzer et al. (2007). Consequently, they advocate for shippers to contemplate the option of outsourcing logistics. For instance, Zhang and Okoroafo (2015) assert that third-party logistics (3PL) firms provide support to shippers by facilitating the utilization of certain resources, such as information technology (IT) tools.

Wu et al. (2006) assert that a growing number of organizations are increasingly dependent on information technology as a means to enhance their operational efficiency within the realm of sustainability. The manufacturing industry has seen notable changes in work processes due to the progress of information systems, namely, manufacturing resource planning (MRP) and enterprise resource planning (ERP). These systems have facilitated the efficient management, storage, and sharing of data, surpassing previous methods. Given the persistent surge in interest in information technology throughout both the industrial and research sectors, it is prudent to include information technology into the third research inquiry. This inclusion has potential ramifications for supply chain management, as highlighted by Hilletofth et al. (2010). Oleskow-Szapka and Lubinski (2016) argue that it is essential for logistics firms to increase their technological investments in order to effectively provide Logistics 4.0 solutions to their clientele.

1.3.3.3 ORDER PROCESSING

The term "customer order processing" pertains to the set of activities included in the execution of a customer's request to acquire goods or services (Benton, 2014). The responsibility for supplying crucial information necessary for managing the interconnections between the logistics department and the rest of the company's departments, both internally and externally, lies with the order processing system (Basheka, 2016). Order fulfillment is often seen as a transactional process that comes under the jurisdiction of the logistics department within an organization. Nevertheless, it is essential for managers to possess a comprehensive comprehension of the strategic elements inherent in the supply chain, alongside a thorough understanding of the cross-functional prerequisites and the pivotal function that the supply chain assumes in the administration thereof. When examining the order fulfillment process from a strategic standpoint, it necessitates the identification of both internal and external needs, along with the assurance that the system has the requisite capabilities. This encompasses the process of identifying the optimal company strategy and customer service demands while concurrently establishing an effective supply chain network capable of efficiently satisfying client expectations. An additional crucial element of the process is the establishment of a responsive system to address situations when demand surpasses supply, resulting in the inability to fulfill certain requests.

The order processing system facilitates the acceptance and processing of customer orders. The delivery is considered incomplete until the purchaser has obtained their acquisition and verified its accurate and complete arrival (Benton, 2014). The initiation of order handling commences upon receiving the customer's order verification and remains unfinished until the customer has obtained the requested products and validated their adherence to the order's specified conditions. One of the fundamental responsibilities of information technology in a corporation is to provide a seamless flow of information that precedes, accompanies, and succeeds the movement of commodities (Bergman and Lundberg, 2013).

1.3.3.4 INVENTORY MANAGEMENT

The requirement for efficient inventory control becomes evident upon contemplation of the detrimental impact that inventories have had on countless firms. The lack of awareness or disregard for inventory costs is a significant contributing factor to the collapse of some enterprises. Inventory, a crucial element in the supply chain, is often seen as a safety measure that facilitates seamless and efficient operations across various components of the chain. In recent times, there has been an increasing notion among scholars and researchers that inventory is seen as a liability (Arthur, 2016). However, it is important to recognize that the major objective of inventory is to achieve cost savings across several domains while also serving as a kind of safeguarding. The challenge is in finding an equilibrium between the need to maintain inventory and the associated expenses incurred in inventory holding. Stockpiling is a prevalent phenomenon seen in organizations operating at different stages of the supply chain, and it is motivated by a multitude of factors. Supply and demand can be balanced, supply and demand risks can be mitigated, regional specialization can be encouraged, and the costs of stockouts may be reduced thanks to inventories, as stated by Bailey (2016). Managing a company's stock of goods and supplies requires careful preparation and attention to detail, which is what inventory management is all about. Hardware and software, together with accompanying processes and procedures, are all part of inventory management's grand scheme for overseeing the tracking and care of stockpiles. Raw materials, supplies, and finished goods are all examples of things that may be sent to vendors and customers. The manufacturing, wholesale, and retail industries all benefit from using an inventory management system (Nasra, 2014). Managing stock is a crucial first step in the commercial logistics process. Because of its importance to business operations, the inventory management system is of tremendous importance in the field of logistics planning and control. Physical inventory on stock or in buffer storage is seen as an inefficient allocation of labor and financial resources in terms of value addition because it is linked to the production process and therefore seen as unnecessary due to the capital it ties up.

1.3.4 RETAIL FIRMS' PERFORMANCE

The role that retail businesses play in their decision-making process is of utmost importance (Li et al., 2018). Successful management within these organizations has a primary obligation to uphold and ensure performance (Katzenbach and Smith, 2015). This field of research has been characterized as profoundly intricate and engrossing because of its crucial role in assessing the effectiveness of organizations (Mone et al., 2018; Steers and Lee, 2017; Brockman et al., 2017) within its wider setting (Haseeb et al., 2019). One of the main areas of focus in the domain of business studies has been extensively explored by Carter et al. (2018), involving both experimental and conceptual investigations. This topic has also been delved into by Ferraris et al. (2018) and Makri et al. (2017). When it comes to the retail sector, the concept of "performance" is commonly used to measure how well a company is effectively achieving its predetermined goals and objectives (Macedo et al., 2016; Jones et al., 2016). The concept of "performance" has been extensively utilized across various management domains for a considerable duration (Schaltegger and Wagner, 2017). Nonetheless, despite its widespread utilization, a universally accepted interpretation of this term remains elusive. The concepts of managing performance, organizational performance, measuring performance, evaluating performance, and appraising performance have been utilized for a considerable period within the realm of management.

Subjective metrics are used by companies to determine the allocation of resources for the purpose of managing their operations and generating profits. The concept of "profit" is often used as a metric for assessing the effectiveness of an organization. This assessment may include comparing the organization's performance to that of comparable firms or may be linked to its commercial endeavors depending upon the specific setting (Aziz et al., 2020). Various methodologies are used in order to measure the financial advantages, although it is consistently observed that each approach yields a comparable outcome. According to Aziz et al. (2020), the computation of operating income and revenue from other sources may be interchanged.

1.3.5 LOGISTICS OUTSOURCING AND RETAIL PERFORMANCE

Sraboti (2012) asserts that the use of Third-Party Logistics (3PL) has enabled shippers to significantly mitigate operational inefficiencies within their logistics systems. This is primarily attributed to the capability of 3PL to effectively guarantee the timely provision of the correct product, in the proper amount and quality, at the designated location. As a consequence, companies have enhanced their customer service and gained a competitive edge as a direct outcome of this phenomenon. In a similar manner, Li (2014) has delineated the whole of the factors that contribute to logistics performance as a notable advantage that shippers get via their engagement with third-party logistics (3PL) providers. According to Zhang and Okoroafo (2015), third-party logistics (3PL) providers have enhanced their ability to provide logistics services that are both efficient and effective due to their technological expertise and industry experience. The advancements seen in this development mostly stem from the information technology and assets possessed by third-party logistics (3PL) providers, together with their skills and practical knowledge (Githinji, 2012).

According to Ross (2003), it is essential for third-party logistics (3PL) providers to possess the requisite skills and practical expertise to effectively address any logistical challenges that may emerge. Moreover, as stated by Sheikh (2012), the integration of logistics resources, logistics expertise, and information technology capabilities held by third-party logistics (3PL) providers empowers them to provide cost-efficient and productive logistics solutions to shippers. The significance of information technology (IT) solutions offered by third-party logistics (3PL) providers cannot be emphasized as they have enhanced shippers' capacity to enhance their "Just In Time" (JIT) service while simultaneously reducing costs associated with inventory management (Zhang and Okoroafo, 2015). Third-party logistics (3PL) providers, in a similar manner, provide information technology (IT) solutions that enable carriers to optimize the utilization of their existing logistical assets. This optimization leads to cost reductions in areas such as depreciation and maintenance charges. Additional benefits of outsourcing may be achieved by using third-party logistics (3PL) providers to reduce costs associated with investing in logistics assets, including material handling and operating equipment (Ross, 2003).

Although it is possible for shippers to own logistics assets, the effectiveness of the logistics asset capabilities offered by third-party logistics (3PL) providers is a crucial determinant of their overall performance. As per Ross (2003:301), third-party logistics (3PL) have historically crafted logistics procedures and frameworks that are aptly designed for the effective warehousing and conveyance of substantial goods throughout the supply network. As indicated by Githinji (2012), tripartite logistics (3PL) can harness economies of scale, leading to the delivery of more budget-friendly logistics solutions to shippers in contrast to their solitary manufacturing capacities.

1.4 THEORETICAL REVIEW

1.4.1 TRANSACTION COST THEORY (TCT)

Organizations are consistently engaged in deliberations over the strategic decision of "make or buy," which pertains to the choice between internal production or external procurement of goods and services (Quin and Hilmer, 1994; Boissinot and Bonet, 2012). The individuals involved are actively seeking the most optimal organizational structure that will provide the highest level of satisfaction. Several theoretical frameworks have been established to provide guidance in making decisions on outsourcing. Theoretical corpus, namely, Transaction Cost Theory (TCT), is extensively used to provide justification for logistics outsourcing. The Transaction Cost Theory (TCT), influenced by Ronald Coase's seminal work in 1937 and further refined by Williamson in 1975 and 1979, posits that every transaction between two parties incurs some costs that need to be accounted for and reimbursed. The aforementioned expenditures are often known as transaction costs. There are many categories of charges including research provider fees (sometimes referred to as information fees), costs related to negotiation and contracting, expenses linked with management control, and costs incurred in monitoring the executed contract (Williamson, 1985). The TCT asserts that the selection of a governance type (hierarchy, market, or hybrid) should be based on the specific characteristics of the transaction that needs coordination. There are four key aspects that should be taken into consideration in this context: the specific nature of assets, uncertainty in transactions, how often they interact with the supplier, and the provider's ability to evaluate their service.

It is advisable to have an internal asset management approach that is very specific in order to mitigate the potential danger of reliance on the Language

Service Provider (LSP) in such circumstances. As a consequence of this inherent risk, there is a likelihood that opportunistic conduct may see an increase in prevalence. In situations characterized by a notable degree of uncertainty, the Theory of Transaction Cost (TCT) suggests that vertical integration is the optimal organizational structure for implementation. In the field of logistics, two distinct forms of uncertainty may arise. The first form, known as "internal" uncertainty, pertains to the challenges faced by shippers in accurately determining future logistics activity management requirements (Stank and Maltz, 1996). The second form, referred to as "external" uncertainty, encompasses the increasing intricacy of the institutional and regulatory landscape, the globalization of markets accompanied by novel organizational practices, and cultural disparities. The frequency of events provides insight into the extent to which the connection exhibits repetition. Ultimately, while making a choice on outsourcing, it is important to evaluate the assessment capabilities of the service provider. Undoubtedly, assessing the performance of a service provider may pose challenges; hence, it is advisable to internalize the transaction for a more comprehensive evaluation. Outsourcing can be considered a favorable option when the organization has a comprehensive comprehension of the functioning and efficacy of the duties being outsourced, along with an uncomplicated ability to assess the skills of the service provider. Valuable insights may be derived from Transaction Cost Theory (TCT) when making decisions on the establishment of an outsourced corporate governance framework. Due to the robustness of its underlying premise, the theoretical framework in question remains widely used for elucidating the concept of logistics outsourcing.

1.5 RESEARCH METHODOLOGY

1.5.1 RESEARCH DESIGN

According to Bansal et al. (2018), there are three distinct forms of quantitative design, namely, correlation, experimental, and quasiexperimental designs. I deliberated over the suitability of experimental and quasiexperimental designs for addressing my research inquiry, ultimately determining that these designs were not well-suited for my purpose. The primary objective of an experimental design is to establish causal links between variables by changing one variable while controlling and evaluating the resulting changes in other variables. We have opted for a correlational research design. Correlational design is a research methodology used by scholars to investigate the association between variables via the utilization of statistical analysis

(Park and Park, 2016). This approach does not include the manipulation of variables (Aggarwal and Ranganathan, 2016). In the context of correlational design, researchers do not anticipate establishing a causal link between variables but rather aim to illustrate the extent of their association (Aggarwal and Ranganathan, 2016). The correlational methodology was used since it aligns with the study objective of investigating the association between logistics outsourcing and retail performance.

1.5.2 RESEARCH STRATEGY

The quantitative technique was selected for this research. The use of the quantitative research approach involves the investigation of the associations between variables via the application of statistical analytic techniques (Park and Park, 2016). The use of quantitative research methods has the potential to enhance the generalizability of study findings to a broader audience (Saunders et al., 2015). According to McCusker and Gunaydin (2019), the use of quantitative data by researchers aims to provide an explanatory framework for observable phenomena. The quantitative technique was chosen since it is seen as most suitable for addressing the research issue as it allows for the analysis of data to elucidate the type and magnitude of correlations between variables.

1.5.3 POPULATION OF THE STUDY

The research used three retail stores located in Tamale, each of which had a workforce size of 150 individuals. The research sample comprises supervisors and associate supervisors within the manufacturing, marketing, and managerial sectors, along with the quartet of employees in the transportation division. This was due to their extensive understanding of outsourcing and their ability to provide the necessary information for the investigation. The investigation included both the management employees and drivers employed by the third-party logistics supplier.

1.5.4 SAMPLE SIZE

Greener (2008) argues that doing a comprehensive examination of an entire population is not feasible in practice. Therefore, it is necessary to choose a representative sample from the population of interest in order to conduct observation and analysis. This procedure is often referred to as sampling. A cohort of fifty (50) individuals in managerial positions was chosen as the sample size for the purpose of completing questionnaires.

1.5.5 DATA COLLECTION

The study used a questionnaire as the research tool. Questionnaires are considered a desirable research tool due to their ability to provide researchers with a broader scope for conducting their studies. Furthermore, the use of surveys is advantageous as it enables participants to provide more sincere and unbiased solutions to inquiries posed in research studies (Munn and Drever, 2014). The research used a questionnaire comprising structured questions. The employment of highly structured questions proved to be advantageous as it minimized the variety in the interpretations associated with different questions. Additionally, they provided methods for guaranteeing the comparability of replies provided by participants. The survey questionnaire had three distinct sections: Category A was created for the purpose of obtaining demographic details, Category B was formulated to amass information regarding the variables not influenced by others, and Category C was employed to assemble data concerning the variables influenced by others. The questionnaires were specially crafted to accumulate quantitative information with the goal of improving understanding. Therefore, the research used Likert scale questions or statements in order to get comprehensive and precise data. This measure also served to guarantee that participants had a comprehensive comprehension of the inquiries and were less inclined to decline providing responses (Allen and Seaman, 2007).

1.5.6 DATA ANALYSIS

The previous part has clarified the approach employed to collect the necessary information for this research undertaking. Consequently, this segment clarifies the approach utilized to scrutinize the accumulated data with the goal of achieving the ultimate result of the study. Zikmund et al. (2013) contend that the procedure of analyzing data entails transforming raw data into polished and meaningful insights. The portrayal of participants' demographic traits was accomplished through descriptive metrics such as frequencies and proportions. An evaluation of hypotheses was conducted to shed light on the influence of 3PL elements on the retail industry's performance.

1.6 RESULTS AND DATA ANALYSIS

1.6.1 DEMOGRAPHIC CHARACTERISTICS

The demographic data encompasses the fundamental attributes of the individuals participating in the study. This research incorporates variables such as gender, age, tenure with the store, and educational attainment.

TABLE 1.1 Gender of Respondents.

Gender	Frequency	Percentage (%)
Male	28	56%
Female	22	44%
Total	**50**	**100%**

Source: Researcher's Field Work, 2021.

Table 1.1 presents the distribution of respondents based on gender. The data indicates that out of a total of fifty (50) participants, twenty eight (28) were identified as men, accounting for fifty-six percent (56%) of the sample. Conversely, twenty-two (22) respondents were classified as females, constituting forty-four percent (44%) of the total population. The participants provide the foundation for our analysis and subsequent discussion of the results throughout our research endeavor.

TABLE 1.2 Educational Background.

Level of Education	Frequency	Percentage (%)
Secondary	20	40%
Tertiary	30	60%
Total	50	100%

Source: Researcher's field work (2021).

Table 1.2 provides the educational background of the respondents, consisting of a sample size of fifty (50) individuals. Among the respondents, twenty (20) individuals had a secondary education, accounting for forty percent (40%) of the sample. Conversely, thirty (30) respondents held a higher degree, representing sixty percent (60%) of the sample.

TABLE 1.3 Number of Years Served in the Organization

Years served	Frequency	Percentage (%)
1-5	10	20
6-12	15	30
12 and abvoe	25	50
Total	**50**	**100**

Source: Researcher's field work (2021).

The data shown in Table 1.3 above illustrates the duration of management's engagement with its outsourcing organizations. The collaborative duration between management and their third-party logistics (3PL) suppliers fosters a conducive environment of mutual understanding and positive relations amongst the involved entities. Table 1.3 illustrates that 50% of the participants had a minimum service duration of 12 years, while 30% had served between 6 and 11 years. Additionally, 20% of the respondents had a service period ranging from 1 to 5 years.

TABLE 1.4 Logisties Activitiesn Performed by Retailers in Tamale.

Logisties activities	Reponses		Percentage (%)	
	Yes	No	Yes	No
Customer service	50	0	100	0
Transportation system	40	10	80	20
Logisties information system	10	40	20	80
Shipment planning	20	30	40	60
Warehousing and storage operations	50	0	100	0
Inventory management	50	0	100	0
Sale	50	0	100	0
Clearance and forwarding	30	20	60	40

Source: Researcher's field work (2021).

Based on the collected data, a higher proportion of the participants expressed a favorable opinion on the company's execution of almost all the aforementioned logistical tasks. The data obtained revealed that all respondents, constituting one hundred percent (100%) of the sample, said that the organization is responsible for customer service, warehouse and storage operations, inventory management, and sales. In relation to the transportation system, a significant majority of the respondents, comprising 80% of the total, expressed their agreement with the company's performance in this domain. Conversely, a minority of 20% of the respondents had a contrasting viewpoint. In the context of logistics and information systems, a minority of respondents, comprising twenty percent (20%) of the sample, indicated that the firm engages in this particular function. Conversely, the majority, accounting for eighty percent (80%) of the respondents, reported that the company does not carry out this activity. In regards to shipment planning, it was found that 40% of the respondents held the perspective that the firm carries out this job, while 60% of them reacted negatively, indicating that the organization does not execute this function. Conversely, the responses regarding clearing and forwarding were the opposite. Based on the data shown in the table, it can be inferred that Tamale retailers mostly engage in doing their main tasks internally rather than outsourcing them to a third-party service provider (3PL).

TABLE 4.5 Has Your Company Ever Out-sourced Any of its Logisties Function?

Response	Frequency	Percentage (%)
Yes	50	100%
No	0	0%
Total	**50**	**100%**

Source: Researcher's field work (2021).

Based on the data shown in Table 1.5, it can be seen that all fifty respondents, accounting for one hundred percent (100%), expressed the belief that the organization has started the practice of outsourcing some logistical operations.

1.6.2 RELIABILITY AND LOADINGS

When evaluating the measurement model, it is important to establish three forms of validity: substantive validity, convergent validity, and discriminatory validity. The substantive validity of the measurements was crafted by incorporating elements from pre-existing gauges. Convergent validity was gauged using Cronbach's alpha, while composite dependability was deduced by extracting the mean variance from the gauges' average variance (AVE). In this specific instance, Fornell and Larcker (1981) defined the threshold values as 0.70 and 0.50, respectively. The investigation produced Cronbach's alpha figures spanning from 0.86 to 0.95, along with composite dependability figures ranging from 0.83 to 0.92. The corresponding AVE values found varied from 0.56 to 0.73. Consequently, all of the data confirmed the soundness of the measures. In addition, it is worth noting that the factor loadings observed in this study, ranging from 0.633 to 0.848, are above the threshold of 0.60. This indicates that the constructs under investigation demonstrated a satisfactory level of individual reliability. Table 1.6 presents the aforementioned information, showcasing the successful outcome of the convergent validity test for the structures under investigation.

TABLE 4.6 Reliability and Loadings.

Constructs	Items	Loadings	CR	α	AVE
Technology			**0.92**	**0.87**	**0.56**
	IT1	0.77			
	IT2	0.85			
	IT3	0.76			
	IT4	0.74			
	IT5	0.75			
Supplier Relationship			**0.88**	**0.86**	**0.72**
	SR1	0.82			
	SR2	0.71			
	SR3.	0.70			
Order Processing			**0.83**	**0.92**	**0.66**
	OP1	0.78			
	OP2	0.73			
	OP3	0.77			
	OP4	0.81			
Inventory Management			**0.91**	**0.95**	**0.73**
	IM1	0.70			
	IM2	0.72			
	IM3	0.77			
	IM4	0.80			
	IM5	0.73			

Source: Researcher's field work (2021).

1.6.3 DISCRIMINANT VALIDITY

Discriminant distinctiveness, as outlined by Henseler et al. (2015), concerns the degree to which a specific underlying concept displays dissimilarity from other latent constructs. Fornell and Larcker (1981) proposed that evaluating discriminant distinctiveness should encompass the utilization of Average Variance (AVE) extracted. This approach involves contrasting the correlations among latent components with the square root of AVE for the corresponding latent structures. Comparable to the validity framework put forth by Voorhees et al. (2016), this form of validity is frequently determined by comparing the loadings of the indicator with those of other reflective markers found in the crossloading matrix. Therefore, the investigation verified the discriminant distinctiveness by utilizing Fornell and Larcker (1981) standards, which necessitate an AVE value of 0.5 or higher on average variance extracted. Furthermore, the square root of the AVE value was demonstrated to exceed the correlations among the latent variables, in accordance with previous findings. The outcomes presented in Tables 1.6 and 1.7 illustrate that the AVE values for the latent variables were above the threshold of 0.50. Additionally, the square root of these AVE values surpassed the correlations among the latent variables. These results signify that the metrics employed in the study possessed satisfactory discriminant distinctiveness. The assessment carried out to establish discriminant distinctiveness encompassed contrasting the indicator loadings with the crossloadings, as depicted in the figure (Henseler et al., 2015). Ensuring proper discriminant distinctiveness requires the indicator loadings to surpass the crossloadings.

TABLE 4.7 Discriminant Validity.

Contructs	AVE	IT	SR	OP	IM
IT	0.56	**0.75**			
SR	0.72	0.65	**0.85**		
OP	0.66	0.56	0.54	**0.81**	
IM	0.73	0.71	0.62	0.615	**0.85**

Source: Researcher's field work (2021).

Note:Technology (IT), Supplier Relationship, Order Processing (OP), Inventory Management (IM) and Retail Performance (RP)

1.6.4 HYPOTHESIS TESTING

Independent t-test results were used to calculate the t-statistic and associated p-value, which were then used to assess the significance of the hypotheses. The t-statistic was used to decide whether or not to accept the null hypothesis. The results of this study were evaluated for statistical significance using the p-value.

TABLE 1.8 Hypothesis Testing.

Hypothesis	Path	Beta (β)	t-values	p-values	Decision
H1	IT→RP	0.354	11.45	0.001	Accepted
H2	SR→RP	0.550	12.16	0.001	Accepted
H3	OP→RP	0.436	12.39	0.000	Accepted
H4	IM→RP	0.630	9.77	0.004	Accepted

Source: Researcher's field work (2021).

This segment delves into the interrelation among the factors impacting the study, namely, logistics outsourcing, encompassing technology, supplier connections, order processing, and inventory management, and their effect on the variable affected by them, which is retail performance. The coefficients of the identified elements, namely, technology, supplier links, order processing, inventory management, and retail performance, alongside their anticipated significance, are displayed in Table 1.8 above.

Once the reliability of the measurement approach is verified, the subsequent phase involves assessing the structural model through the standard bootstrapping technique. This procedure involves generating 500 bootstrap samples and analyzing 50 instances to establish the significance of the path coefficients. Moreover, these 50 cases are employed to validate the measurement model. These steps were executed following the guidelines outlined by Hair et al. (2016). The structural model and the corresponding estimates are elaborated in Table 1.8.

The data in Table 1.8 furnishes evidence of the validation of four aspects of logistics outsourcing. The order processing system operates as a communication network that facilitates the exchange of information necessary to manage the connections between logistics and other operational domains within retailers, as well as within the logistics department itself. According to participants, this particular aspect exerted the most pronounced influence on retailers' performance, as evidenced by the strongest effect ($t = 12.39$; $\beta = 0.436$; and $p = 0.000$) observed.

A significant correlation was established between the application of technology, specifically information systems, in logistics and merchants' performance ($t = 11.45$; $\beta = 0.354$; and $p = 0.001$). A hypothesis concerning the presence of a statistically substantial correlation between inventory management and performance was put forth and verified through statistical analysis ($t = 9.77$; $\beta = 0.630$; and $p = 0.004$). The previous analysis of supplier relationships revealed a consistent pattern, signifying a statistically meaningful positive correlation between supplier relationships and retailers' performance ($t = 12.16$; $\beta = 0.550$; and $p = 0.001$).

Based on the information provided in the above-mentioned tables, it can be deduced that each of the four predictors had a statistically significant positive impact on the merchants in the Tamale-Ghana region. The findings of this study validate all four hypotheses. Consequently, it is anticipated that this framework will possess the capability to comprehensively assess the factors in operation.

1.7 SUMMARY OF THE RESEARCH FINDINGS

In conclusion, it is essential to acknowledge that the utilization of outsourcing businesses, namely, third-party logistics (3PL) providers, as contractual services, has shown a notable level of stability in industrialized nations like the United States. In the context of developing countries like Ghana, there is a notable trend of fast expansion and emergence. The use of outsourcing is gaining significance as organizations want to enhance their competitiveness via the strategic deployment of their knowledge and resources, hence attaining heightened operational efficiency. Achieving success in the practice of logistics outsourcing may provide significant advantages for enterprises.

All four variables had a statistically significant favorable impact on shopkeepers in Tamale, Ghana. The findings of the present investigation provide support for all four theories. Hence, it is anticipated that this module would possess the capability to fully assess the factors. The findings of the research have validated hypotheses H1, H2, H3, and H4, which establish a statistically significant positive correlation between supplier relationships, inventory management, technology, order processing, and the performance of retailers.

1.8 CONCLUSIONS

The results of the study examination suggest that the factors of innovation, supplier relationship, order handling, and stock control greatly influenced the effectiveness of retailers operating within three well-known retail establishments. This assertion is supported by the findings of the correlation and hypothesis analyses presented earlier. The variable of information systems warrants more attention due to its essential role in corporate operations.

Surprisingly, the respondents, who are workers of three retail outlets, do not see it as a necessary component.

Based on the research conducted, it was found that the variable pertaining to supplier connection got favorable feedback. Consequently, the study reached the conclusion that retailers have shown satisfactory performance in this aspect, although acknowledging the need for further improvement. The variable that had the greatest impact on merchants' success was order processing. The conclusion might be drawn that either the aforementioned regions include hidden depths beyond first observations or that the workers lack comprehensive knowledge of the shops' systems. The merchants seem to be proficient in inventory management, while there is a need for ongoing development in order to reduce the proportion of values falling within the neutral range.

1.9 RECOMMENDATIONS

Prior to engaging in outsourcing arrangements with third-party service providers, merchants should have a mutual understanding and consensus over certain quality requirements. These criteria should be effectively communicated to the service providers. Third-party service providers are likely to exhibit more commitment to the terms of agreements or contracts when they have mutually agreed upon certain quality criteria. This will aid in guaranteeing the provision of products and services of superior quality.

Retail management should refrain from outsourcing service providers who are engaged in several contracts. The practice of corporations outsourcing to service providers engaged in several contracts has the inherent danger of confidential information being exposed to the public. Due to the negative consequences of information leakage, such as financial losses and diminished confidence, it is essential for organizations to engage service providers that are not concurrently participating in numerous contracts. This strategic approach aims to mitigate both financial and reputational damages.

Retail firms exhibit reluctance to outsource to third parties primarily due to the presence of substantial switching costs associated with this practice. While it is indeed accurate that a majority of enterprises would choose to outsource to third parties when the expenses associated with transitioning are minimal, this scenario does not often occur. The following personnel needs to be reallocated: There exists the potential for the displacement of human resources engaged in certain organizational responsibilities due to the decision to outsource those duties to external service providers. Instead of implementing workforce reductions, it is advisable to consider reallocating personnel to other areas within the organization as a means to support the company's growth efforts.

KEYWORDS

- **logistics**
- **outsourcing**
- **retail**
- **supply chain**
- **management**
- **outlets**

REFERENCES

Abban, R. Firm Characteristics, Business Environment, and Performance of Non-Traditional Agricultural SME Exporters in Ghana. Unpublished Thesis, Wageningen University, 2020.

Achuora, J.; Arasa, R.; Ochiri, G. Precursors to Effectiveness of Public Procurement Audits for Constituency Development Funds (CDF) in Kenya. *Eur. Sci. J.* **2014,** *8* (25), 198–214.

Agaba, E.; Shipman, N. Public Procurement Reform in Developing Countries: The Ugandan Experience; Pr Academics Press: USA, 2014.

Aggarwal, R.; Ranganathan, P. Common Pitfalls in Statistical Analysis: The Use of Correlation Techniques. *Perspect. Clin. Res.* **2016,** *7,* 187–190.

Ali, A.; Namusonge, G.; Sakwa, M. Effect of Firm Managerial Risk Aversion on Corporate Hedging of Listed Firms in Nairobi Securities Exchange in Kenya. *J. Bus. Manag.* **2016,** *2* (7), 45–64.

Amit, R.; Schoemaker, P. J. H. Strategic Assets and Organizational Rent. *Strat. Manag. J.* **2013,** *14*, 33–46.

Andrew, A. Strategic Sourcing Process Model. *J. Bus. Ind. Lab. Relat. Rev.* **2016,** *17*, 99–120.

Araz, C.; Ozkarahan, I. Supplier Evaluation and Management System for Strategic Sourcing Based on a New Multicriteria Sorting Procedure. *Int. J. Prod. Econ.* **2017,** *106* (2), 585–606.

Armstrong, M. In *Handbook on Personnel Management and Practice*, 6th Ed.; Korgan Page Limited, London, 2016.

Arthur, P. An Overview of EC Policy on Procurement: Current Position and Future Prospects, Procurement Law Review, 2016; vol *1* (1), pp 28–39.

Aseka, J. Supplier Selection Criteria and Performance of Manufacturing Firms Listed in the Nairobi Stock Exchange. Unpublished MBA Project, University of Nairobi: Nairobi, Kenya, 2014.

Bai, C.; Sarkis, J. Supplier Selection and Sustainability: A Grey Rough Set Evaluation; Working Paper No. 2013 -05, 2013.
Bailey, S. In *Public Sector Economics: Theory and Practice*; Macmillan: London, 2016.
Bailey, P.; Farmer, D.; Jessop, D.; Jones, D. In *Purchasing Principles and Management*, 8th Ed.; Financial Times Prentice Hall: Great Britain, 2016.
Bali O.; Kose, E.; Gumus, S. Green Supplier Selection Based on IFS and GRA Grey Ssystems. *Theory Appl.* **2013,** *3* (2), 58–176.
Bansal, H. S.; Irving, P. G.; Taylor, S. F. A Three-Component Model of Customer Commitment to Service Providers. *J. Acad. Mark. Sci.* **2014,** *32* (3), 234–250.
Barsemoi, H.; Mwangagi, P.; Asienyo, B. O. Factors Influencing Procurement Performance in Private Sector in Kenya. *Int. J. Innov. Appl. Stud.* **2014,** *9* (2), 632–641.
Barth, M. E.; Beaver, W. H.; Landsman, W. R. Relative Valuation Roles of Equity Book Value and Net Income as a Function of Financial Health. *J. Account. Econ.* **2013,** *25*, 1–34.
Bartik, L. Supply Chain Management Practices in Institutions. *Procurement J.* **2016,** *28*.
Basheka, B. Procurement Planning and Local Governance in Uganda: A Factor Analysis Approach. Uganda Management Institute, 2016.
Basheka, D.; Tumutegyereize Access to Health Care in a System Transition: The Case of Bulgaria. *Int. J. Health Plann. Manag.* **2016,** *17*, 377–395.
Beatty, R. P.; Ritter, J. R. Investment Banking, Reputation, and Underpricing of Initial, 2016.
Benton, W. C. Power Influences in the Supply Chain. *J. Bus. Logist.* **2014,** *21* (1), 49–73.
Bergman, M. A.; Lundberg, S. Tender Evaluation and Supplier Selection Methods in Public Procurement. *J. Purch. Supply Manag.* **2013,** *19* (2), 73–83.
Butler-Knight, M.; ElSafty, S. Critical Success Factors of Six Sigma Implementation in Automotive Industry in Egypt. SAE Technical Paper, 2015. 2016- 01-1270.
Chalotra, V. Inventory Management and Small Firms Growth: An Analytical Study in Supply Chain. *Vision* **2013,** *17 3* (20-23), 213–222.
Chen, J.; Liang, L.; Yao, D. Q. Factory Encroachment and Channel Selection in an Outsourced Supply Chain. *Int. J. Prod. Econ.* **2018,** *215*, 73–83.
Choi, T.; Wallace, S. W.; Wang, Y. Risk Management and Coordination in Service Supply Chains: Information, Logistics and Outsourcing. *J. Oper. Res. Soc.* **2016,** *67* (2), 159–164.
Creswell, J. In *Research Design: Qualitative, Quantitative, and Mixed Methods Approaches*, 4th Ed.; Sage Publications, Thousand Oaks, 2013.
Davis, F.; Cobb, A. Resource Dependence Theory: Past and future. *Res. Sociol. Organ.* **2010,** *28* (1), 21–42.
Evans, M. M. Impact of Supply Chain Integration Strategies on Performance of Pork Processing Industry in Rwanda (Case of German Butchery in Kigali). European Centre for Research Training and Development UK, 2015. (www.eajournals.org).
Farahani, R. In *Logistics Operations and Management: Concepts and Models*, 1st Ed.; Elsevier Inc.: London, 2011.
Fatiha, N. Customer Service in Supply Chain Management: A Case Study. *J. Enterp. Inf. Manag.* **2014,** *27* (6), 786–801.
Fornell, C.; Larcker, D. F. Evaluating Structural Equation Models with Unobservable Variables and Measurement Error. *J. Mark. Res.* **1981,** *18* (1), 39–50.
Fugate, B. S.; John, T. M.; Stank T. P. Logistics Performance: Efficiency, Effectiveness and Differentiation. *J. Bus. Logist.* **2010,** *31* (1), 43–62.

GaneshKumar, C.; Nambirajan, T. Supply Chain Management Components, Competitiveness and Organisational Performance: Causal Study of Manufacturing Firms. *Asia-Pacific J. Manag. Res. Innov.* **2013,** *9* (4) 399–412.

Gikonyo, N. Performance Monitoring and Quality Outcomes in Contracted Services. *Int. J. Qual. Reliab. Manag.* **2016,** *19* (4), 396–413.

Hair, J. F. Jr.; Hult, G. T. M.; Ringle, C.; Sarstedt, M. In *A Primer on Partial Least Squares Structural Equation Modeling (PLS-SEM)*; Sage Publications, 2016.

Henseler, J.; Ringle, C. M.; Sarstedt, M. A New Criterion for Assessing Discriminant Validity in Variance-Based Structural Equation Modelling. *J. Acad. Mark. Sci.* **2015,** *43* (1), 115–135.

Kamande, M. W. The Impact of Clean Production on the Performance of Kenya Manufacturing Firms, Ph.D. (Economics). Dissertation, University of Dar es Salaam, Tanzania, 2011.

Kilasi, L. B.; Juma, D.; Mathooko, P. M. The Impact of Outsourcing of Logistics on the Competitive Advantage Strategy of East African Breweries Limited. *Int. J. Soc. Sci. Entrepreneurship* **2013,** *1* (3), 521–552.

Kogoh, Z. B. K. Effect of Outsourcing on Performance of Logistics Industry in Kenya. Doctoral Dissertation, Strathmore University, 2015.

Kothari, C. In *Research Methodology: Methods and Techniques*, 2nd Ed., 2011.

Kyusya, J. M. (2015). Effect of Logistics Outsourcing on the Operational Performance of Shipping Industry in Kenya. Doctoral Dissertation, University of Nairobi, 2015.

Lacity, M. C.; Willcocks, L. P. Business Process Outsourcing Studies: A Critical Review and Research Directions. In *Formulating Research Methods for Information Systems*; Palgrave Macmillan: UK, 2015; pp 169–251.

Langley, J. 2016 Third Party Logistics Study. The State of Logistics Outsourcing; New Age Tecno Press: New Delhi, Feb 15, 2015.

Li, J.; Xia, J.; Zajac, E. J. On the Duality of Political and Economic Stakeholder Influenceon Firm Innovation Performance: Theory and Evidence from Chinese Firms. *Strat. Manag. J.* **2018,** *39* (1), 193–216.

Liu, W.; Wang, D.; Shen, X.; Yan, X.; Wei, W. The Impacts of Distributional and Peer-Induced Fairness Concerns on the Decision-Making of Order Allocation in Logistics Service Supply Chain. *Transp. Res. E-Logist. Transp. Rev.* **2018,** *116*, 102–122.

Lou, Y.; Feng, L.; He, S.; He, Z.; Zhao, X. Logistics Service Outsourcing Choices in a Retailer-Led Supply Chain. *Transp. Res. E Logist. Transp. Rev.* **2020,** *141*, 101944. DOI: 10.1016/j.tre.2020.101944

Lysons K.; Farrington, B. In *Purchasing and Supply Chain Management*, 8th Ed.; Pearson Education Limited, 2012.

Makabira, D. K.; Waiganjo, E. Role of Procurement Practices on the Performance of Corporate Organizations in Kenya: A Case Study of Kenya National Police Service. *Int. J. Acad. Res. Bus. Soc. Sci.* **2014,** *4* (10), 369–384.

Margetta, J. The Power of Virtual Integration. *J. Supply Chain Manag.* **2008,** *35* (9), 149–152.

McCusker, K.; Gunaydin, S. Research using Qualitative, Quantitative, or Mixed Methods and Choice based on the Research. *Perfusion* **2019,** *30* (7), 537–542. DOI: 10.1177/0267659114559116

Oleskow-Szłapka, J.; Lubinski, P. In *New Technology Trends and Solutions in Logistics and their Impact on Processes*, 3rd International Conference on Social Science, 2016; pp 408–413.

Papadopoulou, C. An Overview of Third Party Logistics Industry. Centre for Transportation Studies, Massachusetts Institute of Technology, 2001.

Park, J.; Park, M. Qualitative Versus Quantitative Research Methods: Discovery or Justification? *J. Mark. Thought* **2016,** *3*, 1–7. DOI: 10.15577/jmt.2016.03.01.1

Saunders, M. N. K.; Lewis, P.; Thornhill, A. In *Research Methods for Business Students*, 7th Ed.; Pearson Education Unlimited: Essex, England, 2015.

Schaltegger, S.; Wagner, M. Eds.; In *Managing the Business Case for Sustainability: The Integration of Social, Environmental and Economic Performance*, Routledge, 2017.

Tang, C. S.; Veelenturf, L. P. The Strategic Role of Logistics in the Industry 4.0 era. *Transp. Res. E Logist. Transp. Rev.* **2019,** *129*, 1–11.

Voorhees, C.M.; Brady, M. K.; Calantone, R.; Ramirez, E. Discriminant Validity Testing in Marketing: An Analysis, Causes for Concern, and Proposed Remedies. *J. Acad. Mark. Sci.* **2016,** *44* (1), 119-134.

, F.; Yang, X.; Zhuo, X.; Xiong, M. Joint Logistics and Financial Services by a 3PL Firm: Effects of Risk Preference and Demand Volatility. *Transp. Res. E Logist. Transp. Rev.* **2019,** *130*, 312–328. https://doi.org/10.1016/j.tre.2019.09.006.

Xin, Y.; Huang, R.; Song, M.; Mishra, N. Pre-Positioning Inventory and Service Outsourcing of Relief Material Supply Chain. *Int. J. Prod. Res.* **2018,** *56* (21), 6859–6871.

Zhang, S.; Dan, B.; Zhou, M. After-Sale Service Deployment and Information Sharing in a Supply Chain Under Demand Uncertainty. *Eur. J. Oper. Res.* **2019,** *279* (2), 351–363.

Zhang, S.; Zhang, J.; Zhu, G. Retail Service Investing: An Anti-Encroachment Strategy in a Retailer-Led Supply Chain. *Omega* **2019,** *84,* 212–231. https://doi.org/10.1016/j.omega.2018.05.005.

Zhou, Y.; Guo, J.; Zhou, W. Pricing/Service Strategies for a Dual-Channel Supply Chain withFree Riding and Service-Cost Sharing. *Int. J. Prod. Econ.* **2017,** *196,* 198–210.

CHAPTER 2

Make-or-Buy Decision Strategy in Critical Procurement and Supply Chain Management with Break-Even Analysis: A Comprehensive Review

SHALOM AKHAI

Department of Mechanical Engineering, Chandigarh Engineering College, Jhanjeri, Mohali, Punjab, India

ABSTRACT

This paper aims to provide a comprehensive review of the make-or-buy decision strategy in critical procurement and supply chain management through break-even analysis. The make-or-buy choice is a crucial strategy that impacts a firm's performance in procurement and supply chain management. The decision involves balancing between in-house production and external sourcing and is based on various factors, including cost, quality, capacity, and expertise. This decision can have a significant impact on a company's financial success and must be made with thorough consideration of internal resources, market conditions, and competition. Literature review shows that the make-or-buy decision is influenced by internal and external factors, including production cost, production volume, production technology, supplier performance, and market conditions. The findings from literature also demonstrate that the make-or-buy choice can significantly impact supply chain efficiency, productivity, quality, and cost-effectiveness. The success of the decision-making process depends on the ability to collect and analyze relevant data and implement effective strategies for procurement and supply chain operations. In conclusion, the make-or-buy decision is an ongoing process that requires businesses to regularly re-evaluate their choices, taking

Essentials of Supply Chain Management: Strategy, Planning and Operations.
Mohammed Majeed, Abdul-Rasheed Akeji Alhassan Alolo, Seidu Alhassan, and S. Sekar (Eds.)

into account changing market conditions and internal considerations to make informed decisions that align with their goals and objectives while staying ahead of the competition. Also, this review highlights the importance of utilizing a break-even analysis in the make-or-buy decision process and emphasizes its significance in ensuring a successful procurement and supply chain management strategy.

2.1 INTRODUCTION

The make-or-buy choice is a significant strategy that plays a vital part in deciding the performance of a firm in the area of procurement and supply chain management (Lee and Billington, 1992). This decision may be summarized as follows: The choice of whether a firm should manufacture a product internally or acquire it from an outside vendor is referred to as the "make-or-buy" decision (Choi and Hartley, 1996). This choice has far-reaching consequences on the operations of a firm, including cost, quality, and efficiency, and is thus an essential component of both procurement and the management of supply chain relationships (Cohen and Roussel, 1989). The decision of whether a company should produce something themselves or purchase it from another source has become an increasingly difficult one over the years (Javalgi and White, 1993). Businesses now have to take into account a plethora of factors, including the ever-shifting conditions of the market, the progression of technology, and the variations in the cost of production (Hamel and Prahalad, 1989). As a direct consequence of this, businesses are now needed to implement a method of decision-making that is both thorough and strategic in order to guarantee that they can continue to be competitive in the market (Zhang and Dilts, 2004).

2.2 SITUATIONS UNDER WHICH "MAKE" OR "BUY" DECISIONS ARISE

In the context of business and project management, the question of whether an organization should produce a component in-house or buy it from an outside vendor is referred to as a "make or buy" choice (Lambert and Stock, 2017). The choice is made after taking into account a number of different variables, including cost, the availability of resources, experience, and strategic considerations (Simchi-Levi et al., 2015). The following are some examples of frequent scenarios in which a choice between making or buying must be made:

- When the business has more capacity than it needs and is looking to make the most of its available resources. When an organization needs complete command over the timing and quality of the supply of a vital component (Tersine, 2014).
- When a corporation wishes to save costs by outsourcing the production of components that are not important to its operations (Lambert and Stock, 2017).
- When the firm does not have the necessary knowledge or equipment to manufacture a certain component (Simchi-Levi et al., 2015).
- When the firm wishes to cut down on either its fixed expenses or its inventory (Tersine, 2014).
- In the end, the choice about whether to manufacture or acquire anything relies on a trade-off between the costs and advantages of each available alternative as well as the company's particular objectives and top priorities (Lambert and Stock, 2017; Simchi-Levi et al., 2015).

2.3 METHODS OF COST ANALYSIS

As shown in Figure 2.1, there are several approaches to cost analysis that may be utilized when deciding whether to create or purchase anything. Some of these approaches, along with others that are addressed further down, are as follows:

1. **Simple Cost Analysis:** This method compares the direct costs of manufacturing and purchasing the product, such as raw materials, labor, and transportation (Choi and Hartley, 1996). It does not consider indirect costs such as overhead and depreciation.
2. **Economic Cost Analysis:** This method takes into account both direct and indirect costs, as well as other factors such as production volume and economies of scale (Cohen and Roussel, 1989). It provides a more comprehensive picture of the total cost of manufacturing versus purchasing the product.
3. **Break-Even Cost Analysis:** This method focuses on calculating the point at which the cost of manufacturing and purchasing the product are equal (Javalgi and White, 1993). It is often used to determine the production volume required to make the manufacturing option economically viable.

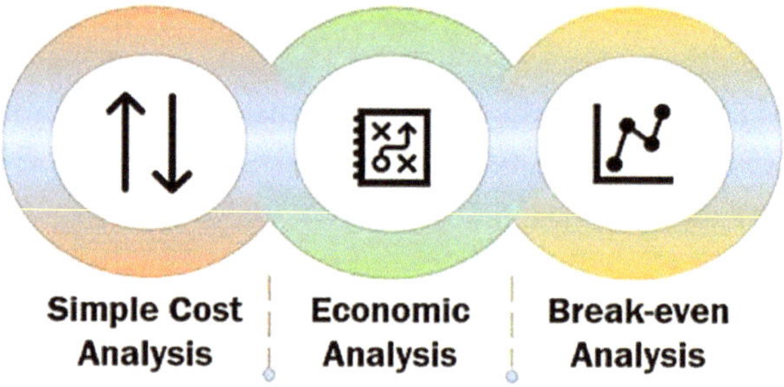

FIGURE 2.1 Methods of cost analysis.

Each of these approaches has some advantages as well as drawbacks (Hamel and Prahalad, 1989), and the most appropriate approach to take will be determined by the particulars of the make-or-buy decision as well as the information that is at hand (Zhang and Dilts, 2004).

The break-even analysis (Lee and Billington, 1992) is a quantitative approach that estimates the point at which the cost of creating a product is equal to the cost of acquiring it. This is a frequent way for making this choice. According to Choi and Hartley (1996), the following procedures are frequently included in the approach for performing a make-or-buy decision break-even analysis:

1. Identify the costs involved in both making and buying the product, including direct costs (e.g., materials, labor) and indirect costs (e.g., overhead) (Cohen and Roussel, 1989).
2. Estimate the production volume required to break even between making and buying (Javalgi and White, 1993).
3. Compare the estimated break-even production volume to the expected demand for the product to determine which option is more cost-effective (Hamel and Prahalad, 1989).

2.4 NAVIGATING THE COMPLEXITIES OF MAKE-OR-BUY DECISIONS IN PROCUREMENT AND SUPPLY CHAIN MANAGEMENT

The make-or-buy choice is a crucial procurement and supply chain management strategy, as it sets the ideal balance between internal production and external sourcing. The selection is based on many variables, including price, quality, capacity, and knowledge. Recent research indicates that a company's financial performance may be considerably affected by its decision to create or acquire a product (Dekker and Javalgi, 2018). For instance, in-house production may result in lower total costs, but it may also result in higher overhead expenditures and less flexibility (Wang et al., 2018). Alternatively, purchasing from an external supplier may result in cheaper costs; however, this may be at the sacrifice of product quality or delivery time (Kopczak and Prabhu, 2019). Organizations must provide carefully consider each of their accessible options in order to reach a judgment based on factual data. To do this, it is required to perform a comprehensive analysis of not just the organization's internal resources and skills, but also the market conditions and the nature of the competitors. In addition, firms are obligated to consider aspects such as the cost of production, the time required to bring a product to market, and the quality level that they can achieve (Al-Tabbaa, 2018). According to the results of a research conducted by Peng and Liang (2018), a variety of internal and external variables impact the choice of whether or not to manufacture or purchase anything. Cost of production, production volume, manufacturing technology, supplier performance, and market circumstances are some of these variables. According to the study's results, the decision of whether to manufacture something oneself or acquire it is typically impacted by the manufacturing cost. This value is determined by factoring in a variety of elements, such as the cost of labor, the cost of raw materials, and the cost of overhead charges. In a similar vein, Zhang and Huang (2017) evaluated the impact of a company's make-or-buy decision on its supply chain efficiency. The results indicated that whether something is created or purchased may have a significant influence on the supply chain's productivity, quality, and cost-efficiency. According to the results of the study, firms who effectively select whether to develop or purchase a product may gain a variety of benefits, such as lower pricing, higher quality, and stronger relationships with their respective suppliers. The decision of whether to manufacture or purchase a product is not a one-time event, but rather a continuing process that requires organizations to often re-evaluate their options in light of changing external market conditions and internal factors. The effectiveness of this decision-making process depends on the company's capacity to gather and evaluate pertinent data, as well as to create and execute successful strategies for managing procurement and supply chain activities. The effectiveness of this decision-making process is contingent on the company's capacity to obtain and evaluate relevant data (Liu et al., 2021).

Thus, the question of whether a company should create something themselves or acquire it is a crucial component of procurement and supply chain management that has far-reaching impacts on the operations of a firm.

In order for businesses to guarantee that they will continue to be competitive in the market, it is imperative that they approach the process of decision-making in a manner that is both thorough and strategic. In order to do this, it is necessary to conduct an in-depth examination not only of the internal resources and capabilities of the organization but also of the circumstances of the market and the nature of the competition. When organizations evaluate a range of aspects, including cost, time, and quality, they are able to make informed choices that are in accordance with their goals and objectives, as well as ones that help them remain ahead of the competition in a fast-changing business climate. Making the appropriate option on whether to create or acquire something may result in financial savings, improvements in quality, and a rise in productivity. Ineffective execution of a decision, on the other hand, may result in greater costs, decreased quality, and decreased efficiency.

2.5 FACTORS AFFECTING THE MAKE-OR-BUY DECISION

The make-or-buy decision refers to the choice companies make between producing goods or services in-house or purchasing them from an external supplier (Dyer, 1986). There are several factors that can impact this decision, including:

1. **Cost:** Companies must compare the cost of producing goods or services in-house to the cost of purchasing them from an external supplier (Ellram and Tate, 1996).
2. **Capacity:** Companies must consider their current production capacity and whether they have the resources to produce goods or services in-house (Hitt et al., 2000).
3. **Quality:** Companies must consider the quality of goods or services that can be produced in-house compared to those that can be purchased from an external supplier (Hayes and Wheelwright, 1984).
4. **Lead time:** Companies must consider the lead time required to produce goods or services in-house compared to the lead time required to purchase them from an external supplier (Schonsleben, 2002a, 2002b).
5. **Expertise:** Companies must consider their expertise in producing goods or services in-house compared to the expertise of external suppliers (Lambert and Cooper, 2000a, 2000b, 2000c).

6. **Flexibility:** Companies must consider their flexibility to change production processes in-house compared to the flexibility of external suppliers (Kerns, 2006a, 2006b. 2006c).
7. **Strategic importance:** Companies must consider the strategic importance of producing goods or services in-house compared to purchasing them from an external supplier (Chen and Paulraj, 2004).
8. **Legal and regulatory requirements:** Companies must consider any legal and regulatory requirements that may impact the make-or-buy decision (Ellram and Li, 1998a, 1998b).
9. **Economic conditions:** Companies must consider the current economic conditions and any trends that may impact the make-or-buy decision (Porter, 1985).

2.6 IMPACT OF TECHNOLOGY ON THE MAKE-OR-BUY DECISION

The impact of technology on the make-or-buy decision strategy has been significant in recent years (Kaufman and Hotchkiss, 2018). The advancement of technology has transformed the way companies approach the decision to produce goods or services in-house or purchase them from an external supplier (Wang and Li, 2020).

- **Automation:** Advances in automation have made it possible for companies to produce goods or services in-house with fewer resources and lower costs, leading to an increase in the number of companies choosing to make rather than buy (Kaufman and Hotchkiss, 2018).
- **E-commerce:** The rise of e-commerce has made it easier for companies to purchase goods or services from external suppliers, allowing them to quickly and easily compare prices, quality, and lead times (Wang and Li, 2020).
- **Globalization:** The growth of the global economy has increased competition among suppliers, making it easier for companies to find external suppliers that offer high-quality goods and services at a reasonable price (Kaufman and Hotchkiss, 2018).
- **Data analytics:** The increasing availability of data analytics tools has made it possible for companies to make more informed decisions

about the make-or-buy decision (Wang and Li, 2020). Companies can now access real-time data on costs, quality, lead time, and other important factors to make informed decisions (Kaufman and Hotchkiss, 2018).

- **Supply chain management:** Advances in supply chain management have made it easier for companies to manage their relationships with external suppliers, reducing the risk of disruptions and ensuring a steady flow of goods and services (Wang and Li, 2020).

2.7 BREAK-EVEN CHARTS IN MAKING MAKE-OR-BUY DECISIONS

The decision to produce a product in-house or to outsource it is a critical one for companies (Schonsleben, 2002a, 2002b). In order to make informed decisions, companies must consider a variety of factors, including costs, quality, and timelines (Lambert and Cooper, 2000a, 2000b, 2000c). One important tool for making these decisions is the break-even chart (Kerns, 2006a, 2006b, 2006c). The break-even chart provides a visual representation of the costs and benefits of outsourcing and helps companies determine the optimal level of outsourcing that will maximize their profits (Chen and Paulraj, 2004). Steps to create a break-even chart for make-or-buy decisions are:

1. **Determine the fixed costs:** These are costs that do not change with the level of production or sales, such as rent, salaries, and insurance.
2. **Determine the variable costs:** These are costs that vary with the level of production or sales, such as raw materials and labor.
3. **Determine the unit price:** This is the selling price per unit of the product.
4. **Calculate the break-even point:** This is the point at which total revenue equals total costs (fixed costs plus variable costs). The formula for this is: break-even point = fixed costs/(unit price − variable costs per unit).
5. **Plot the fixed costs and variable costs on the chart:** Fixed costs are represented as a horizontal line, while variable costs are represented as a downward-sloping line.
6. **Plot the revenue line:** This line shows the total revenue generated at different levels of production. It is calculated by multiplying the unit price by the number of units sold.

7. **Draw the break-even point:** This is the point at which the revenue line intersects the sum of the fixed and variable cost lines.
8. **Analyze the chart:** The chart will show the level of production or sales needed to cover all costs and start generating a profit. It will also show the impact of changes in unit price, variable costs, and fixed costs on the break-even point.

Basically, a break-even chart is a visual representation of the point at which the cost of producing goods or services in-house is equal to the cost of purchasing them from an external supplier (Porter, 1985). It is a useful tool in make-or-buy decisions as it helps companies compare the costs of both options over a specified range of production. The break-even chart consists of two lines: the cost line and the revenue line. The cost line represents the total cost of producing goods or services in-house and includes both fixed costs (e.g., equipment, labor) and variable costs (e.g., raw materials, energy). The revenue line represents the total revenue generated by the sale of goods or services and is equal to the unit price multiplied by the number of units sold. The point at which the two lines intersect is the break-even point. At this point, the cost of producing goods or services in-house is equal to the cost of purchasing them from an external supplier. If the cost line is above the revenue line, it means that it is more expensive to produce goods or services in-house, and it is more cost-effective to purchase them from an external supplier. Conversely, if the cost line is below the revenue line, it means that it is less expensive to produce goods or services in-house, and it is more cost-effective to produce them in-house. With this information, one can make informed decisions about whether to make the product in-house or buy it from an external supplier (Ellram and Li, 1998a, 1998b).

Figure 2.2 shows how the chart provides a clear visual representation of the costs and benefits of outsourcing and helps firms to make informed decisions about whether to outsource or to keep production in-house. The use of a break-even chart in making effective make-or-buy decisions has been widely researched and documented in the literature.

- One of the key studies in this area is by Chawla and Gupte (2009), who used a break-even analysis to assess the economic viability of outsourcing decisions in an Indian firm. They found that the break-even chart provided a clear visual representation of the costs and benefits of outsourcing and helped the firm to make informed decisions about whether to outsource specific activities or to keep them in-house.

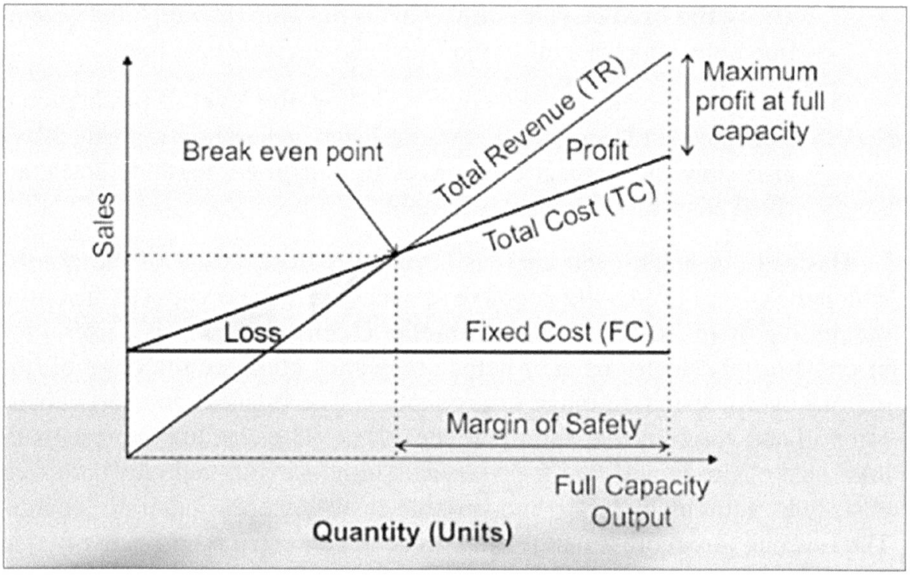

FIGURE 2.2 Make-or-buy decision based on break-even chart.

- Another study by Kato and Takahashi (2011) explored the use of a break-even chart in the Japanese automotive industry. They found that the break-even chart was an effective tool for evaluating the costs and benefits of outsourcing and helped the firms to determine the optimal level of outsourcing that would maximize their profits.
- A more recent study by Li et al. (2019) focused on the use of a break-even chart in the Chinese manufacturing industry. The authors found that the break-even chart was a useful tool for decision-making, as it provided a clear visual representation of the costs and benefits of outsourcing. This helped the firms to make informed decisions about whether to outsource or to keep production in-house, based on the costs and benefits of each option.

The literature reviewed on the use of break-even charts in make-or-buy decisions includes studies from various industries, including the Indian, Japanese, and Chinese manufacturing industries. The findings of these studies indicate that the use of break-even charts is an effective tool for making informed decisions about outsourcing and production processes.

2.8 CONCLUSIONS

This paper provides a comprehensive overview of the literature on the use of break-even charts in make-or-buy decisions and highlights their effectiveness as a decision-making tool. The following conclusions can be drawn on the basis of literature:

- The make-or-buy decision is a critical strategy in procurement and supply chain management that determines whether a company should produce a product in-house or purchase it from an external supplier. The decision is based on a number of factors, including cost, quality, capacity, and expertise, and is influenced by technology. A well-executed make-or-buy decision can lead to cost savings, improved quality, and increased efficiency, while a poorly executed decision can lead to increased costs, decreased quality, and reduced efficiency.
- The make-or-buy decision is a complex one that requires companies to weigh a variety of factors to determine the best course of action. Companies must consider cost, capacity, quality, lead time, expertise, flexibility, strategic importance, legal and regulatory requirements, and economic conditions to make an informed decision.
- Technology has had a profound impact on the make-or-buy decision. Companies are now able to make more informed decisions about whether to produce goods or services in-house or purchase them from an external supplier, thanks to advances in automation, e-commerce, globalization, data analytics, and supply chain management.
- A break-even chart has proven to be a useful tool for companies in make-or-buy decisions as it allows them to compare the costs of both options and make informed decisions about which option is more cost-effective. By considering both fixed and variable costs, the break-even chart provides a comprehensive view of the cost implications of each option. In conclusion, the use of a break-even chart has been shown to be an effective tool for making make-or-buy decisions in various industries.

2.9 FUTURE SCOPE

Future directions in make-or-buy decision research could include the integration of additional variables such as delivery time, product quality, and the impact on the company's overall supply chain. Additionally, considering new technologies such as advanced automation and 3D printing could impact the cost–benefit analysis of making versus buying a product.

KEYWORDS

- **make-or-buy decision strategy**
- **procurement**
- **supply chain management**
- **decision making**

REFERENCES

Al-Tabbaa, O. Make-or-Buy Decision: A Review of the Literature. *Int. J. Prod. Res.* **2018,** *56* (7), 2111–2126. https://doi.org/10.1080/00207543.2017.1395161

Chawla, D.; Gupte, P. Outsourcing Decisions: An Empirical Study of Indian Firms. *Int. J. Inf. Technol. Bus. Manag.* **2009,** *8* (1), 1–16.

Chen, Y. R.; Paulraj, A. Strategic Outsourcing: A Review and Future Directions. *Int. J. Manag. Rev.* **2004,** *6* (1), 47–61.

Choi, T. Y.; Hartley, J. L. The Impact of External and Internal Factors on the Make-or-Buy Decision. *J. Supply Chain Manag.* **1996,** *32* (3), 46–56.

Cohen, S.; Roussel, J. Make-or-Buy Decisions in Manufacturing Firms. *Int. J. Prod. Econ.* **1989,** *18* (1), 25–37.

Dekker, R.; Javalgi, R. G. The Impact of Make-or-Buy Decisions on Firm Financial Performance: An Empirical Analysis. *J. Bus. Econ. Res.* **2018,** *16* (6), 567–576. https://doi.org/10.19030/jber.v16i6.10423

Dyer, J. H. Quality, Time, and Cost Trade-Offs in Make-or-Buy Decisions. *Acad. Manag. J.* **1986,** *29* (2), 275–291.

Ellram, L. M.; Li, Y. The Make-or-Buy Decision: An Empirical Study. *Int. J. Purch. Mater. Manag.* **1998a,** *34* (1), 16–22.

Ellram, L. M.; Li, Y. Factors Influencing Make or Buy Decisions in US and Chinese Manufacturing Firms. *Int. J. Purch. Mater. Manag.* **1998b,** *34* (2), 2–8.

Ellram, L. M.; Tate, W. L. Characteristics of Firms Using Outsourcing. *J. Supply Chain Manag.* **1996,** *32* (3), 16–22.

Hamel, G.; Prahalad, C. K. In *Strategic Intent*; Harvard Business Review, 1989; vol *67* (3), pp 63–76.

Hayes, R. H.; Wheelwright, S. C. In *Restoring our Competitive Edge: Competing Through Manufacturing*; John Wiley & Sons: New York, NY, 1984.

Hitt, M. A.; Ireland, R. D.; Hoskisson, R. E. In *Strategic Management: Concepts and Cases: Competitiveness and Globalization*; Houghton Mifflin: Boston, MA.

Javalgi, R. G.; White, D. S. The Impact of Political and Cultural Factors on the Make-or-Buy Decision. *Int. J. Purch. Mater. Manag.* **1993,** *29* (1), 2–9.

Kato, M.; Takahashi, K. The Use of Break-Even Charts in the Japanese Automotive Industry. *Int. J. Automot. Technol. Manag.* **2011,** *11* (2), 127–142.

Kaufman, G. F.; Hotchkiss, J. The Strategic Management of the Make-or-Buy Decision. *Bus. Horiz.* **2018,** *61* (4), 459–468.

Kerns, C. Outsourcing and Offshoring in a Global Economy. *Manag. Res. News* **2006a,** *29* (6), 450–459.

Kerns, C. Outsourcing Logistics Functions: Key Considerations and Decision Factors. *Int. J. Phys. Distrib. Logist. Manag.* **2006b,** *36* (1), 47–62.

Kerns, C. D. Make or Buy Decisions: A Review of the Literature and Implications for Future Research. *J. Supply Chain Manag.* **2006c,** *42* (4), 5–17. https://doi.org/10.1111/j.1745-493X.2006.tb00192.x

Kopczak, L. R.; Prabhu, J. C. Make-or-Buy Decisions in the Public Sector. *Public Adm. Rev.* **2019,** *79* (5), 833–844. https://doi.org/10.1111/puar.13143

Lambert, D. M.; Cooper, M. C. Issues in Outsourcing. *Int. J. Phys. Distrib. Logist. Manag.* **2000a,** *30* (4), 286–306.

Lambert, D. M.; Cooper, M. C. Issues in Supply Chain Management. *Ind. Mark. Manag.* **2000b,** *29* (1), 65–83.

Lambert, D. M.; Cooper, M. C. Issues in Make-or-Buy Decisions. *Int. J. Purch. Mater. Manag.* **2000c,** *36* (2), 2–12.

Lambert, D. M.; Stock, J. R. In *Strategic Logistics Management*, 5th Ed.; Cengage Learning: Boston, MA, 2017.

Lee, H. L.; Billington, C. The Make-or-Buy Decision in Strategic Supplier Selection. *Int. J. Purch. Mater. Manag.* **1992,** *28* (2), 2-10.

Li, R.; Rong, X.; Han, H. The Use of Break-Even Charts in the Chinese Manufacturing Industry. *J. Manuf. Operat. Manag.* **2019,** *21* (4), 231–240.

Liu, J.; Wang, Q.; Gao, Y.; Chen, J. A Comprehensive Review of the Make-or-Buy Decision: A Supply Chain Management Perspective. *Front. Bus. Res. China* **2021,** *15* (1), 1–32. https://doi.org/10.1186/s11782-021-00172-y

Peng, Y.; Liang, H. The Impact of Internal and External Factors on the Make-or-Buy Decision. *Int. J. Prod. Econ.* **2018,** *194*, 8–16. https://doi.org/10.1016/j.ijpe.2017.07.022

Porter, M. E. In *Competitive Advantage: Creating and Sustaining Superior Performance*; Free Press: New York, NY, 1985.

Schonsleben, P. In-House Production Versus Outsourcing: A Review of the Literature. *Int. J. Oper. Prod. Manag.* **2002a,** *22* (2), 195–214. https://doi.org/10.1108/01443570210412918

Schonsleben, P. Make-or-Buy Decisions in German SMEs: An Empirical Investigation. *Eur. Manag. J.* **2002b**.

Simchi-Levi, D.; Kaminsky, P.; Simchi-Levi, E. In *Designing and Managing the Supply Chain: Concepts, Strategies, and Cases*, 3rd Ed.; McGraw-Hill Education: New York, NY, 2015.

Tersine, R. J. In *Principles of Supply Chain Management: A Balanced Approach*, 3rd Ed.; South-Western Cengage Learning: Mason, OH, 2014.

Wang, Y.; Li, X. The Impact of Technology on the Make-or-Buy Decision. J. *Supply Chain Manag.* **2020,** *56* (2), 72–79.

Wang, Y.; Lu, Y.; Liu, Y.; Huang, J. The Impact of Make-or-Buy Decisions on Firm Performance: Evidence from China. *Int. J. Procurement Manag.* **2018,** *11* (1), 25–49. https://doi.org/10.1504/IJPM.2018.093906

Zhang, Q.; Dilts, D. A. A Strategic Decision Model for the Make-or-Buy Decision. *Int. J. Oper. Prod. Manag.* **2004,** *24* (7), 773–794.

Zhang, X.; Huang, X. The Impact of Make-or-Buy Decision on Supply Chain Performance: Evidence from the Chinese Electronics Industry. *Int. J. Inf. Manag.* **2017,** *37* (1), 54–64. https://doi.org/10.1016/j.ijinfomgt.2017.04.001.

CHAPTER 3

The Role of Industry 4.0 Software Tools in Creating Sustainable Supply Chain Management in Emerging Markets

KETAN RATHOR

GyanSys Inc., Carmel, IN, United States

ABSTRACT

In the context of Industry 4.0, sustainable supply chain management may be one of the technology applications that drives the industry's development; however, it is also one of the most significant barriers to the sector's performance in terms of its competitiveness, environmental impact, and social impact. A future picture of the production system is "Industry 4.0," also known as the "Fourth Industrial Revolution." With the intention of raising the overall degree of automation found within the manufacturing sector, the German government initially suggested and then embraced the concept of Industry 4.0 in the year 2011. In order to make the world a more sustainable place, the objective of the Fourth Industrial Revolution, also known as Industry 4.0, is to fully automate and link all of the systems that are a part of the manufacturing process. The Internet of Things (IoT) is the only example of a technology that may be disruptive. This means that all components of the supply chain are now online and share data in real time. IoT is composed of a combination of a wide range of computer hardware and software, including a variety of sensors, networks, algorithmic frameworks, and application programs (IoT). With the assistance of the IoT, businesses may be able to improve their levels of production and simplify their supply chains.

Essentials of Supply Chain Management: Strategy, Planning and Operations.
Mohammed Majeed, Abdul-Rasheed Akeji Alhassan Alolo, Seidu Alhassan, and S. Sekar (Eds.)

The innovations of today have profound impact, not just on the day-to-day lives of individuals but also on the very fabric of our civilization as a whole. Changes in the climate, loss of resources as a result of increasing output, and waste generated by industries are only some of the environmental challenges that have been brought on by Industry 4.0. The current research aims to show how Industry 4.0 might affect the functioning of a sustainable supply chain and the advantages it could bring about. Individuals, nongovernmental organizations, and governments have banded together to demand that businesses modify how they run their supply chains in order to better adhere to the sustainability principle of "filling today's requirements without sacrificing the capacity of future generations to meet their own needs." At first, a high-level summary of the three major industrial revolutions and an explanation of the fourth iteration of industry were provided.

The present age, which was brought about by advancements in dynamic data processing and cyber-physical systems that link the actual world to the web, has resulted in value chains being connected from the very beginning to the very end. Formerly human-managed functions in "smart factories" are being taken over by robots instead, including production scheduling and inventory management, for example. The fundamental objective of this line of study is to get an understanding of the relevance of Industry 4.0 software tools in the development of sustainable supply chain management in developing countries such as India. The findings of this study emphasize many critical components of sustainable development, including the preservation of the environment, increased collaboration and integration of supply chain systems, and decision-making that is driven by data.

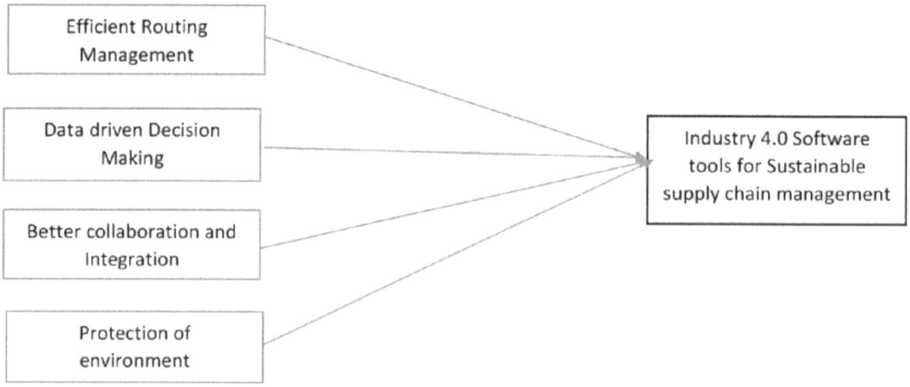

FIGURE 3.1 Conceptual model.

3.1 INTRODUCTION

The most significant advantages that have resulted from the digitalization of processes in recent years have been for private, professional, and creative endeavors. The manufacturing sector is one of the most essential sectors that must be successful for Industry 4.0 to be implemented. The usage of this information is very beneficial to the choices about investment, production, costs, marketing, and distribution. In addition to this, it improves both the performance of processes and the efficiency of activities throughout supply chains, which ultimately leads to improved resource utilization optimization (Legenvre, 2020). This helps to outline a new paradigm for the industrial revolution. Implementing practices of circular economies and operating under moral principles that direct the chain's participants in what and how to maintain value and reciprocity relationships in order to gain a competitive edge in the global market are central to the sustainable supply chain management's optimization of resource consumption.

Industry 4.0 is an initiative that combines infrastructure design and technical improvements to allow the interconnection and integration of processes. At its core, sustainable regional supply chain performance is at the center of this initiative. Those industries that have not yet adopted these innovations will face increasing disadvantages in the global competitive landscape, while industrial ecosystems that are committed to the initiatives of Industry 4.0 will thrive. As more industries adopt these innovations, those that have not yet done so will face increasing disadvantages in the global competitive landscape. Because of the burden that this places on both industrial organizations and the countries in which they operate, it is important to determine what is preventing the full adoption of these technological advancements in order to boost logistics and commercial performance. This will allow for greater efficiency in both areas. Because of the constantly changing nature of the system, it is common knowledge that not all manufacturing organizations are now in a position to apply technology 4.0 at the same time (Yavas, 2020). From the commencement of the industrial revolution, companies have placed an emphasis on maximizing their profits as their primary objective. In the early days of industrialization, increasing production alone was all that was necessary to increase profits since there was such a huge demand for goods and there was so little competition. Yet in the years that have passed since then, quite a bit has changed (Bag et al., 2018). Several companies are searching for cost-cutting strategies in order to raise their profitability in the face of increasing competition and a corresponding increase in the number of suppliers available to satisfy customer demand. This is because there are now more suppliers available to fulfill customer demand. When undercutting the competition only via lower pricing was not enough, more flexible production processes were developed, and new management practices were used in order to further reduce costs, while simultaneously increasing production flexibility and quality. Since then, companies that are part of the supply chain often collaborate, making use of technology and making purposeful attempts to increase both their productivity and their profits (Chalmeta, 2020).

The influence that modern society has had on the natural environment has a number of repercussions, one of which is climate change. The increased use of natural resources has led to a growth in the amount of trash produced by industries, which has prompted reactions from people, nongovernmental organizations, governments, and enterprises alike (Gupta et al., 2020). As a result of the development of systems that can satisfy an endless amount of demand, it is no longer practical to manage activities in the supply chain with simply financial objectives in mind. As the world struggles to keep up with its present demands (Palladino et al., 2020). These issues have recently gained prominence as the world struggles to keep up with its present demands. As a result, companies have begun placing a higher priority on the environmentally friendly aspects of sustainability.

In order to accomplish monetary, ecological, and social goals, sustainable supply chain management must cater to the requirements of all parties involved in the chain's production and distribution, beginning with the producers and ending with the customers (Osterrieder et al., 2020). The term "supply chain" refers to the whole process, beginning with the conception of an idea and continuing through the procurement of raw materials, the production of completed items, distribution, consumption, and finally disposal. New regulations are being passed that are in line with concerns about carbon emissions, ecological footprints, and other issues of a similar kind in order to prevent pollution that is the result of inappropriate waste management and recycling programs (Yadav et al., 2020). The concept of Industry 4.0 centers on the integration of digital infrastructure with more conventional methods of production. This approach for industrial integration involves a great deal more than just the internal automation of value chains as an element of its scope. This system is both intelligent and adaptable since all of the actions that take place along the value chain are interacting with one another and adapting to one another in real time. It will be possible to integrate environmentally friendly management procedures all the way through the supply chain if the concept of Industry 4.0 is updated to include the most cutting-edge technological advancements (Manavalan and Jayakrishna, 2019).

Smart factories are able to maintain a continuous flow of products because the interdependence of their automated equipment and the storage of crucial data by sensors makes it possible for them to do so. Companies have been sluggish to accept this notion because they have struggled to locate the proper integrated solution that would give them with a larger return (Wang et al., 2020). This has caused the adoption rate to be slower than it otherwise would have been. Unmanned aerial delivery, sometimes known as "drone" delivery, is a concept that has applications in the last mile of supply chain delivery. This idea comes under the purview of Industry 4.0 and is sometimes referred to as "drone" delivery. The problem of city logistics, which entails the movement of goods inside a metropolis, may be helped by the development of this new piece of technology, which may be of assistance to companies (Bai et al., 2020). The traditional means of automobile distribution are being phased out in favor of delivery through unmanned aircraft. Deliveries that are not only effective but also kind to the environment have emerged as a top focus for a variety of businesses. Customers who purchase products from Amazon with a total weight that does not exceed 5 kg are eligible for the new 30-min delivery option. Companies like as Google and DHL are exerting a lot of effort to deliver this technology to the market as soon as possible. The German manufacturing industry has been an early user of these technologies, and numerous companies, notably Volkswagen, BMW, and Daimler, have started to effectively implement and utilize them in their products (Raj et al., 2020).

The governments of several nations, such as India, have started programs such as "Made in India" in an effort to increase output via sectoral digitalization In today's economy, which is more linked on a worldwide scale, businesses are coming under growing pressure to prioritize sustainable development from the perspectives of economics, ecology, and society. As a strategic and competitive advantage, organizations actively endeavor to strengthen the long-term viability of their business operations (Palmaccio et al., 2021). It is for this reason that it is of the utmost importance that digital manufacturing systems enable firms to innovate and be environmentally responsible. These are two aspects that are generally accepted as being the driving forces behind the rise of the global economy. As a result, manufacturers of all sizes are working to develop solutions that will make the environmental impact of their manufacturing processes much lower. Nevertheless, the level of knowledge and skills that are now accessible is not adequate to properly integrate sustainability into the process of supply chain management. The production of greenhouse gases has a pattern of increasing in line with the advancement of technology (Weking et al., 2020). A direct result of this is a quickening of the warming of the planet. Yet, the broad use of these cutting-edge technologies helps solve the difficulties associated to sustainability by reducing the amount of time needed for lead times and maximizing the use of all resources that are accessible (Meneghello et al., 2019).

Over the course of the last 10 years, some of the most innovative companies in the world have been exploring the potential benefits of digitally transforming conventional manufacturing companies. Research into the advances was also required because of the potentially enormous influence they may have on the market. The implementation of these technologies into the distribution network poses a substantial obstacle for companies operating in the manufacturing industry. Yet, a number of studies have previously broken out what "Industry 4.0" is, what its fundamental principles are, and how those ideas connect to preexisting industrial organizations.

3.2 LITERATURE REVIEW

The goal of the "Industry 4.0" initiative is to integrate digital technology into manufacturing processes that are already well-established. This kind of industrial integration goes far beyond the simple automation of enterprises since it is both intelligent and has the capacity to improve itself over time. As a direct result of this, it ensures that connections at all points throughout the value chain are kept active and current at all times. The eventual result of implementing Industry 4.0 will be to have completely automated factories that are continually interacting with one another and coordinating the activities of their many machinery, integrated computer systems, and sensors (Feng, 2020). If robots and computers could simultaneously share data and make choices, manufacturing would use less time, energy, raw materials, and labor to produce bigger quantities of better quality things, while at the same time creating higher quality goods at a higher volume. It is possible to discover where an item came from by using either its one-of-a-kind serial number or any other identifying information. The internet always provides access to the tools as well as the final goods that are used in the manufacturing process of these items. They will be equipped with sensors that allow them to react properly to their surroundings, and they will be able to communicate in real time with other Internet-connected devices situated anywhere on the planet (Bezai et al., 2021). When it is fully implemented, the Fourth Industrial Revolution will have an effect not only on individuals and society as a whole, but also on factories, industries, and all other kinds of enterprises. Because Industry 4.0 was responsible for making these advancements possible, we owe it a tremendous lot of gratitude.

Because of the Internet of Things (IoT), machines and other cyber-physical systems now have access to distributed databases that include information about suppliers, manufacturers, and distributors (Mani et al., 2018). As a result of this, it is now feasible to link all of the stages of the supply chain. By way of illustration, owing to the IoT, depleted raw material stockpiles for a product may be automatically refilled from sources located in other countries. This ensures that a quantity of raw materials that is estimated, used in an appropriate manner, and utilized effectively throughout the production process. There is yet another illustration of this in the realm of business. It discusses how the internet and other services are being included in the manufacturing process as well as the distribution of finished products (Govindan et al., 2020).

Processing techniques are required for the analysis of large data collections. The term "big data" refers to data sets that are either too extensive or too complicated to be adequately analyzed using the methods that are more traditionally used. The day-to-day operations of an organization are susceptible to being impacted by a variety of outside factors. There are several examples, some of which include production logs, financial accounts, and studies based on market research (Sony and Naik, 2020). Nontraditional sources such as the Internet, search engines, social media, and the sensors integrated into smart things (in part because of the IoT) are some examples of where we may now get the information that is necessary for us to make choices (e.g., Google, Facebook, and Twitter). Big data is a word that is used to describe the massive quantities of data that have been lately collected and stored from a variety of kinds of digital media. These data are referred to as "big" data. As a consequence of developments in information technology and declining prices associated with data storage, an increasing number of individuals are ingesting and analyzing enormous amounts of data. While doing strategic planning and evaluation, having the ability to anticipate fluctuations in consumer demand via the analysis of enormous data sets may be valuable.

3.3 ROBOTICS

Robots are adaptable robots that can move or remain still under the supervision of prestored computer programs in their onboard processors. These programs are run by the robots' onboard processors. It is possible that the software created by humans and already installed on robots holds the key to solving their difficulties. Intelligent robots, on the other hand, may alter their programming in response to the lessons that they have gained from the mistakes that they have made. In addition, students often provide fresh points of view and methods for approaching problems that need to be solved (Mangla et al., 2018).

Make sure that both the horizontal and the vertical axis of integration are considered: for the vertical integration concept of Industry 4.0 to be put into practice, all machines, workstations, computers, and other pieces of production equipment, in addition to all of the company's internal business operations, need to be connected to one another and able to communicate in both directions (including product design, procurement, production, marketing, and distribution, among other things). Companies in the value chain should engage in horizontal integration, which entails digitally coordinating their production and planning processes with those of other companies in the value chain, in order to ensure that all unnecessary steps are removed and flow is optimized. This can be accomplished by coordinating their production and planning procedures with those of other companies in the value chain. The successful operation of the value chain will be ensured as a result of this (Culot et al., 2020). The procedure of developing a product that functions as a whole entity is referred to as "whole engineering." Connecting the digital engineering systems used in the factory with those used by other stakeholders, including the end users, requires the usage of interfaces and systems that are analogous to those used by those stakeholders. Integration on both the vertical and the horizontal planes might be incorporated in an alternative formulation.

3.4 CLOUD COMPUTING

Due of computing in the "cloud," a company's information may be kept privately and safely on a distant server and accessible from any location in the world with an Internet connection. Hackers have the ability to target gadgets that are linked to the internet. Each and every financial transaction is secured using encryption, and only authorized computers are permitted to access to the network. There is a level of cyber-security risk associated with both horizontal and vertical integration techniques, especially with respect to the theft or manipulation of personal or commercial data and information.

Cyber-interventions in manufacturing processes and equipment also pose a threat since they might result in a halt in output or perhaps the cessation of all manufacturing altogether.

It is essential for supply chains that are committed to sustainability to pay particular attention to the design of their goods in order to guarantee that the manufacturing process does not include the use of any chemicals that are hazardous to either human or environmental health. Since the product has a lengthy lifetime, less of the resources that go into making it will be wasted after they have accomplished their function. It is very necessary for these raw materials and their suppliers to adhere to the 6R principles. This is especially the case in terms of reuse and remanufacturing. Reducing the total quantity of material used in manufacturing and packaging is just as important as making use of environmentally friendly items. Redesign projects reduce the negative effects of production on the environment by reusing resources that are already in use.

It will be possible to monitor the state of a product at every step of its manufacturing and distribution with the help of IoT, a technology that is part of the Industry 4.0 initiative. This will make it much simpler to adopt 6 Sigma and other practices that are analogous to it. Creating intelligent objects that are able to connect with one another across the IoT calls for further thought. By the use of simulation, one is able to evaluate the compatibility of materials with the practices as well as their impact on human health and the environment. Because of the horizontal and vertical integration, information about the design of products that comply with the standard may be supplied to internal processes. Sharing one's knowledge about one's own design processes with other partners in the supply chain helps to ensure the effectiveness of sustainability components that can be performed with closed-cycle product life cycles, such as reduction and reuse. Integration on both the horizontal and the vertical planes necessitates the use of precursor technologies such as cloud computing, big data, and analytics in order to guarantee the confidentiality of all data that is exchanged.

3.5 GATHERING DATA AND INFORMATION FROM DECISION-MAKING

Acquiring, shopping, and gathering information: Throughout the stages of sourcing and procurement, it is essential for a sustainable supply chain to choose suppliers that engage in environmentally friendly production practices and make use of environmentally friendly products. When it comes to procuring raw materials and components, it is best to utilize techniques that are favorable to the environment, and the same can be said for the manufacturing process itself. The highest priority should be placed on machines and systems that reduce waste, electricity consumption, and emissions of carbon dioxide. It is crucial to put the 6 Sigma concepts at the center of your decision-making when it comes to making purchases. For example, if raw materials and supplies are recovered, recycled, or reused, this may prolong the product's lifetime while simultaneously reducing the total resource consumption and waste production of the supply chain as a whole. In order to advance the cause of social sustainability, businesses should be selected based on their ability to meet the sustainability standards for working conditions, and the terms of the contracts for purchasing goods and services should make specific reference to the working conditions of the workforce.

Integration of technology from the Fourth Industrial Revolution in both horizontal and vertical directions has a significant impact on the performance of sustainability measures throughout the procurement process. If suppliers are subjected to frequent monitoring of both the safety of the raw materials used and the things produced, as well as the safety of the working circumstances of the workers who make those items, then the suppliers may be compelled to improve their own working conditions in order to satisfy the requirements of the monitoring. It is possible that the use of technology for additive manufacturing might assist economically developing nations by enabling commerce with suppliers who were previously inaccessible. Businesses will be able to assess a broad range of possible suppliers and resources thanks to the use of big data and analytics. This will enable the firms to make choices that are more economically sound and will result in cost savings. Vertically integrated manufacturers will be able to inform their horizontally integrated suppliers of the time and amount of the needed material by keeping track of raw material and supply utilization in real time through the IoT. This will allow horizontally integrated suppliers to operate with less stock and speed up delivery times. Vertically integrated manufacturers will be able to inform their suppliers of the time and amount of the needed material.

Researchers intend to maximize the environmental element of supply chain sustainability by thinking up and implementing techniques and technologies that minimize waste output, energy use, and raw material utilization. This will allow us to maximize the sustainability of the supply chain. The decreased use of resources like energy, raw materials, and supplies will bring about cost reductions, which will be beneficial to the enterprise as a whole. The management of production in the vast majority of supply chains is primarily focused with either boosting productivity or cutting expenditures, with little consideration for the health and safety of the people who are actually carrying out the work. As part of the social pillar of sustainability, efforts are made to increase access for employees to things like fair pay, safe working conditions, and health safeguards. In order to ensure the continued viability of society over the long term, it is imperative that all members of society have access to equal work opportunities, regardless of criteria such as gender, age, or any other personal traits. While developing their industrial workforces, companies should keep in mind the requirement to offer diverse social groups with equal job opportunities, fair pay, and other social rights. This obligation should be a priority for businesses. For the nation as a whole to have sustainable development economically, the distribution of income and chances for employment must be equitable.

Now that we have intelligent robots and automated production lines, potentially dangerous industrial processes that would have previously put people in risk may be carried out without the need for human involvement. Because of this, reducing the amount of wasted resources is one of the most significant things that can be done to safeguard the environment. Businesses are able to adapt production and are ready for expected fluctuations in demand with the help of real-time data from smart industrial applications. This enables firms to substantially reduce the amount of stock they have on hand. Because of advancements in additive manufacturing technology, it is becoming more unnecessary to complete all stages of production in a single site. This might result in some manufacturing being relocated to less developed regions or countries.

3.6 BETTER DISTRIBUTION

The distribution function of the supply chain is responsible for the shipment of products and services from the various suppliers to the various production facilities and then from the manufacturing facilities to the various distributors, retailers, consumers, and end users. One of the most useful functions is making sure that products are distributed through supply chains that are beneficial to the environment. Traditional supply chains prioritize cost reduction by selecting the method of distribution that results in the least amount of environmental damage. In contrast, sustainable supply networks place a higher priority on finding solutions that will have the opposite effect. Driving in a way that is less harmful to the environment should be a top concern since there is a clear link between the kind of gas used in automobiles and the amount of damage they do to the environment. Since the number of distribution trips has a direct influence on the amount of gasoline that is used, many participants in the supply chain utilize mathematical models for precise planning in order to reduce the total number of distribution trips.

The IoT enables the whole distribution network to maintain visibility over all of the resources and components that will be put to use. Because of horizontal integration and cloud computing, all of the partners in a distribution chain now have access to the data, which enables businesses to make use of distribution channels. Since these technologies allow the simultaneous interchange of data on demand and production at all stages of the supply chain, it is now possible to both anticipate and factor future needs into distribution planning. This was previously impossible. There is a possibility that cyber-physical systems, such as the navigational software that is put in delivery trucks, may be able to cut down on the amount of time that is spent traveling.

The client was successful in transitioning the supply chain from one based on conventional practices to one that is sustainable by requiring sustainable business practices throughout all stages of the product's life cycle. Customers have the ability to play an important role in the policing of unsustainable business practices in the supply chain by choosing to purchase only products that are made with nonhazardous materials, remaining loyal to brands that are committed to social sustainability practices such as providing decent working conditions and avoiding companies that use processes that are in question.

3.7 DISCUSSION

This section involved in presenting the critical analysis based on the data sourced from the respondents, the focus of the study is to understand the importance of using Industry 4.0 tools in creating sustainable supply chain management in emerging markets. The data are mainly sourced from the respondents who are working in supply chain industry. The analysis involves in presenting the demographic variables through frequency analysis, and further analysis is performed using tools like correlation, regression, and chi-square test.

3.7.1 *FREQUENCY ANALYSIS*

TABLE 3.1 Frequency Analysis.

Gender	**Frequency**	**Percent**
Male	95	56.9
Female	72	43.1
Age	**Frequency**	**Percent**
Less than 30 years	52	31.1
31–40 years	54	32.3
41–50 years	22	13.2
Above 50 years	39	23.4
Current position	**Frequency**	**Percent**
Lower level management	76	45.5
Middle-level management	60	35.9
Top-level management	31	18.6
Type of family	**Frequency**	**Percent**
Nuclear family	98	58.7
Joint family	69	41.3
Education	**Frequency**	**Percent**
Completed UG	77	46.1
Completed PG	39	23.4
Completed professional course	29	17.4
Others	22	13.2
Work experience	**Frequency**	**Percent**
Less than 5 years of experience	45	26.9
5–10 years	45	26.9
10 15 years	30	18
15–20 years	33	19.8
Above 20 years	14	8.4
Total	**167**	**100**

Based on analysis from Table 3.1, it is noted that nearly 56.9% were male respondents and 43.1% were female respondents, 31.1% were in the age group of less than 30 years, 32.3% were between 31 and 40 years, 13.2% were in the age group between 41 and 50 years, and 23.4% were above 50 years, 45.5% were in the lower level management, 35.9% were in middle-level management and remaining 18.6% were in top-level management.

Furthermore, it is identified that 58.7% were living in a nuclear family and the remaining 41.3% were living in a joint family, 46.1% of the sample population have completed under graduation course, 23.4% have completed postgraduation course, 17.4% have completed professional course, and remaining 13.2% have done other courses. Lastly, 26.9% were having experience of little less than five years.

3.7.2 RELIABILITY ANALYSIS

The next step in the analysis is to test whether the data are reliable and valid; for this purpose, Cronbach's alpha is used. The researcher considers four key independent variables: efficient routing management, data-driven decision-making, better collaboration, and integration and protection of environment, whereas the dependent variable is sustainable SCM.

TABLE 3.2 Test of Reliability.

Variables	Cronbach's alpha
Efficient routing management	0.859
Data-driven decision-making	0.853
Better collaboration and integration	0.833
Protection of environment	0.813
Sustainable SCM	0.842

From Table 3.2, it is noted that the value of Cronbach's alpha is more than 0.700; hence, it can be stated that the data are highly reliable and valid.

3.7.3 CORRELATION ANALYSIS

The researcher is then poised to understand the nature of relationship between independent and dependent variables for this purpose correlation analysis is applied.

Based on Table 3.3 of the correlation analysis, it is noted that all the independent variables possess a significant positive correlation toward the dependent variable. It is further noted that environment protection possesses a high positive correlation toward sustainable supply chain management with a coefficient value of 0.900, followed by decision-making with nearly 0.886, efficient routing management possesses a coefficient of 0.870 toward sustainable supply chain management, and lastly, collaboration, and integration possess a coefficient of 0.834 toward the dependent variable: sustainable supply chain management.

TABLE 3.3 Correlation Analysis.

Correlations	Efficient routing management	Decision–making	Collaboration	Environment protection	Sustainable SCM
Efficient routing management	1	0.893**	0.834**	0.948**	0.870**
Decision-making	0.893**	1	0.859**	0.944**	0.886**
Collaboration	0.834**	0.859**	1	0.895**	0.834**
Environment protection	0.948**	0.944**	0.895**	1	0.900**
Sustainable SCM	0.870**	0.886**	0.834**	0.900**	1

Note: **Correlation is significant at the 0.01 level (2-tailed).

3.7.4 *CHI-SQUARE ANALYSIS*

This section is involved in testing the hypothesis.

3.7.4.1 HYPOTHESIS 1

Null: There is no significant difference between efficient routing management and Industry 4.0 software tools for sustainable supply chain management.

TABLE 3.4 Chi-Square Analysis between Efficient Routing Management and Industry 4.0 Software Tools for Sustainable Supply Chain Management.

Efficient routing management	Value	df	P value
Pearson chi-square	312.072a	16	0.00
Phi	1.369		0.00
Cramer's *V*	0.684		0.00

Note: **Correlation is significant at the 0.01 level (2-tailed).

Based on Table 3.4, it is noted that the *P* value is 0.00. Furthermore, the value of phi is 1.36 which states that the variables possess a positive relationship, also the value of Cramer's *V* is 0.684, usually the value ranges between 0 (no association) and 1 (perfect association). Since the value is nearly 0.684, it can be stated that the association is strong among the variables; hence it can be concluded that there is a significant difference between efficient routing management and Industry 4.0 software tools for sustainable supply chain management.

3.7.4.2 *HYPOTHESIS 2*

Null: There is no significant difference between data-driven decision-making and Industry 4.0 software tools for sustainable supply chain management.

TABLE 3.5 Chi-Square Analysis between Data-Driven Decision-Making and Industry 4.0 Software Tools for Sustainable Supply Chain Management.

Data-driven decision-making	Value	df	P value
Pearson chi-square	254.739a	16	0.00
Phi	1.235		0.00
Cramer's *V*	0.618		0.00

Based on Table 3.5, it is noted that the *P* value of chi-square is 0.00; hence, the null hypothesis is rejected and the alternate hypothesis is accepted. Furthermore, the value of phi is 1.23 which states that the variables possess a positive relationship, also the value of Cramer's *V* is 0.618, usually the value ranges between 0 (no association) and 1 (perfect association). Since the value is nearly 0.618, it can be stated that the association is strong among the variables; hence, it can be concluded that there is a significant difference between data-driven decision-making and Industry 4.0 software tools for sustainable supply chain management.

3.7.4.3 *HYPOTHESIS 3*

Null: There is no significant difference between better collaboration and integration and Industry 4.0 software tools for sustainable supply chain management.

TABLE 3.6 Chi-Square Analysis between Better Collaboration and Integration and Industry 4.0 Software Tools for Sustainable Supply Chain Management.

Better collaboration and integration	Value	df	P value
Pearson chi-square	216.982a	16	0.00
Phi	1.14		0.00
Cramer's *V*	0.57		0.00

Note: ** Correlation is significant at the 0.01 level (2-tailed).

Based on Table 3.6, it is noted that the *P* value of chi-square is 0.00; hence, null hypothesis is rejected and alternate hypothesis is accepted.

Furthermore, the value of phi is 1.14 which states that the variables possess a positive relationship, also the value of Cramer's *V* is 0.570, usually the value ranges between 0 (no association) and 1 (perfect association). Since the value is nearly 0.570, it can be stated that the association is strong among the variables; hence, it can be concluded that there is a significant difference between better collaboration and integration and Industry 4.0 software tools for sustainable supply chain management.

3.7.4.4 HYPOTHESIS 4

Null: There is no significant difference between protection of environment and integration and Industry 4.0 software tools for sustainable supply chain management.

TABLE 3.7 Chi-Square Analysis between Protection of Environment and Industry 4.0 Software Tools for Sustainable Supply Chain Management.

Protection of environment	Value	df	P value
Pearson chi-square	379.606a	16	0.00
Phi	1.508		0.00
Cramer's *V*	0.754		0.00

Note: **Correlation is significant at the 0.01 level (2-tailed).

Based on Table 3.7, it is noted that the *P* value of chi-square is 0.00; hence, null hypothesis is rejected and alternate hypothesis is accepted. Furthermore, the value of phi is 1.50 which states that the variables possess a positive relationship, also the value of Cramer's *V* is 0.754, usually the value ranges between 0 (no association) and 1 (perfect association). Since the value is nearly 0.754, it can be stated that the association is strong among the variables; hence, it can be concluded that there is a significant difference between protection of environment and Industry 4.0 software tools for sustainable supply chain management.

3.8 IMPLICATIONS

Industry 4.0 is bringing a variety of benefits to businesses thanks to the digitization of activities involved in supply chains. It is possible that the findings of this analysis will be beneficial to researchers, lawmakers, and the administration of corporations. According to the published research, the SC process is still being automated and the vast majority of businesses, especially small and medium-sized firms (SMEs), are resistant to change. In order to assist companies in making the transition from a traditional to a digital supply chain, managers are required to provide guidance and instruction to their task forces, employees, and workers. Companies should collaborate with educational institutions such as universities and research institutes in order to get knowledge about the possible technological breakthroughs that may make SC processes viable. This report should be read in its entirety if Industry 4.0 has not yet been implemented at your organization. This article provides a framework that managers and policymakers may use to understand the purpose of technology related to Industry 4.0 at different points throughout the supply chain.

3.9 CONCLUSIONS

Consolidating sustainable supply chains requires management in which public–private support mechanisms are reflected in territorial and individual-level policies and financing options, as well as a better understanding of the benefits of technological applications related to Industry 4.0 and the significance of exchange and collaboration for more efficient utilization of the capabilities and resources of the various actors. In addition, a better understanding of the benefits of Industry 4.0 technological applications is required. A sustainable supply chain can improve its economic, environmental, and social performance by enhancing its coordination, delivery, error reduction, and waste prevention, as well as by developing ethical practices in which transparency, collaboration, and data traceability are prioritized, and by incorporating gap aware practices. The use of technology 4.0 into the process of managing the sustainability of supply chains highlights a distinction.

3.10 FUTURE STUDIES

In spite of the fact that it is helpful, a systematic evaluation of the relevant literature has critical limitations that need to be taken into consideration. The academic journals were the only sources that were considered for the literature review in this work; however, the research may have also included conference papers and books. In addition, the scope of this inquiry is limited to only five different breakthroughs related to Industry 4.0. A wide array of resources, such as the online databases ScienceDirect, IEEE Explore, and Scholar, are used to compile the data that is used in this study. Yet, there is a possibility that significant articles were missed since they were not included in the database search. This might have been a significant oversight. The selection of keywords used in the publication is another shortcoming, since it may have required researchers to limit the scope of their search. Other criteria for the selection of keywords may be used in future studies in order to locate material that is both more comprehensive and relevant. The gathering of manuscripts may also make use of several other databases, such as Scopus and Web of Sciences. It is possible that the amount of time spent on literature reviews by future researchers will be a role in driving this process. Big data, blockchain, and RFID are three other examples of Industry 4.0 technologies that have the potential to be used in the supply chain in the near future. Developing countries, where SMEs represent the backbone of the economy, may be the focus of future research that investigates the framework in context and looks at context-specific applications. We have shown that proprietors of small and medium-sized companies do not consider Industry 4.0 to be an indication of long-term prosperity.

KEYWORDS

- **sustainable supply chain management**
- **data-driven decision-making**
- **routing management**
- **chi-square analysi**

REFERENCES

Bag, S.; Telukdarie, A.; Pretorius, J.; Gupta, S. Industry 4.0 and Supply Chain Sustainability: Framework and Future Research Directions. *Benchmarking Int. J.* **2018,** *28*, 1410–1450.

Bai, C.; Dallasega, P.; Orzes, G.; Sarkis, J. Industry 4.0 Technologies Assessment: A Sustainability Perspective. *Int. J. Prod. Econ.* **2020,** *229*, 107776.

Bezai, N. E.; Medjdoub, B.; Al-Habaibeh, A.; Chalal, M. L.; Fadli, F. Future Cities and Autonomous Vehicles: Analysis of the Barriers to Full Adoption. *Energy Built Environ.* **2021,** *2*, 65–68.

Chalmeta, R.; Santos-Deleón, N. J. Sustainable Supply Chain in the Era of Industry 4.0 and Big Data: A Systematic Analysis of Literature and Research. *Sustainability* **2020,** *12*, 4108

Culot, G.; Nassimbeni, G.; Orzes, G.; Sartor, M. Behind the Definition of Industry 4.0: Analysis and Open Questions. *Int. J. Prod. Econ.* **2020,** *226*, 107617.

Feng, L. Integration of Industry 4.0 Related Technologies in Construction Industry: A Framework of Cyber-Physical System. *IEEE Access* **2020,** *8*, 122908–122922.

Govindan, K.; Rajeev, A.; Padhi, S. S.; Pati, R. K. Supply Chain Sustainability and Performance of Firms: A Meta-Analysis of the Literature. *Transp. Res. E Logist. Transp. Rev.* **2020,** *137*, 101923.

Gupta, R.; Tanwar, S.; Kumar, N.; Tyagi, S. Blockchain-Based Security Attack Resilience Schemes for Autonomous Vehicles in Industry 4.0: A Systematic Review. *Comput. Electr. Eng.* **2020,** *86*, 106717.

Legenvre, H.; Henke, M.; Ruile, H. Making Sense of the Impact of the Internet of Things on Purchasing and Supply Management: A Tension Perspective. *J. Purch. Supply Manag.* **2020,** *26*, 100596.

Manavalan, E.; Jayakrishna, K. A Review of Internet of Things (IoT) Embedded Sustainable Supply Chain for Industry 4.0 Requirements. *Comput. Ind. Eng.* **2019,** *127*, 925–953.

Mangla, S. K.; Luthra, S.; Rich, N.; Kumar, D.; Rana, N. P.; Dwivedi, Y. K. Enablers to Implement Sustainable Initiatives in Agri-Food Supply Chains. *Int. J. Prod. Econ.* **2018,** *203*, 379–393.

Mani, V.; Gunasekaran, A.; Delgado, C. Enhancing Supply Chain Performance through Supplier Social Sustainability: An Emerging Economy Perspective. *Int. J. Prod. Econ.* **2018,** *195*, 259–272.

Meneghello, F.; Calore, M.; Zucchetto, D.; Polese, M.; Zanella, A. Internet of Threats? A Survey of Practical Security Vulnerabilities in Real IoT Devices. *IEEE Internet Things J.* **2019,** *6*, 8182–8201.

Osterrieder, P.; Budde, L.; Friedli, T. The Smart Factory as a Key Construct of Industry 4.0: A Systematic Literature Review. *Int. J. Prod. Econ.* **2020,** *221*, 10747.

Palladino, R.; Hassan, R.; Escobar, O. Artificial Intelligence and Business Models in the Sustainable Development Goals Perspective: A Systematic Literature Review. *J. Bus. Res.* **2020,** *121*, 283–314.

Palmaccio, M.; Dicuonzo, G.; Belyaeva, Z. S. The Internet of Things and Corporate Business Models: A Systematic Literature Review. *J. Bus. Res.* **2021,** *131*, 610–618.

Raj, A.; Dwivedi, G.; Sharma, A.; Jabbour, A. B. L. D. S.; Rajak, S. Barriers to the Adoption of Industry 4.0 Technologies in the Manufacturing Sector: An Inter-Country Comparative Perspective. *Int. J. Prod. Econ.* **2020,** *224*, 107546.

Sony, M.; Naik, S. Industry 4.0 Integration with Socio-Technical Systems Theory: A Systematic Review and Proposed Theoretical Model. *Technol. Soc.* **2020,** *61*, 101248.

Wang, J.; Lim, M. K.; Zhan, Y.; Wang, X. An Intelligent Logistics Service System for Enhancing Dispatching Operations in an IoT Environment. *Transp. Res. E Logist. Transp. Rev.* **2020,** *135*, 101886.

Weking, J.; Stöcker, M.; Kowalkiewicz, M.; Böhm, M.; Krcmar, H. Leveraging Industry 4.0—A Business Model Pattern Framework. *Int. J. Prod. Econ.* **2020,** *225*, 107588.

Yadav, G.; Luthra, S.; Jakhar, S. K.; Mangla, S. K.; Rai, D. P. A Framework to Overcome Sustainable Supply Chain Challenges through Solution Measures of Industry 4.0 and Circular Economy: An Automotive Case. *J. Clean. Prod.* **2020,** *254*, 120112.

Yavas, V.; Ozkan-Ozen, Y. D. Logistics Centers in the New Industrial Era: A Proposed Framework for Logistics Center 4.0. *Transp. Res. E Logist. Transp. Rev.* **2020,** *135*, 101864.

CHAPTER 4

The Effect of Supply Chain Integration on Financial Performance: A Case Study of Hospitals in Northern Region

MOHAMMED MAJEED[1], ABAAH AKANSAKE JOSEPH[2], and JONAS YOMBOI[3]

[1]*Marketing Department, Tamale Technical University, Tamale, Ghana*

[2]*Tamale Technical University, Tamale, Ghana*

[3]*University for Developing Studies, Tamale, Ghana*

ABSTRACT

This research aims to investigate how the integration of supply chains impacts the financial performance of hospitals in Ghana. The study used a quantitative methodology, which included a sample of 139 hospitals located in the northern area. This sample included 17 district/municipal hospitals as well as metropolitan hospitals. The data that was gathered was subjected to analysis via Smart-PLS. The financial performance of the hospitals was positively influenced by each of the three predictors, indicating their significance. This finding provides support for the validation of all three hypotheses proposed in this research. In conclusion, the results confirm the validity of hypotheses H1, H2, and H3, demonstrating a statistically significant and positive association between supply chain integration and financial success.

4.1 BACKGROUND OF THE STUDY

Recently, there has been significant attention placed on the concept of supply chain integration (SCI) from both professionals and scholars (for

Essentials of Supply Chain Management: Strategy, Planning and Operations.
Mohammed Majeed, Abdul-Rasheed Akeji Alhassan Alolo, Seidu Alhassan, and S. Sekar (Eds.)

a comprehensive overview, consult Fabbe-Costes and Jahre (2008); Van der Vaart and van Donk (2008)). Huo (2012), Van der Vaart and van Donk (2008) SCI refers to a company's capacity to collaborate strategically with members of its supply chain and effectively manage internal and external procedures to deliver maximum value to customers with optimal efficiency and speed (Bagchi et al., 2005; Childerhouse and Towill, 2011; Huo, 2012; Kim, 2006). It is argued that the establishment of SCI empowers a central firm to access and leverage the resources and expertise within the supply chain. This perspective underscores SCI as a tool for integrating internal and external aspects, leading to enhanced financial performance. However, the direct correlation between higher levels of SCI and improved financial outcomes remains unclear.

For a more comprehensive understanding of SCI's impact on financial success, it is crucial to examine potential risks and unfavorable consequences. Certain researchers (Das et al., 2006; Enkel et al., 2005; Ertimur and Venkatesh, 2010; Hertz, 2001) caution that SCI could potentially hinder financial success in specific scenarios. Given the substantial investment made by focal companies in developing SCI, its implementation could significantly strain management resources. Gunasekaran and Ngai (2004) discovered that SCI might lead to redundancy and opportunistic behavior. Ertimur and Venkatesh (2010) and Lui et al. (2006) hold similar viewpoints. Consequently, higher levels of SCI could potentially represent a misallocation of resources and detrimentally impact an organization's financial health.

In our research, we aim to merge both favorable and unfavorable outcomes of SCI into a unified model, transcending the narrow focus on SCI's positive influence on financial performance. We concur with Huo (2012) and Kim (2006) that SCI indeed exerts a positive effect on financial success, provided that it remains within reasonable limits. Nevertheless, it is plausible to enhance this line of thinking by considering that the benefits derived from augmenting SCI may possess inherent limitations. In simpler terms, should the risks and costs associated with SCI escalate, its overall value might begin to diminish.

4.2 PROBLEM STATEMENT

The need for coordinating internal operational activities with supply chain partners becomes evident to management due to heightened competition and a company's internal integration challenges. The concept of supply chain integration becomes imperative in achieving this coordination (Palma-Mendoza et al., 2014). Earlier research (Jie et al., 2013; Mackelprang et al., 2014; Xu Huo et al., 2014) has established a positive correlation between organizational levels and both external and internal integration (Tseng and Liao, 2015). Another study indicates that enhanced customer service and cost reduction lead to improved company performance. Supply Chain Integration involves tasks such as enhancing supplier relationships, updating the business network, and implementing programs to expedite service product procurement and delivery to customers. Although the company acknowledges the necessity of such projects, their execution lacks substantiation (Danese and Romano, 2011).

Supply chain integration offers two advantages: (1) It enables companies to concentrate on core competencies and existing internal and external strengths to optimize productivity and profits. It also adds tangible values to organizational, supplier, and customer activities (Jin et al., 2013; Klueber and Okeefe, 2013). Numerous studies in supply chain management (Elmuti et al., 2008; Gibson et al., 2005) emphasize the importance of closely integrating the supply chain to enhance financial performance, as highlighted by Zhao et al. (2008). The dwindling lifespan of products due to global competition necessitates a shift from a competitive, single-supplier model to collaborative supplier relationships, according to Lambert and Cooper (2000), Wisner and Tan (2000). To remain competitive, a company's supply chain must align with its partner's supply chain strategy (Richey et al., 2009). This alignment is feasible when internal processes and external partners collaborate to establish efficient supply chain partnerships (Qi et al., 2011; Narasimhan and Kim, 2002).

Frohlich and Westbrook (2001) and Zailani and Rajagopal (2005) argue that a company's sustained success hinges on integrating its processes with those of its customers and suppliers. Several studies underscore the positive impact of overall supply chain integration on company's performance (Bagchi and Chun Ha, 2005; Flynn et al., 2010; Kim, 2006; Zailani and Rajagopal, 2005). Other research reveals favorable effects on supply chain performance (Lee et al., 2007; Narasimhan and Kim, 2002). Flynn et al. (2010), Frohlich and Westbrook (2001) suggest that supply chain integration reduces costs while enhancing company, shareholder, and supply chain partner value. Yeung et al. (2009) assert that the primary aim of supply chain integration is to confer a competitive advantage to each participant in the chain. Consequently, there remain unexplored opportunities for supply chain enhancement, particularly concerning the interplay between external and internal aspects of the company (Evans, 2015). Vaart and van Donk (2018) contend that insufficient research exists on the impact of internal variables, supplier integration, and customer integration on financial performance. As previously mentioned, this study will delve into the influence of internal, supplier, and customer integration on a business's financial prosperity.

4.3 RESEARCH OBJECTIVES

4.3.1 MAIN OBJECTIVE

The purpose of this study is to examine the effect of supply integration on financial performance of hospitals in Ghana.

4.3.2 SPECIFIC OBJECTIVES

The specific objectives to help achieve the main objectives are as follows:

1. To examine the effect of supply integration on financial performance of hospitals in Ghana.
2. To investigate the effect of customer integration on financial performance of hospitals in Ghana.
3. To find out the effect of internal integration on financial performance of hospitals in Ghana.

4.4 LITERATURE REVIEW

4.4.1 SUPPLY CHAIN INTEGRATION IN HEATH SECTOR

With the aim of advancing our collective comprehension of the integration of healthcare supply chains in Ghana, this study will focalize on Ghana's district, metropolitan, and municipal hospitals (inclusive of general medical and surgical hospitals). It will delve into the connection between the inner and outer dimensions of integration, alongside diverse facets of financial effectiveness. Within Ghanaian medical institutions, the supply chain performs two primary functions: a tangible role mainly centered on managing inventory and transportation, and a market-intermediary role that harmonizes supply and demand.

The foundational element for electronic data interchange (EDI), facilitating computer-based data exchange and trade among members, lies in the realm of inventory and logistics management within hospitals. This area places significant emphasis on the interplay between suppliers and purchasers. Hospitals need to grasp patient requirements and establish systems to fulfill client appeals to maintain an equilibrium between supply and demand. From this perspective, Akkermans et al. (2003) perceive the supply chain as an interconnected network comprising three core constituents: the operational tier, members, and pillars.

The operational tier encompasses the financial, informational, and material streams that hospitals undergo. Financial flows encompass payment schedules, credit terms, and title ownership agreements. Information flows encompass order monitoring, order transmission, and coordination of material movement. Material flows indicate the tangible progression of products from suppliers to customers, inclusive of reversed flows for product returns, servicing, and recycling. The network comprises a consortium of customers, manufacturers, distributors, retailers, and suppliers.

4.4.2 UNDERPINNING THEORY

4.4.2.1 RESOURCES-BASED VIEW

As per the findings of Cao and Zhang in 2011, the Resource-Based View (RBV) has garnered increased attention for elucidating the dynamics of collaboration and integration within supply chains. In alignment with this notion (Penrose, 1959; Barney, 1991), fluctuations in a company's performance can be clarified by the effective utilization of its assets. The assets alluded to encompass "every form of possession, capacities, internal processes, attributes, data, understanding, etc., under a firm's control" (Barney, 1991, p. 101). The RBV posits that through investment in assets tailored to specific relationships, partnered enterprises can cultivate distinctive, valuable, irreplaceable, and arduous-to-duplicate resources, thus attaining a competitive advantage (Barney, 1991). Furthermore, as per the RBV, engagement in supply chain collaboration not only fosters the evolution of these invaluable resources but also empowers businesses to focus on their fundamental activities, thereby enhancing firm-specific proficiencies and enabling the realization of economies of scale and learning effects, thereby bolstering their competitive stance (Park et al., 2004).

4.4.3 SUPPLY CHAIN INTEGRATION (SCI)

As per Flynn et al. (2010), supply chain integration (SCI) pertains to the level of cooperation with significant associates in the supply chain. Such collaboration, according to Wiengarten et al. (2014), enhances the efficiency and effectiveness of resource utilization among all contributors in the supply chain. SCI can manifest in various forms, spanning from internal fusion (within divisions or functions) to external fusion (with entities upstream or downstream) (Frohlich and Westbrook, 2001). In practical application, establishing a standard gauge for SCI and pinpointing the optimal degree of SCI can be challenging (Madzimure, 2019). As per Whipple et al. (2015), supply chain integration entails merging internal and external resources from supply chain collaborators of both businesses. SCI embodies a multi-dimensional concept comprised of variables related to internal and external fusion, according to Wong et al. (2011). Conversely, internal integration denotes the interconnection of all cross-functional components within an organization's context (Wiengarten et al. 2016). An organization's upstream (customers) and downstream (suppliers) commercial associates are fused as part of external integration, in contrast (Wong et al., 2011).

To attain an optimal competitive advantage, supply chain integration endeavors to cultivate efficient synergy and collaboration in operational processes (Kumar et al. 2017). Thus, rather than segregating into discrete functions, the notion leans toward an interactive approach encompassing diverse supply chain networks (Ataseven and Nair 2017; Whipple et al. 2015). It could be argued that SCI is a strategic undertaking that amplifies competitive performance within SMEs. As outlined by Madzimure (2019), the efficiency of hospital operations correlates with their ability to merge their internal logistics and network activities. The extent of information, financial, and material flows exchanged between the focal company and its associates can serve as a metric for gauging integration throughout the supply chain (Rai et al., 2006). In this context, implementing digital information systems to creatively link supply chains can facilitate information exchange (Kim and Schoenherr, 2018). Swift technological advancements also empower businesses to seamlessly connect certain internal operations with third parties, enhancing performance through effective coordination of activities and material flows (Ellram and Cooper, 2014). Given the escalating complexity of supply chains crossing international boundaries due to heightened globalization, SCI holds paramount importance within the industrial sector (Moyano-Fuentes et al., 2016).

4.5 DIMENSIONS OF SCI

The extent to which various organizational operations, the undertakings of suppliers, engagements of customers, and interactions among other members of the supply chain are harmonized to achieve the objectives of each company serves as the precursor to achieving supply chain integration. The degree to which businesses cooperate with external partners to formulate strategies encompassing organizational aspects, practices, and cooperative procedures to attain synchronization is referred to as external integration, also identified as customer and supplier integration (Belvedere and Grando, 2017; Stank et al., 2001). While supplier integration encompasses fundamental proficiencies associated with harmonizing activities with key suppliers, customer integration incorporates fundamental proficiencies derived from the consequences of coordinating with clients (Kim, 2006).

4.5.1 SUPPLIER INTEGRATION

Flynn et al. (2010) and Shou et al. (2018) propose that supplier collaboration entails cooperative interactions between a company and its vital suppliers, facilitating the exchange of information, joint planning, and a collaborative approach. This approach encompasses shared product development, strategic alliances, interdisciplinary teamwork, and collaborative issue resolution (Wong et al., 2011; Yu et al., 2017). According to Echtelt et al. (2008), supplier integration is defined by diverse elements and activities, including the sharing of information, cooperation, trust establishment, utilization of shared technology, incorporation of unified processes, establishment of long-term agreements, aiding suppliers in enhancing their production methods, fostering quality enhancement, investing in supplier assets like novel service offerings, enhancing the capacity of all partner suppliers, and resource pooling. The outcomes of supply chain integration comprise enhanced decision-making, augmented knowledge dissemination, heightened competencies, cultivation of learning behaviors, and enhanced performance of supply chain collaborators. Sahay (2003) further contends that nurturing trust among suppliers, customers, and other business associates heightens commitment levels, diminishes transaction expenses, encourages deeper collaboration, elevates individual contentment, and reduces the necessity for formal agreements and disputes. Frohlich and Westbrook (2001) describe supplier integration as the procedure of engaging and cooperating with suppliers to optimize inventory flow efficiency (Zhao et al., 2011).

4.5.2 CUSTOMER INTEGRATION

Customer integration refers to the collaborative efforts made by a company and its main clientele. As stated by Flynn et al. (2010), this framework allows the fusion of strategies, methods, and practices between organizations, resulting in harmonious and synchronized procedures. The inclusion of customers enables manufacturers to attain a deeper comprehension of consumer needs, market dynamics, and potential opportunities. This inclusion also assists manufacturers in improving their ability to respond to client appeals (Afshan and Motwani, 2018; Wong et al., 2011). Furthermore, the integration of customers offers the possibility of enhancing cooperative procedures, along with aiding in cost reduction, value generation, and prompt identification of market demand shifts for organizations. The notion of customer integration is closely linked to customer satisfaction (Homburg and Stock, 2004), and it also indirectly affects the development and innovation of service products (Koufteros et al., 2007; Song and Di Benedetto, 2008).

4.5.3 INTERNAL INTEGRATION

Internal integration can be described as how extensively a manufacturer combines its own organizational tactics, procedures, and methods into unified and synchronized operations to meet consumer requirements with minimal expenditure (Wong et al., 2011; Flynn et al., 2010). The concept of internal integration underscores the necessity of cultivating a united approach across diverse sections within a company, motivating them to function as a unified entity instead of working in seclusion. Internal integration pertains to the level of a company's ability to devise organizational tactics and implement them collaboratively, resulting in coordination to meet customer contentment and enable efficient interaction with supplier associates (Flynn et al., 2010). Internal integration signifies the procedure of amalgamating information and communication pathways among various divisions within an organization. This facilitates access to management information related to service products, enables the development of easily accessible integrated data sources that encompass essential operational data, and facilitates the integration of production processes through the use of information systems. Additionally, internal integration involves connecting the production and marketing departments through the utilization of digital planning systems (Lee et al., 2007; Belvedere and Grando, 2017).

4.6 FINANCIAL PERFORMANCE

The complete achievement of a corporation is encapsulated via indicators of its financial performance. The customary indicators employed to evaluate a firm's financial achievement encompass yield on holdings, yield on capital outlay, yield on vending, gainfulness, and portion of the market. As per the findings of Vickery et al. (2003), this analysis employs three factors to gauge financial performance: yield on vending, pre-tax yield on holdings, and holdings' yield.

4.6.1 SUPPLY CHAIN INTEGRATION AND FINANCIAL PERFORMANCE

Instead of merely operating within the functional framework of historically linked departments or areas of expertise, which are meant to establish connections and enhance corporate performance, internal integration has the capability to transcend hierarchical barriers and amplify collaboration in fulfilling customer requirements. Organizations now possess a broader spectrum of information due to internal integration (Muntaka et al., 2015). Furthermore, frequent exchanges occur among individuals with differing viewpoints, which can reduce mistakes and inefficiencies while also uncovering fresh possibilities for streamlining. As evidenced by the preceding details, internal integration serves as the cornerstone of supply chain amalgamation and exhibits a favorable correlation with the operational and financial achievements of a business. In line with prior research (Scott et al., 2002; Rosenzweig et al., 2003; Vickery et al., 2003; Belvedere and Grando, 2017), elements of internal integration such as cooperation and the assimilation of multifunctional management systems for handling service-related products yield a positive impact on a company's performance.

4.6.2 SUPPLIER INTEGRATION AND FINANCIAL PERFORMANCE

As per Flynn et al. (2010), the practice of integrating suppliers plays a pivotal role in enhancing the performance of companies. Establishing integration with suppliers fosters collaboration and regular joint issue-solving, which contributes to improved management of supply chain activities (Zhang et al., 2019). In line with findings by Sukoso et al. (2018) and the work of Zhang et al. (2018), supplier integration involves incorporating suppliers into both the production and procurement processes. This action leads to reduced transaction expenses, cycle durations, and time required to bring products to market, thereby leading to better company performance. Involving suppliers from the initial stages of product development also results in accelerated product creation and introduction times. The integration of suppliers aids in decreasing administrative, production, and transportation overheads, thereby reducing overall operational costs (Zhang et al., 2019). Zhang et al. (2019) highlight that supplier integration contributes to an enhancement in time-related performance metrics, encompassing procurement lead duration, product development speed, and market entry swiftness. Strategic supplier integration, as presented by Huang et al. (2014) and further supported by Zhang et al. (2018), empowers suppliers to effectively adapt to evolving manufacturer requisites and produce components of superior quality. Hence,

H1: Supplier integration has significant positive relationship with financial performance.

4.6.3 CUSTOMER INTEGRATION AND FINANCIAL PERFORMANCE

Enhancing the degree of fusion between a company and its primary patrons has been shown to generate multiple advantages, such as enhanced precision of demand data, decreased time necessary for production scheming and product conceptualization, and heightened receptiveness to customer requisites (Flynn et al., 2010; Afshan and Motwani, 2018). As per Zhang et al. (2019), constructing a resilient patron affiliation operates as a preemptive strategy against quality concerns, minimizes stock obsolescence, and alleviates the costs linked with product malfunction. The application of patron amalgamation enables enterprises to efficiently harness each other's capacities to optimize the advantages and worth that both sides acquire (Jajja et al., 2018). Numerous studies have evaluated the correlation between patron amalgamation and fiscal performance, exposing diverse discoveries. To illustrate, Zhao et al. (2015) uncovered a straight correlation, whereas Afshan and Motwani (2018) and Zhang et al. (2019) recognized an indirect correlation. Conversely, Seo et al. (2014) documented no substantial correlation between patron amalgamation and fiscal performance. Based on the inconsistent results reported in the existing body of research, we put out our second hypothesis in the following manner:

H2: Customer integration has significant positive relationship with financial performance.

4.6.4 INTERNAL INTEGRATION AND FINANCIAL PERFORMANCE

The process of internal integration promotes improved communication among different divisions of an organization, leading to the optimization of efficiency and effectiveness in the realm of in-house production (Jajja et al., 2018). According to Zhang et al. (2019), this phenomenon results in enhanced lucidity in both strategic and operational decision-making processes, facilitating the harmonization of goals across functional departments. In organizations characterized by a heightened degree of internal integration, different departments engage in collaborative efforts to improve processes and products, rather than operating in isolation. Chang et al. (2016) argue that internal integration plays a crucial role in facilitating external supply chain integration, leading to streamlined processes for developing new goods and improving product quality. According to Huang et al. (2014), the implementation of internal integration facilitates the development of resilient mechanisms for the exchange of information and the building of effective governance systems. According to the findings of Munir et al. (2020), internal integration has been shown to have a positive effect on a company's operational performance. This includes improvements in logistics, process efficiency, accelerated new product development, and an increased range of products offered. Furthermore, there is a positive relationship between increased internal integration and enhanced performance in terms of "time-to-product" and "time-to-market" metrics. According to the study conducted by Droge et al. (2004), multiple studies have emphasized the impact of internal integration on the functioning of organizations (Droge et al., 2004). Internal integration, when implemented via the main channel, leads to rapid improvements in performance. These improvements include increased responsiveness, decreased time-related performance limitations, cost control, and enhanced productivity. According to previous studies conducted by Droge et al. (2004) and Huang et al. (2014), it has been shown that the immediate performance results have a beneficial influence on financial prosperity. Multiple research (Zhu et al., 2018; Zhang et al., 2019) provide support for the concept of indirect relationships between internal integration and financial performance. Several studies (Flynn et al., 2010; Zhao et al., 2015) have shown empirical data supporting the notion that internal integration has a direct and beneficial influence on financial performance. Given these different results in the research, we offer the following as our third hypothesis:

H3. The relationship between internal integration and financial performance.

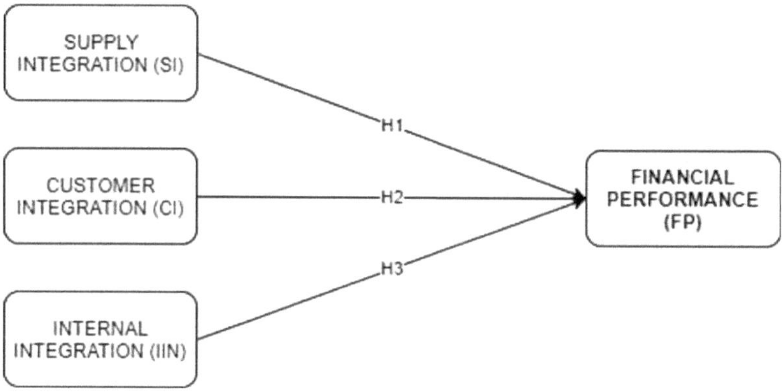

FIGURE 4.1 Conceptual framework.

4.7 RESEARCH METHODOLOGY

4.7.1 STUDY AREA AND HEALTH CARE SITUATION IN GHANA

Ghana, situated along the Gulf of Guinea and positioned between Cote d'Ivoire and Togo, possesses a populace of approximately 30 million individuals. Starting from 1992, when a constitutional democratic system was established, the country has maintained political stability and tranquility, gaining recognition as a prototype of democracy in its neighboring area. Since then, a span of 25 years has witnessed proficient economic administration, a competitive commercial environment, a gradual reduction in poverty ratios, and an overall enhancement in the economic state. If you are seeking investment prospects, Ghana stands out as the sole African nation worth contemplating due to its market-oriented economy and minimal trade and investment constraints. The significant contributors to this scenario are modest landholders, who constitute more than half of the workforce and about 20% of the gross domestic product (GDP). Vital sources of foreign revenue include gold, cocoa, and oil, while other exports consist of timber, tuna, aluminum, manganese ore, diamonds, and agricultural products.

Human economic and industrial activities are detrimental to the environment's health, necessitating swift global action to curtail further harm. The 1987 report from the Brundtland and Khalid Commission played a pioneering role in examining climate change and its effects on global resources. The commission underscored the necessity for sustainable economic growth that avoids excessive depletion of natural resources or undue strain on the environment. The healthcare domain is characterized by substantial risks, financial investments, and intricate operations. This sector confronts obstacles such as remote locations, marginal oilfields, emerging global business trends, novel technological advancements, and fluctuating oil and gas prices. These factors impede the formulation and implementation of innovative approaches for procurement of goods and services. To ensure prudent economic advancement, nations often progress in tandem with an augmented demand for sustainable procurement practices, exemplified by the establishment of dedicated regulations governing these sectors. By concentrating on procurement and supply chain management in healthcare, governments can expedite the fulfillment of their prolonged economic development objectives.

Hospitals, as defined by the World Health Organization, serve as healthcare establishments that deliver round-the-clock inpatient services, staffed by skilled medical professionals, alongside related services. In Ghana, healthcare institutions encompass public and private clinics, primary care centers, as well as secondary and tertiary/referral hospitals (WHO, 2016). Similar to numerous other developing countries, Ghana encompasses three distinctive healthcare systems: the public system managed by the National Health Insurance Scheme (NHIS), commercial and nonprofit healthcare frameworks, and traditional medicine along with self-medication. Despite the acknowledged fundamental right to quality healthcare access, merely a fraction of Ghana's populace benefits from this privilege (MoH, 2007). Generally, the northern region of Ghana faces a scarcity of healthcare facilities, leading to challenges in obtaining medical services and elevating the risk of self-medication prior to the NHIS implementation.

4.7.2 RESEARCH DESIGN

Researchers chose a design after careful consideration of its compatibility with the intended audience (Robson and McCartan, 2016). As outlined by Gabbiadini and Greitemeyer (2017), quantitative methodologies consist of experimental, quasiexperimental, and nonexperimental designs, encompassing correlational, descriptive, and evaluative techniques. Qualitative methodologies, such as grounded theory, ethnography, phenomenological investigation, narrative analysis, and case study methodologies, comprise another facet of research approaches (Ahmed and Ahmed, 2014). In this study, a correlational framework proved to be the most fitting quantitative method. When assessing multiple quantitative variables within the same participant group, the recommendation from Bettany-Saltikov and Whittaker (2014) is to employ correlational designs, unveiling potential associations between the variables. Hence, I utilized this strategy to explore the connection between the self-governing variable of financial success and the reliant variable of SCI (integrations involving customers, internal processes, and suppliers).

The experimental, quasi-experimental, and evaluative approaches were among the alternative quantitative designs that were not selected for this investigation. The experimental design has elements of manipulation, control, and random selection (Delost and Nadder, 2014). Fischer et al. (2014) claim that one or both of the crucial components of randomization and a control group are missing from the quasiexperimental design. Because there was no manipulation or control of the research in this study, experimental and quasiexperimental approaches were inappropriate.

4.7.3 RESEARCH STRATEGY

A researcher must choose the appropriate methodology for the line of inquiry in order to produce relevant results (Yin, 2018). Qualitative, quantitative, and mixed techniques are the three options for conducting research; each method generates a distinct kind of data (McLaughlin et al., 2016; Yin, 2018).

The objective of this study is to establish relationships, so the researchers determined that a quantitative approach would be appropriate. According to McCusker and Gunaydin (2015), a number of study components in quantitative research are designed before the data collection procedure. The researcher is capable of maintaining objectivity by being aware of the research objective (McCusker and Gunaydin, 2015). Quantitative data are accurate but lack contextual information (McCusker and Gunaydin, 2015), which hinders the researcher's ability to fully comprehend a problem. According to Marshall and Rossman (2016), qualitative researchers study an issue's complexity or evaluate it from a different angle. By allowing participants to express their experiences in their own words, a qualitative technique makes it possible to collect detailed data (Marshall and Rossman, 2016). A data-gathering technique that aids in identifying and exploring the underlying dynamics of a problem is necessary when using a qualitative approach (Merriam and Tisdell, 2015). The credibility of a qualitative study is enhanced when a mixed-methods approach is used, integrating both qualitative and quantitative procedures. However, it should be noted that the researchers did not specifically intend to gather extensive data or request participants to provide detailed explanations of their experiences. The researcher did not use either mixed or qualitative methodologies in their study.

4.7.4 *POPULATION AND SAMPLING*

To verify my hypotheses, I gathered data from medical institutions in Ghana. I specifically opted for the northern territories of Ghana (comprising 17 urban areas, municipalities, and districts) to encompass a broad array of geographical and economic options. Within the urban vicinity surrounding Tamale, there is observable economic advancement and the emergence of marketplaces. In the Eastern Corridor, the typical process of economic restructuring and market expansion includes Yendi and Bimbilla, as well as Wulensi, Gushegu, and Karaga. Saveligu, situated in the northwest, embodies an initial phase of market development and economic transformation. Kpandai, a significant agricultural region, remains in the preliminary stages of economic restructuring and market progression. A variety of distinct supply chain procedures are operational within these MMDs (Metropolis, Municipalities, and Districts) hospitals. Hence, these locations offer a valuable setting to assess the viability of SCI (supply chain integration). As advised by local scholars and governmental representatives, the study's participants were selected (Feng et al., 2010). This approach enhances the precision and comprehensiveness of the sampling data. Leading executives (including the CEO, president, vice president, and supply chain manager) were identified as the primary sources of information for each organization. Our on-site interviews indicate that these managers possess a strong grasp of SCI practices. While the researcher distributed 250 questionnaires, only 139 were ultimately returned with completed responses.

4.7.5 *MEASURES AND QUESTIONNAIRE*

The assessment of all items was carried out with a five-point Likert scale. The scale used in this study had a range from 1 to 5, with 1 representing "strongly disagree" and 5 representing "strongly agree." This scale was employed for both the operational performance components and the IT competency constructs. The scale for the SCI constructs varied from 1, representing the absence of the construct, to 5, representing a high level of the construct. The constructs and their respective components were obtained from the already published literature sources, as seen in Table 4.1.

TABLE 4.1 Measures.

Supplier integration (SI): Flynn et al. (2010), Narasimhan and Kim (2002), Zhao et al. (2011)
Our level of information exchange with our major supplier through information network
The establishment of a quick ordering system with our major supplier
The extent of our strategic partnership with our major supplier
Stable procurement through networking with our major supplier
The participation level of our major supplier in our procurement and production processes
We share our demand forecast with our major supplier
Customer integration (CI): Flynn et al. (2010), Narasimhan and Kim (2002), Zhao et al. (2011)
The extent of our linkage with our major customer through information network
The extent of sharing of market information by our major customer
Our level of communication with our major customer
Our follow-up with our major customer for feedback
The frequency of our contacts with our major customer
Our major customer shares demand forecast with us
Internal integration (IIN): Flynn et al. (2010), Narasimhan and Kim (2002), Zhao et al. (2011)
The use of periodic interdepartmental meetings among internal functions
The use of cross functional teams in new product development
The extent of strategic partnership among different internal functions
Different internal functions jointly develop strategic plans in collaboration with each other
Different internal functions monitor business processes together
Different internal functions jointly develop and maintain measurement systems
Financial performance: Zhao, Feng, & Wang, (2015)
Our return on investment (ROI) is high
Our return on sales is high
Our growth in sales is high
Our growth in profit is high
Our growth in market share is high

4.7.6 DATA COLLECTION

The participants were sent with a cover letter that accompanied the questionnaire, which outlined the goals and objectives of the study. According to Frohlich (2002), those who were specifically selected as responders but did not provide a response were contacted through phone calls and letters as part of our subsequent endeavors to elicit their participation. The managers and experts of these companies were surveyed in order to get information regarding their particular work functions. The survey was conducted within each organization, including participation from managers, retail proprietors, accountants, operations personnel, and supply chain experts.

4.7.7 DATA ANALYSIS

The present study used structural equation modeling (SEM) as a method for data analysis, specifically using the partial least-squares (PLS) technique. When comparing software options for covariance-based structural equation modeling (SEM), such as LISREL (Chin et al., 2003) or AMOS (Goodhue et al., 2012), it has been noted that partial least-squares structural equation modeling (PLS-SEM) necessitates a lower sample size (Hair et al., 2011). The use of SmartPLS 3.2.7 enabled the analysis of data. The elements underwent normalization, resulting in a mean of zero and a variance of one. The researchers used a bootstrapping methodology to create a total of 300 random samples from the original dataset. The present study used the aforementioned approach to assess the statistical significance of route coefficients and item loadings, following the recommendations of Chin (1998) and Efron and Tibshirani (1994).

4.8 DATA ANALYSIS AND RESULTS

4.8.1 DEMOGRAPHIC DATA

The study employed a survey approach for data collection. A questionnaire mainly consisting of closed-ended queries, along with a few open-ended questions, was used. To maintain the study's scope, communication was restricted to individuals working in the oil and gas sector. Participant information covered various demographics including age, sex, education, job background, and area of specialization. Precise and thorough data from 139 respondents were gathered for analysis and later conversation.

4.8.2 GENDER

The research aimed to assess the gender composition within the study participants with the goal of investigating the presence of any gender disparity in information gathering and ensuring an equitable representation of both genders aligned with the objectives of the study. The outcomes are outlined in Table 4.2.

TABLE 4.2 Gender of the Respondent.

	Frequency	Percentage
Male	75	53.9
Female	64	46.1
Total	**139**	**100.0**

Source: Researcher's field work (2021).

According to the data shown in Table 4.2, it can be seen that out of the total participants, 64 individuals, accounting for 46.1% of the sample, were identified as women, while 75 individuals, representing 53.9% of the sample, were identified as males. This suggests that the study did not demonstrate any gender bias, since the observed gender inequalities were not significant enough to raise suspicions of favoritism toward a certain gender. This indicates that the Ghana Electricity Generating Company complied with the requirement set by oil and gas companies, which mandates that an organization's staff shall not surpass a two-third representation from any one gender.

4.8.3 AGES OF THE RESPONDENTS

The study's objective was to determine the respondents' age. Table 4.3 presents the findings.

TABLE 4.3 Ages of Respondents.

Ages of respondents in years	Frequency	Percentage (%)
21–25	10	7.2
36–40	17	12.2
26–30	33	23.7
31–35	32	23.1
41–44	28	20.1
45 and above	19	13.7
Total	139	100.0

Source: Researcher's field work (2021).

As shown in Table 4.3, 33 (23.7%) of the respondents were between the ages of 26 and 30, 17 (12.2%) were between the ages of 21 and 25, and 10 (7.2%) were between the ages of 21 and 25. Another 32 (23.1%) were between the ages of 31 and 35, 28 (20.1%) were between the ages of 41 and 44, and 19 (13.7%) were over the age of 44. This meant that most of the people who answered were in their middle years and were ready to take part in the study. Also, the ages of the people who took part in the study were important because opinions from people of different ages were collected.

4.8.4 RESPONDENTS' WORK EXPERIENCE

The goal of the study was to find out how long each responder had worked at his or her own organization. This was done to see how much their answers could be trusted to draw conclusions about the study problems based on their work experience at the organization. In Table 4.4, the results are shown.

Nineteen (13.6%) of the participants who provided responses indicated they had been employed for under 5 years. Thirty-five (25.2%) had a work tenure ranging from 6 to 10 years, while forty-six (33.1%) had job experience spanning 11–15 years. Additionally, thirty-nine (28.1%) had accumulated over 16 years of work experience. Table 4.4 visually illustrates that a substantial portion of the survey respondents had a work history of 11–15 years. Work experience is important for them to fully understand how the organization works, which helps them answer the questions. These results back up what Braxton (2008) said about how people with more work experience give more reliable data on the study problem because they know more about how the problem works. The study's results showed that most of the people who answered the questions had worked for their organizations for a long time and knew how e-procurement adoption affected procurement performance.

TABLE 4.4 Respondents Work Experience.

Respondents Work Experience	Frequency	Percentage (%)
Less than 5 year	19	13.6
6-10 years	35	25.2
11-15 years	46	33.1
16 years and above	39	28.1
Total	**139**	**100.0**

Source: Researcher's field work (2021).

4.8.5 LEVEL OF EDUCATION OF RESPONDENTS

Determining the educational background of the participants was crucial in order to determine whether they possessed the necessary competencies to assess the impact of e-procurement adoption on procurement performance.

Based on the educational attainment of the participants, the data reveals that out of the total respondents, 45 individuals (32.3%) possessed a diploma qualification, 77 individuals (55.4%) held a bachelor's degree, 14 individuals (10.1%) had a master's qualification, and 3 individuals (2.2%) possessed a PhD qualification. Hence, it may be deduced that a significant proportion of the participants possess the requisite qualifications necessary to comprehend the intricacies of the research subject.

Moreover, the investigation of performance dimensions through factor analysis indicated that certain items had substantial loadings on a singular factor, implying that these items are likely to represent a distinct performance dimension. In this study, it was found that product modification and the launch of new products in response to evolving client needs were strongly associated with the product-mix flexibility dimension.

TABLE 4.5 Level of Education of Respondents.

Respondents Work Experience	**Frequency**	**Percentage (%)**
Diploma Holder	45	32.3
Bachelor Degree	77	55.4
Master Degree	14	10.1
Degree of Doctorate Philosophy	3	2.2
Total	**139**	**100.0**

Source: Researcher's field work (2021).

The loadings of factors and the values of Cronbach's alpha for each construct are provided in Table 4.6. The alpha values, indicating scale reliability, vary between 0.623 and 0.910, surpassing the commonly accepted threshold of 0.60 (Flynn et al., 1990; Nunnally and Bernstein, 1994). Factor analysis was used to evaluate the single dimensionality of measures. Accordingly, certain aspects of customer integration and one item related to supplier integration were removed due to low factor loadings. Moreover, an item concerning cross-functional application and two items associated with internal integration were excluded as they cross-loaded on multiple constructs. The results of repeated factor analysis confirmed the one-dimensional nature of all six factors, as items loaded exclusively on one factor. All factor loadings exceed 0.7.

Item loadings were assessed to test convergent validity, composite reliability (CR), and average variance extracted (AVE), as indicated in Table 4.6. Both the CR and AVE values surpass the baseline thresholds of 0.60 and 0.50, respectively (Bagozzi and Yi, 1988; Fornell and Larcker, 1981; Hair et al., 1998; Nunnally and Bernstein, 1994), demonstrating convergent validity.

TABLE 4.6 Loadings and Reliability.

Construct	Item	Loadings	CR	Alpha	AVE
Supply integration (SI)		0.72	0.92	0.89	0.65
	SI1	0.80			
	SI2	0.70			
	SI3	0.77			
	SI4	0.73			
	SI5	0.82			
Customer integration (CI)			0.88	0.92	0.71
	CI1	0.71			
	CI2	0.70			
	CI3	0.77			
	CI4	0.72			
Internal integration (IIN)			0.90	0.95	0.68
	IIN1	0.81			
	IIN2	0.76			
	IIN3	0.70			
	IIN4	0.71			
	IIN5	0.71			
			0.91	0.92	0.58
	FP1	0.81			
Financial Performance (FP)	FP2	0.70			
	FP3	0.77			
	FP4	0.76			
	FP5	0.82			

Additionally, significant t-values at $p < 0.001$ support convergent validity of measurement tools. Following the approach outlined in Fornell and Larcker (1981), the model's discriminant validity was examined. In Table 4.7, all scales exhibit square root AVE values notably higher than their relationships with other constructs, indicating discriminant validity.

TABLE 4.7 Discriminant Validity.

Construct	Mean	SD	AVE	SI	CI	IIN	FP
SI	4.20	0.98	0.65	**0.81**			
CI	4.32	0.93	0.71	0.45	**0.84**		
IIN	3.95	1.05	0.68	0.56	0.52	**0.82**	
FP	3.88	1.19	0.58	0.48	0.64	0.36	0.76

The mean values, reflecting the descriptive statistics of the measures, indicate favorable rankings. For instance, SI = 4.20, CI = 4.32, IIN = 3.95, and FP = 3.88, placing them toward the middle and upper ends of the 5-point semantic differential scale. In each case, the standard deviation ranges from 0.93 to 1.19, indicating moderate variability.

The data from Table 4.8 was employed to deduce the conjectures. The correlation between incorporating supply and achieving financial results (SI FP [= 0.52 and p = 0.000]) was notable and favorable; thus, the initial hypothesis (H1) was validated within this investigation. The findings also indicate a substantial and beneficial connection between supply integration and financial achievement (CI FP [= 0.43 and p = 0.001]), implying the accuracy of the second hypothesis (H2). Lastly, a substantial and advantageous correlation existed between internal integration and financial accomplishment (IIN FP [= 0.60 and p = 0.000]). Hence, the third hypothesis (H3) held true in this particular study.

TABLE 4.8 SEM (Hypotheses Results).

Hypothesis	Path	β	p-value	Decision
H1	SI → FP	0.52	0.000	Accepted
H2	CI → FP	0.43	0.001	Accepted
H3	IIN → FP	0.60	0.000	Accepted

Source: Field work (2021).

4.8.6 SUMMARY OF FINDINGS

The research findings unfold a compelling narrative, shedding light on the intricate relationship between different variables. Through a meticulous examination of the data presented in Table 4.8, the study unraveled a series of significant revelations that provide valuable insights into the world of business dynamics.

Firstly, the investigation delved into the correlation between supply integration and financial performance. The results spoke volumes, unveiling a robust and encouraging connection between these two realms. The numerical depiction of this relationship, denoted as SI FP [= 0.52 and p = 0.000], underscores the substantial impact of supply integration on enhancing financial outcomes. As a result, the initial hypothesis (H1) gained solid ground, standing validated within the context of this study.

Secondly, the study expanded its scope to encompass the nexus between supply integration and financial success. The exploration bore fruit as it brought to the fore a noteworthy correlation, characterized by its positive nature. The statistical representation, encapsulated as CI FP [= 0.43 and $p = 0.001$], serves as a testament to the constructive influence of supply integration on achieving financial prosperity. This finding lent unequivocal support to the veracity of the second hypothesis (H2), validating its relevance and significance.

Lastly, the investigation turned its gaze toward the link between internal integration and financial accomplishment. The results left an indelible mark, revealing a robust and advantageous connection between these two dimensions. The numerical portrayal, articulated as IIN FP [= 0.60 and $p = 0.000$], illuminated the pivotal role of internal integration in fostering financial achievements. As a consequence, the third hypothesis (H3) emerged triumphant, its validity firmly established within the contours of this study.

4.9 DISCUSSIONS

The outcomes of this investigation support the findings of Droge et al. (2004), Germain and Iyer (2006), and Stank et al. (2001). There is no uncertainty that internal coordination plays a significant role in determining financial effectiveness. The study's outcomes illustrate the crucial nature of internal integration in enhancing a company's financial performance. The significance of this study's findings lies in its novel approach to Supply Chain Integration research, where Internal Integration's influence as a catalyst is often overlooked. The results demonstrated a robust link between Customer Integration and Corporate Achievement. This aligns with analogous discoveries (Germain and Iyer, 2006; Koufteros et al., 2005).

However, this study's discoveries counter the research outcomes of Devaraj et al. (2007), who suggest that customer integration indirectly affects operational efficiency. The findings suggest a favorable association between supplier integration and specific facets of financial effectiveness. These conclusions coincide with the inferences drawn by Stank et al. (2001), while conflicting with the study conducted by Devaraj et al. (2007), which indicated an adverse relationship between supplier integration and financial effectiveness.

4.10 CONCLUSION

The data presented in this study demonstrate a clear and direct correlation between the level of supplier integration and the financial performance of the organization, so providing empirical support for Hypothesis 1. Further research has uncovered evidence of a clear correlation between customer integration and financial performance. This correlation is observed in the frequent encounters with customers, which aim to uphold reliability, responsiveness, and other necessary factors in achieving customer expectations. Consequently, these findings lend support to Hypothesis 2 as proposed in the study. The internal integration remains unaffected. Hypothesis 3 posits that there exists a relationship between internal integration and financial performance.

The study utilized the theory of supply chain integration as a framework for examining the hospitals in North Ghana. Theoretical frameworks propose that conducting empirical evaluations to examine the association between Antecedents of Supply Chain Integration and financial performance could potentially contribute to the improvement of current literature. The findings unveiled a robust correlation between financial performance and the levels of internal integration and customer integration. The prioritization of Supply Chain Integration is crucial in attaining the desired objectives of a company, encompassing customer engagement with boundless expectations, regular customer follow-up to gather feedback on the quality of the company's service offerings, and periodic cross-functional department meetings that incorporate integrated product and service management. The financial performance of every organization is influenced by the interplay between Supply Chain Integration and its collaborative relationships with supply chain partners. Supply Chain Integration is considered a crucial organizational asset that enhances financial performance and enables companies to effectively navigate the intensifying competition within the healthcare industry. The findings of the study indicate the following.

4.11 RECOMMENDATION

Foremost and primarily, it is crucial that managers possess an extensive comprehension of the potential risks and monetary ramifications linked with the application of SCI. In the modern corporate environment, it is vital for supply chain managers to grasp thoroughly how supply chain integration (SCI) can effectively contribute to enhancing their firms' financial performance and empower them to surmount limitations in resources. Caution should be exercised by the manager of a specialized healthcare facility concerning the notion of declining returns when there is an escalation in the degrees of integration with suppliers and clients, surpassing a certain threshold.

Vigilant monitoring of any deviations from the optimal integration level is imperative for supply chain managers. Maintaining a moderate level of supplier integration ensures a well-balanced cost-benefit association in the specific facets. Over 50% of the examined organizations allocated either excessive or insufficient resources in terms of time and financial commitment to the integration of their suppliers. When considering consumer integration, practitioners are advised to adopt a measured approach. There are still opportunities for enhancing the financial performance of nearly 60% of enterprises. Managers also need to explore methods for adapting the extent to which each integration practice is utilized.

It is suggested that hospitals prioritize process integration over alternative integration forms. The findings of the study indicate that organizations should contemplate expanding their engagements with customers and suppliers, shifting their focus from internal to external contexts.

KEYWORDS

- **supply chain integration**
- **financial performance**
- **customer**
- **industrial sector**
- **hospital**

REFERENCES

Ataseven, C.; Nair, A. Assessment of Supply Chain Integration and Performance Relationships: A Meta-Analytic Investigation of the Literature. *Int. J. Prod. Econ.* **2017,** *185*, 252–265.

Barney, J. B. Firm Resources and Sustained Competitive Advantage. *J. Manag.* **1991,** *17* (1), 99–120.

Ellram, L. M.; Cooper, M. C. Supply Chain Management: It's all about the Journey, Not the Destination. *J. Supply Chain Manag.* **2014,** *50* (1), 8–20.

Flynn, B. B.; Huo, B.; Zhao, X. The Impact of Supply Chain Integration on Performance: A Contingency and Configuration Approach. *J. Oper. Manag.* **2010,** *28* (1), 58–71. doi:10.1016/j.jom.2009.06.001.

Frohlich, M. T.; Westbrook, R. Arcs of Integration: An International Study of Supply Chain Strategies. *J. Oper. Manag.* **2001,** *19* (2), 185–200. DOI: 10.1016/S0272-6963(00)00055-3.

Ghana's Ministry of Health. Health Sector 5 year Programme of Work, 2002–2006: Independent Review of POW-2006, Health, Editor, 2007.

Kim, Y. H.; Schoenherr, T. The Effects of Supply Chain Integration on the Cost Efficiency of Contract Manufacturing. *J. Supply Chain Manag.* **2018,** *54* (3), 42–64. DOI: 10.1111/jscm.12168.

Madzimure, J. The Influence of Strategic Networks and Logistics Integration on Firm Performance among Small and Medium Enterprises. *South. Afr. J. Entrep. Small Bus. Manag.* **2019,** *11* (1), 1–7. https://doi.org/10.4102/sajesbm.v11i1.282

Moyano-Fuentes, J.; Sacristán-Díaz, M.; Garrido-Vega, P. Improving Supply Chain Responsiveness through Advanced Manufacturing Technology: The Mediating Role of Internal and External Integration. *Prod. Plan. Control* **2016,** *27* (9), 686–697. DOI: 10.1080/09537287.2016.116 6277.

Narasimhan, R.; Kim, S. W. Effect of Supply Chain Integration on the Relationship between Diversification and Performance: Evidence from Japanese and Korean Firms. *J. Oper. Manag.* **2002,** *20* (3), 303–323.

Park, N. K.; Mezias, J. M.; Song, J. A Resource-Based View of Strategic Alliances and Firm Value in the Electronic Marketplace. *J. Manag.* **2004,** *30* (1), 7–27.

Rai, A.; Patnayakuni, R.; Seth, N. Firm Performance Impacts of Digitally Enabled Supply Chain Integration Capabilities. *MIS Quart.* **2006,** *30* (2), 225–246. DOI: 10. 2307/25148729

Rosa H.; Reza Saeidi S. |Supply Chain Integration and Firm Performance: The Moderating Role of Demand Uncertainty. *Cogent Bus. Manag.* **2020,** *7* (1). DOI: 10.1080/23311975.2020.1760477

Whipple, J. M.; Wiedmer, R.; Boyer, K. K. A Dyadic Investigation of Collaborative Competence, Social Capital, and Performance in Buyer-Supplier Relationships. *J. Supply Chain Manag.* **2015,** *51* (2), 1–20.

WHO. Hospital. [Online] [2016 12/10]. http://www.who.int/topics/hospitals/en/ 22.

Wiengarten, F.; Humphreys, P.; Gimenez, C.; McIvor, R. Risk, Risk Management Practices, and the Success of Supply Chain Integration. *Int. J. Prod. Eco.* **2016,** *171* (3), 361–370.

Wiengarten, F.; Pagell, M.; Ahmed, M. U.;Gimenez, C. Do a Country's Logistical Capabilities Moderate the External Integration Performance Relationship?" *J. Oper. Manag.* **2014,** *32* (1), 51–63. DOI: 10.1016/j.jom.2013. 07.001.

Wong, C. Y.; Boon-Itt, S.; Wong, C. W. The Contingency Effects of Environmental Uncertainty on the Relationship between Supply Chain Integration and Operational Performance. *J. Oper. Manag.* **2011,** *29* (6), 604–615.

Zhou, H.; Benton, W. C. Jr. Supply Chain Practice and Information Sharing. *J. Oper. Manag.* **2007,** *25* (6), 1348–1365.

Zhao, G.; Feng, T.; Wang, D. Is More Supply Chain Integration Always Beneficial to Financial Performance? *Ind. Mark. Manag.* **2015,** *45,* 162–172.

Zhao, X.; Huo, B.; Selen, W.; Yeung, J. H. Y. The Impact of Internal Integration and Relationship Commitment on External Integration. *J. Oper. Manag.* **2011,** *29* (1-2), 17–32.

Appendix: Questionnaire
Tamale Technical University
Center for Professional Studies (CPS)

THE EFFECT OF SUPPLY CHAIN INTEGRATION ON FINANCIAL PERFORMANCE (A CASE STUDY OF HOSPITALS IN NORTHERN REGION)

We are final year Advanced Diploma in Chartered Institute of Logistic and Transport (CILT) of Tamale Technical University undertaking a research on the topic: *the effect of supply chain integration on financial performance (a case study of hospitals in northern region).*

This study serves in partial fulfillment for the award of Chartered Institute of Logistic and Transport. All information provided by the respondent will be used for academic purpose and their privacy is highly guaranteed. Kindly provide the researchers with the needed information.

Thank you.

INSTRUCTION: Please tick (√) in the box and write where necessary.

Section 1

Gender	Please tick
Male	
Female	
Age	
21–25	
36–40	
26–30	
31–35	
41–44	
45 and above	
Working experience	
Less 5 years	
6–10 years	
11–15 years	
18 and above years	
Education	
Diploma	
Degree	
Masters	
PhD	

Section 2

Please, in the following table indicate your level of agreement or disagreement with the statement relating to e-procurement and procurement performance.

	1	2	3	4	5
Supplier Integration (SI)					
Our level of information exchange with our major supplier through information network					
The establishment of a quick ordering system with our major supplier					
The extent of our strategic partnership with our major supplier					
Stable procurement through networking with our major supplier					
The participation level of our major supplier in our procurement and production processes					
We share our demand forecast with our major supplier					
Customer Integration (CI)					
The extent of our linkage with our major customer through information network					
The extent of sharing of market information by our major customer					
Our level of communication with our major customer					
Our follow-up with our major customer for feedback					
The frequency of our contacts with our major customer					
Our major customer shares demand forecast with us					
Internal Integration (IIN)					
The use of periodic interdepartmental meetings among internal functions					
The use of cross functional teams in new product development					
The extent of strategic partnership among different internal functions					
Different internal functions jointly develop strategic plans in collaboration with each other					
Different internal functions monitor business processes together					
Different internal functions jointly develop and maintain measurement systems					
Financial Performance					
Our return on investment (ROI) is high					
Our return on sales is high					
Our growth in sales is high					
Our growth in profit is high					
Our growth in market share is high					

Note: 1 = Strongly Disagree, 2 = Disagree, 3 = neutral, 4 = agree, and 5= Strongly agree.

CHAPTER 5

A Study of the Relationship among Supply Chain Performance Management Factors and Organizational Performance of Manufacturing Industries

K. BHAVANA RAJ[1], S. SREENIVASA MURTHY[2], DIVYESHKUMAR JITENDRAKUMAR GANDHI[3], and SUNIL ADHAV[4]

[1]*Department of Management Studies, Institute of Public Enterprise, Hyderabad, India*

[2]*Institute of Public Enterprise (IPE), Hyderabad, Telangana, India*

[3]*Naran Lala School of Industrial Management & Computer Science, Navsari, Gujarat, India*

[4]*Faculty of Management (PG), School of Management (PG), Dr. Vishwanath Karad MIT World Peace University, Pune, India*

ABSTRACT

Purpose: The paper's aim is to outline the key elements that will shape the new supply chains (SCMs) brought about by the adoption and acceleration of industry. Examining how strategic supply chain management strategies enhance organizational performance is the main goal.

Design/methodology/approach: The study has been carried with a sample of 250 respondents who are randomly selected. The practice of supply chain management and its impact on the performance of the company (performance based on sales) is observed from the respondents through the questionnaire.

Research limitations/implications: Overall, effective SCPM is crucial for manufacturing industries to achieve organizational performance and maintain

Essentials of Supply Chain Management: Strategy, Planning and Operations.
Mohammed Majeed, Abdul-Rasheed Akeji Alhassan Alolo, Seidu Alhassan, and S. Sekar (Eds.)

a competitive edge in the marketplace. By measuring and managing key factors such as quality, speed, cost, and flexibility, manufacturing companies can optimize their supply chain performance and meet the demands of their customers.

Findings: The results demonstrated a strong statistical correlation between dimensions of supply chain management.

Practical implications: The suggested methodology enables purchasing participants to examine essential SCM aspects both before and during SCM system operation.

Originality/value: The report offers helpful information regarding the function of SCM systems by examining SRM-related operations holistically and offering suggestions and guidelines.

5.1 INTRODUCTION

The SCM is crucial to a company's ability to create and keep a competitive advantage. It boosts total business efficiency by raising the quality of all outputs, services, and answers (Spohrer, 2006). Hence, in order for the organization to stay competitive, it must acknowledge the importance of SCM and implement its practices. An organization's value is raised via the supply chain, which links the provider company to its end users. An organization's supply chains are made up of the departments and processes involved in accepting, processing, and finishing customer orders. These departments and processes might cover customer support, sales, logistics, and R&D (Makena and Mike, 2014). Only with carefully controlled supply chains can a company give its products and services (Akyuz et al., 2010). This involves measuring and managing the key factors that impact supply chain performance, including quality, speed, cost, and flexibility. Manufacturing industries, in particular, rely heavily on SCPM to maintain operational efficiency and meet customer demands (Rao, 2006). Organizational performance, which is closely tied to SCPM, is a measure of how well a company is meeting its strategic objectives and financial goals (Kroes and Ghosh, 2010). In a theoretical sense, this research contributes to the existing body of work on topics such as knowledge management methods, organizational performance, and supply chain management strategies. Businesses that possess resources, such as the supply chain management strategies investigated in this study, might provide an advantage to their organizations in terms of competitiveness and have an effect on how well they function. In addition, the knowledge-based theory

(Zenger, 2004) places an emphasis on the aspects of knowledge that apply to its development, dissemination, and application and permit an organization to use it to improve organizational performance (Bengtsson et al., 2010). Knowledge may promote organizational effectiveness in several ways. The study adds to the knowledge of how successful supply chain management techniques affect organization performance, particularly in manufacturing (Kroes and Ghosh, 2010). Some academics have found a correlation between knowledge management methodologies, organizational performance, and supply chain management, but no research has directly linked these factors. The study's findings may help verify the manufacturing industry's link. This research provides a roadmap for firms to plan and execute knowledge collection, sharing, and application in supply chain management. This will boost company performance. According to Claycomb (2001), more academics are recognizing knowledge management (KM) as an essential supply chain management issue. SCM also manages supplier-to-customer processes. In competitive business environment, firms must properly manage their supply chain knowledge. The study may help Malaysian manufacturing organizations understand how vital knowledge management is applied to the company to properly manage the knowledge they have gained through supply chain management methods. This information may assist these firms understand how critical knowledge management is to the organization (Goyal, 2008). Several factors can impact the effectiveness of SCPM and organizational performance in manufacturing industries. These include:

1. Technology adoption: Manufacturing companies that invest in new technologies, such as automation and digitalization, can improve SCPM and organizational performance by increasing efficiency, reducing costs, and enhancing product quality.
2. Supply chain collaboration: Collaboration between supply chain partners can improve SCPM and organizational performance by enabling better communication, more efficient processes, and faster decision-making.
3. Risk management: Effective risk management strategies, such as contingency planning and supplier diversification, can help manufacturing companies mitigate the impact of supply chain disruptions and maintain organizational performance.
4. Customer focus: Manufacturing companies that prioritize customer satisfaction can improve SCPM and organizational performance by delivering products that meet customer's needs and expectations.

5.2 SUPPLY CHAIN MANAGEMENT AND ORGANIZATIONAL PERFORMANCE

Supply chains (SCs) and industrial logistics procedures are crucial to many modern activities, including professional and personal ones. Global economic progress depends on them. Because of rapid change in many markets and economic, financial, social, and technical sectors, SCs are continually changing (Kroes and Ghosh, 2010). SCs expand and alter in size, form, configuration, coordination, management, and control. This model will include additional players and roles along with Industry's major components and aspects (Rao, 2006). This work aims to improve the SC model theory and architecture by surveying the literature. Manufacturing organizations use supply chain management to gain a competitive edge (SCM). It includes purchasing, sourcing, conversion, logistics management, planning, and administration. Due to the global business environment, organizations have been exposed to several technological innovations during the previous several decades. Market integration and networking are the biggest changes. Latest transformation. Hence, supply networks currently dominate competition between corporations. SCM researchers prioritize customer value research because it is important to good company marketing (Goyal, 2008). Many organizations consider their customers a competitive asset. Businesses must retain high customer levels while cutting expenses and boosting profit margins due to revenue enhancement, suppliers obtaining access to customer information, market access, product ideas, or technology, or suppliers earning revenue-enhancing revenue. Commercial initiatives now prioritize consumers and their worth. The research examined supply chain performance and how manufacturing organizations might increase value creation.

5.3 MANAGEMENT OF THE SUPPLY CHAIN AND THE GENERATION OF VALUE

The process of taking input from a company's suppliers, adding value to it, and then distributing it to clients is the core concept behind the activities that make up supply chain operations. A consumer is just one link in the supply chain, which also includes the manufacturer, the supplier, the carrier, the warehouse, the retailer, and so on. Among these functions are the creation of new products, promotion of those products, operations of the business, distribution of goods, financing of the business, and customer service, as well as other responsibilities associated with satisfying the needs of customers. Information management

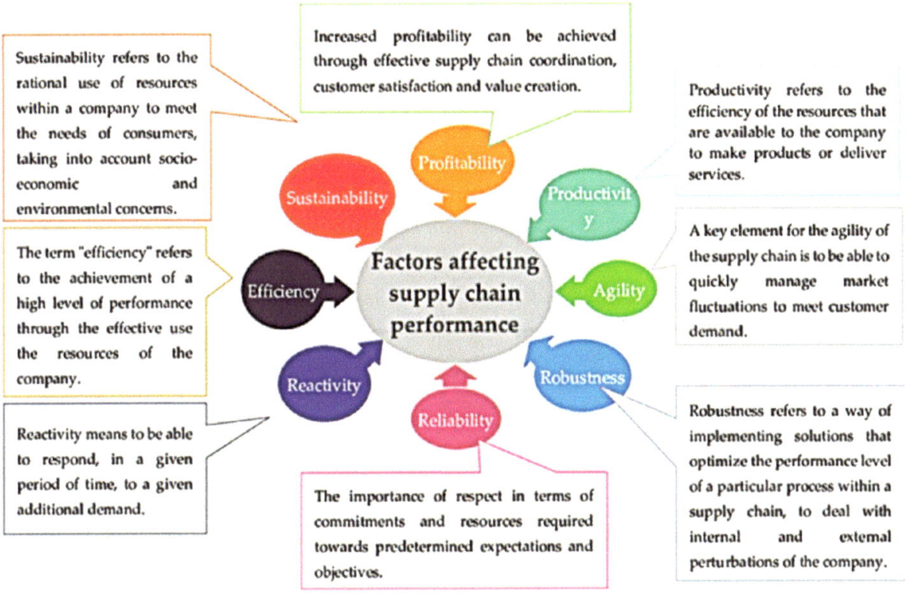

FIGURE 5.1 Management of the supply chain and the generation of value.
Source: Reprinted from Jelti et al. 2021. https://creativecommons.org/licenses/by/4.0/

and integration affect supply chain efficiency. Information technology will help organizations integrate the supply chain. Kristensen and Górecka (2008) define SCM as the management function that oversees an organization's supply chain operations from upstream to downstream. This was done to boost client happiness (Jain et al., 2009). Supply chains must maximize value to create and offer value to consumers, increase chain profit, and minimize supply chain profitability. This project also aims to maximize chain profit and lower supply chain profitability. This creates value for the client, which sustainably benefits all chain stakeholders (Kroes and Ghosh, 2010).

Valuation practitioners and marketing professionals have rediscovered value in recent years. This is because value-centered management increases the likelihood of short-term and long-term success and a competitive edge. Previous experiments have supported the customer value strategy. Customer loyalty improves firm success, according to Fredericks et al. (2001). Industry professionals are struggling to define consumer value, which is gaining attention. Customer value constructs are poorly articulated and operationalized. It is the problem. Operationalizing customer value has two main approaches. These two view consumer value differently, whether from a rational, emotive, or balanced standpoint. Supply chain management connects a company's internal operations with those of external parties like consumers and suppliers, improving competitiveness (SCM) (Bengtsson et al., 2010). Supply chain integration may succeed if various supply chain methods are applied appropriately and integrated. A corporation must integrate both its internal cross-functional barriers and its external supplier and consumer integration to get great supply chain outcomes (Narasimhan, 1997). Several studies have shown the importance of organizational supply networks and supply chain management. OSC impact production agility. Hence, industrial supply chain management methods are fascinating to investigate. Supply chain managers have historically exchanged data, coordinated on product development, negotiated terms and price, questioned potential partners about their product needs, and reviewed demand estimates with customers and suppliers (Kroes and Ghosh, 2010). Cooperation will determine the organization's success. Knowledge management (KM) provides collaborative processes that make the supply chain more adaptable and sensitive to information changes from various working units. Knowledge management involves transforming unstructured data from several sources into usable information. Employees and SCM must be able to easily access and document employees' skills, knowledge, and experiences. Knowledge management predicts organizational performance improvement.

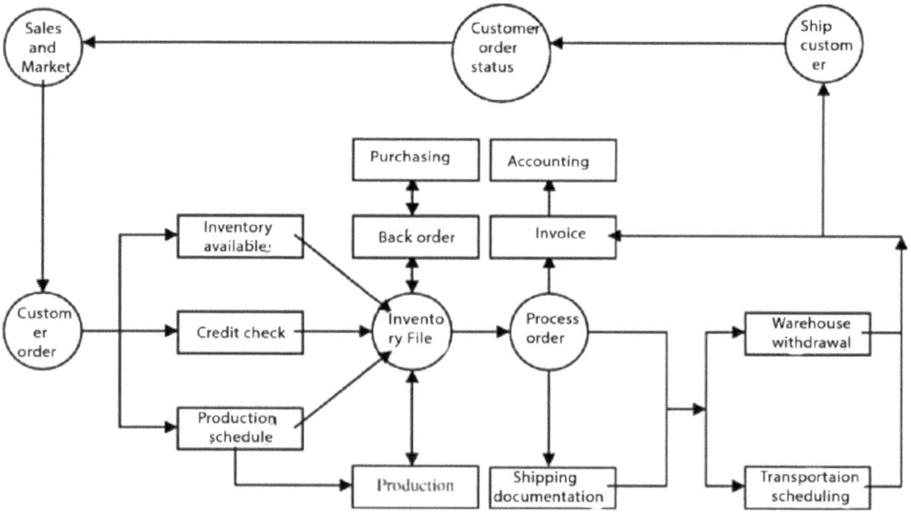

FIGURE 5.2 Performance measurement of supply chain management: A balanced scorecard approach.

Source: Reprinted with permission from Saini et al. 2020. Copyright © 2020, Springer Nature Switzerland AG

5.4 A PARADIGM ANALYSIS OF THE SCM

Throughout the course of the past 30 years or more, the business world has been subjected to a significant amount of upheaval and uncertainty. The changes in consumer expectations, the globalization of markets, and the complexity of product components have combined to make supply chain efficiency an essential component of an organization's ability to compete in its industry. In response to this, a number of companies have implemented new organizational structures, such as supply chains, supply chain alliances, and supply chain networks, which currently serve as the key organizational units in a number of different sectors (Duclos et al., 2003). The focus is on the development of businesses and their ability to work together in a positive manner over the long term. As a result of the fact that they are complimentary to one another, these two may be merged to produce a third paradigm that is known as co-coopetition (Kroes and Ghosh, 2010). The cohabitation of collaboration and rivalry among firms is highlighted by a concept that was coined relatively recently and given the name "coopetition." Coopetition is a compound term that can be broken down into its component parts. Although coopetition is not a paradigm in the same sense that cooperation or rivalry is, it may be considered a paradigm that is complementary to those two.

5.5 DIMENSIONS OF SCM

(SCM) is a complex and multifaceted discipline that encompasses various activities and functions aimed at optimizing the flow of goods, services, and information from suppliers to customers. SCM involves the coordination and integration of multiple stakeholders, processes, and systems, and requires a holistic approach to achieve success. The following are the dimensions of SCM:

- Planning: Planning is a critical dimension of SCM that involves the creation of a comprehensive strategy to manage the supply chain effectively. This includes activities such as demand forecasting, production planning, and inventory management.
- Sourcing: Sourcing involves identifying, selecting, and managing suppliers and other partners that contribute to the supply chain. This includes activities such as supplier evaluation, contract negotiation, and supplier relationship management.
- Production: Production involves the creation of goods and services through various processes, including manufacturing, assembly, and packaging. Effective SCM requires organizations to optimize

production processes to meet customer demand efficiently and cost-effectively.

- Logistics: Logistics is a critical dimension of SCM that involves the transportation, storage, and distribution of goods and services. This includes activities such as transportation planning, inventory management, and order fulfillment.
- Customer service: Customer service involves activities aimed at meeting customer needs and expectations, including order processing, delivery tracking, and returns management. Effective SCM requires organizations to prioritize customer service to maintain customer satisfaction and loyalty.
- Performance measurement: Performance measurement involves the creation and monitoring of metrics that evaluate supply chain performance. This includes measures such as delivery time, inventory turnover, and order accuracy. Effective SCM requires organizations to continuously monitor and improve performance to optimize supply chain efficiency and effectiveness.

5.5.1 A REVIEW OF THE RELEVANT PREVIOUS RESEARCH

The study sought to determine if and how supply chain management strategies affect supply chain performance. Three notions were needed to understand these goals: supply chain management techniques include lean, agile, and hybrid supply chains, and practices include supplier alliances, customer interactions, and information exchange. Supply chain management techniques include lean, agile, and hybrid. Supply chain integration, flexibility, and customer response time. As competition has increased, supply network management has grown more important. A corporation needs a supply chain management plan to compete. For supply chain actors to be more efficient, the strategy must incorporate collaboration and integration across the chain.

Vonderembse et al. (2006) investigated whether it was necessary to use standard, creative, in order to match the requirements of three distinct categories of products. They demonstrate how a lean distribution system should be utilized to produce conventional goods, which are often uncomplicated and provide little space for variety. Techniques for continuous improvement are utilized in lean supply chains, and the reduction of waste is the primary focus of these systems. Yet, innovative products that have the potential to make use of cutting-edge technology require a supply chain that is adaptable. Supply chains that are agile are adaptable and dynamic across organizations, which allows them to respond effectively to rapidly evolving worldwide marketplaces. Hybrid products have several parts and supply chain partners. Hybrid goods may need several supplier agreements. This makes their supply chains hybrids. Hybrid supply networks integrate lean and agile supply chains to address complex product needs. Supply chain management involves several strategies and procedures that link suppliers, manufacturers, distributors, and consumers. These methods increase the company's long-term performance and supply chain. This research found that supply chain management strategies include a number of management efforts to improve supply chain efficiency (Wong's 2005).

Strategic supplier alliances need better supplier collaboration. Long-term supplier connections benefit companies. Vijay Kumar (2013) argued that supply chain management was crucial to a company's success. Enterprises use several goal-oriented methods to find the best way to transport commodities. Today's corporations use the latest scientific methods to meet customer demand for high-quality items. The manufacturing sector has been the main study focus despite the supply chain being separated into outward and inward chains. Supply chain performance, efficiency, and analysis have improved. In today's hypercompetitive environment, supply chain management is increasingly complicated since organizations must monitor hundreds of external data points and respond quickly and automatically along the supply chain (Garul Goyal, 2009). As a result of their growing significance in today's highly competitive business climate, academics and industry professionals are devoting a greater amount of attention to supply chain management modeling and integration. If the value chains of all of an organization's business partners are connected and coordinated, then the supply chain process will be able to transport things, money, value, data, and information more swiftly. This results in increased levels of customer satisfaction as well as increased returns on investment by offering logistical services of a higher quality and lower cost everywhere. The supply chain of a company is said to be optimized when the company has linked its own value chain with those of its business partners in order to increase the value it delivers to its customers by means of improved cooperation, trust, and loyalty as well as the rapid and transparent sharing of confidential information. According to Mahamani and Rao (2010), channel partners and suppliers enable the efficient extension of an integrated supply chain and logistical operations coordination to cover the processes of sourcing, manufacture, and delivery. This is accomplished by extending the scope of the integrated supply chain. It is possible for a corporation to increase its responsiveness to shifts in the market by better coordinating its internal procurement, production, and logistical processes.

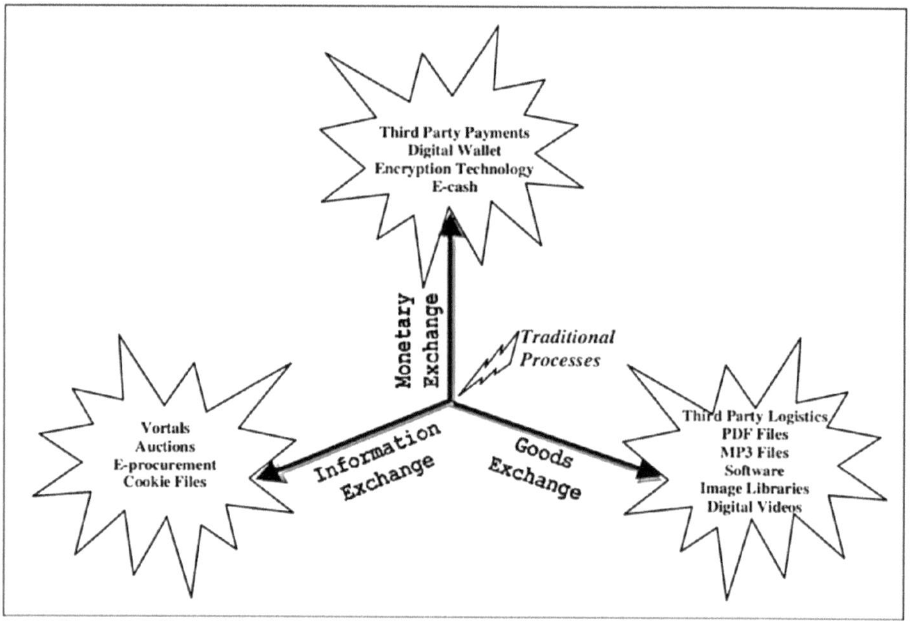

FIGURE 5.3 The effectiveness of organizations performance.

Source: Redrawn from Christopher, 1992.

5.5.2 THE EFFECTIVENESS OF ORGANIZATION'S PERFORMANCE

Organizational performance is an organization's ability to improve its finances and compete with others. This study divides organizational performance into financial and nonfinancial areas. Comparing an organization's results to its goals might indicate its performance. It is crucial and required to investigate numerous facets of organizational performance evaluation before selecting the organizational performance indicator that is most appropriate for your company. Supply chain management (SCM) is an essential function for organizations that rely on complex networks of suppliers, manufacturers, distributors, and retailers to deliver goods and services to customers. Effective SCM requires organizations to coordinate and integrate various processes, from procurement to delivery, in order to optimize performance and minimize costs. The effectiveness of organizations in SCM can be measured in several ways. One key metric is supply chain performance, which reflects how well an organization is able to meet customer's demand while maintaining operational efficiency. Supply chain resilience, which assesses an organization's capacity to recover from unforeseen disruptions, and supply chain agility, which refers to an organization's capacity to adapt swiftly to changes in demand or supply chain interruptions, are other crucial variables.

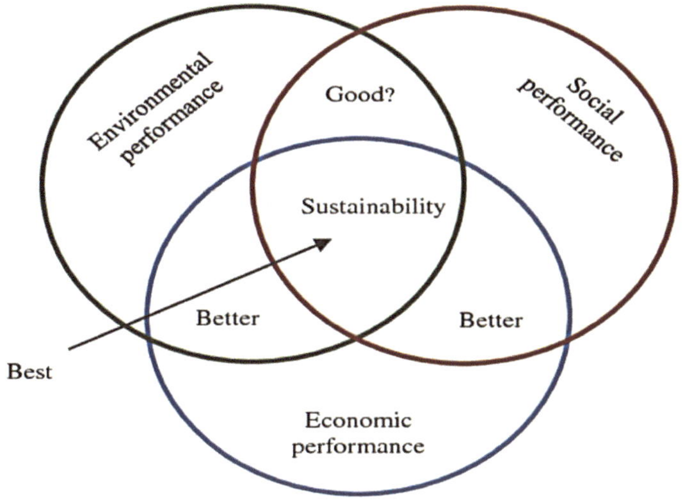

FIGURE 5.4 Effective organizations in SCM tend to exhibit several key characteristics.

Effective organizations in SCM tend to exhibit several key characteristics. These include:

1. Collaboration: Organizations that foster strong relationships and open communication channels with their partners are more likely to achieve optimal performance.
2. Integration: Integration of multiple systems and processes throughout the whole supply chain is necessary for successful SCM. Organizations that invest in technology and tools to facilitate this integration are better equipped to optimize performance and respond quickly to changes.
3. Continuous Improvement: Effective organizations in SCM are committed to continuous improvement, regularly evaluating and refining their processes and systems to optimize performance and reduce costs.
4. Risk Management: Companies that are successful in supply chain management typically have robust risk management methods in place, which allows them to lessen the impact of supply chain interruptions and keep their operations running smoothly.

5.6 SIGNIFICANCE OF THE RESEARCH

Implementing a strategy into operations is the biggest issue for firms. Recent study shows that supply chain efficiency and strategy are completely unrelated. Smart supplier alliances, customer interactions, and information exchange can predict effective supply chain performance, according to this research. If not implemented, a supply chain management plan will not improve performance. The paper suggests integrating supply chain management methods and procedures to achieve this aim (Akyuz et al., 2010). A company's bottom line depends on its supply network's efficiency. Supply chain management is more important than ever for firms to increase output, meet consumer expectations, and enhance efficiency. Supply chain management research aims to enhance corporate value by enhancing resource usage and distribution efficiency. The companies are becoming more and more aware of the intense rivalry that exists among their many different supplier networks. In order to raise their overall productivity, businesses are placing a significant amount of emphasis on consistently improving their supply networks. Linkages between a successful company's internal operations and those of its external suppliers and consumers are typically seen as extremely successful by all parties involved. This is especially true of those relationships that are maintained between the organization and its most important stakeholders. In addition, in an effort to assure the highest possible level of performance, they place a significant emphasis on monitoring and researching supply chain indicators. One method that can be used to evaluate the performance of an organization is to examine how well it performs in comparison to its competitors and how well it maintains its competitiveness in the market. Both these factors are important to the organization's ability to continue existing and expanding in the market.

5.7 THE IMPORTANT OF SCMP

A company may use technology to control the rate of change as well as the outcomes of a number of supply chain factors, including quality, cost, flexibility, delivery, and profit. As has been found, the importance of supply chain efficiency will be significantly impacted by information technology. They even went so far to claim that giving IT R&D and maintenance more of a priority will increase businesses' long-term profitability, shareholder value, and market share. The bottom lines of organizations may benefit from using a more integrated approach to IT infrastructure, which in turn improves the efficacy and efficiency of their supply chains. The increased level of international competition mostly favors consumers. Because he has so many possibilities, he can pick and choose what he wants to buy and establish his own criteria. In an effort to attract customers, businesses launch products with distinctive qualities, yet this results in short product lifespans. If a firm wants to introduce new models rapidly, having trusted suppliers that can give speedy assistance is vital. As the producer now needs to rely on so many different suppliers to provide the necessary components, the overall system has grown complicated. Businesses have started implementing innovative tactics in an effort to lower costs and compete with rates offered elsewhere (Spohrer, 2006). It is recommended that businesses reorganize. Multinational corporations are using their own R&D and design studios and offshore manufacturing to other parts of the world. Businesses increasingly focus on their capabilities and outsource everything else to save money. Supply chain management is a critical function for organizations that rely on complex networks of suppliers, manufacturers, distributors, and retailers to deliver products and services to customers. Effective supply chain management requires coordination and integration of various processes, from procurement to delivery, in order to optimize performance and minimize costs. Supply chain management performance (SCMP) plays an important role in achieving this optimization, as it measures how well an organization manages its supply chain processes and systems.

The importance of SCMP can be summarized as follows:

1. Cost reduction: An effective SCMP helps organizations reduce costs associated with supply chain processes, such as procurement, production, transportation, and inventory management. By optimizing these processes, organizations can lower costs while maintaining or improving quality.
2. Improved customer satisfaction: A well-managed supply chain can help organizations meet customer demands more efficiently and effectively. This results in improved customer satisfaction, which can lead to increased loyalty and repeat business.
3. Increased efficiency: Effective SCMP can improve efficiency by reducing lead times, minimizing inventory levels, and optimizing transportation routes. This results in reduced waste, improved resource utilization, and increased productivity.
4. Competitive advantage: Organizations that excel in SCMP can gain a competitive advantage by delivering products and services faster

and more cost-effectively than their competitors. This can lead to increased market share and profitability.

5. Risk management: Effective SCMP can also help organizations mitigate supply chain risks, such as supply disruptions, quality issues, and transportation delays. By proactively managing these risks, organizations can maintain operational continuity and minimize the impact of disruptions.

5.8 OBJECTIVES OF THE STUDY

The research aimed to ascertain the selected supply chain management strategies has an effect on the performance of the firm (Sukati et al., 2006). The study also hopes to ascertain whether the presence of a whole knowledge management process (including information acquisition, knowledge exchange, and knowledge application) mediators this connection.

The aims of the research are as follows:

1. To examine the relationship between the nature of the respondents and their opinion toward (SCM) practices.
2. To study the impact of SCM and chain management methods.
3. To find out dimensions of supply chain management.

5.8.1 RESEARCH APPROACH

The study has been carried with a sample of 250 respondents who are randomly selected. The practice of supply chain management and its impact on the performance of the company (performance based on sales) is observed from the respondents through the questionnaire (SCM) practices implemented in the organization.

5.9 ANALYSIS, FINDINGS, AND CONCLUSION

5.9.1 RELATIONSHIP BETWEEN THE NATURE OF THE RESPONDENTS AND THEIR OPINION TOWARD (SCM) PRACTICES

It is an attempt to study the relationship between the nature of the respondents and their opinion toward (SCM) practices. For this, the age and the

TABLE 5.1 Age of the Respondents and their Opinion on SCMP.

Variables	Age group	N	Mean rank	Chi-square value (df-2)/Sig.
Holding safety stock	Young	82	124.57	0.234/0.983
	Middle	88	125.38	
	Old	80	126.59	
Strategic planning	Young	82	128.57	0.033/0.785
	Middle	88	121.54	
	Old	80	124.32	
Supply chain benchmarking	Young	82	125.19	0.384 / 0.613
	Middle	88	122.35	
	Old	80	128.69	
Outsourcing	Young	82	127.46	0.156/0.735
	Middle	88	124.96	
	Old	80	123.77	
Subcontracting	Young	82	119.72	0.912/0.634
	Middle	88	129.18	
	Old	80	127.11	
E-procurement	Young	82	115.50	0.382/0.169
	Middle	88	125.30	
	Old	80	132.58	
	Total	250		

income of the employees are considered important characters influencing their behavior. It is discussed one by one in detail as below.

The result from the above table shows that young-aged respondents have preferred more strategic planning (128.57) and outsourcing (127.46). The middle-aged respondents like subcontracting (129.18) and E-procurement (125.30) as better practices for SCMP. The old-aged respondents opined that supply chain benchmarking (128.69) and E-procurement (132.58) are SCMP.

The result from the Kruskal–Wallis test indicates insignificant relationship between the opinion of the respondents about the different SCMP and the age of the respondents. The calculated Chi-Square values are less than table value for the degree of freedom 2. Hence, the values of probability are more than 0.05. It is concluded that the opinion of the respondents about the difference of their opinion on SCMP does not vary according to the age of the respondents.

5.9.2 DIMENSIONS OF SUPPLY CHAIN MANAGEMENT

SCMP is a critical component of effective supply chain management, enabling organizations to reduce costs, improve customer satisfaction, increase efficiency, gain competitive advantage, and mitigate supply chain risks (Makena and Mike, 2014). Organizations that prioritize SCMP are better equipped to optimize supply chain performance and achieve long-term success in the marketplace.

TABLE 5.2 Dimensions of Supply Chain Management.

Dimensions	Mean	Std. deviation	Mean rank
Customer relationship	3.17	1.276	6.41
Information sharing	3.52	1.055	6.32
Information technology	3.24	1.141	6.75
Internal operation	3.08	1.167	6.29
Strategic supplier partnership	3.01	1.414	6.63
Training	3.25	1.237	6.31
Collaborative distribution	3.83	1.072	6.59
Distribution flexibility	3.48	1.925	6.58
IT-enabled distribution	3.37	1.118	6.56
Inventory management	3.45	1.235	6.87
Order commitment	3.21	1.240	6.52
Transparency in the distribution process	3.19	1.084	6.01

The result shows that inventory management (6.87) is the most impressive dimension in the supply chain management. Information technology (6.75) is another dimension to find a successful one. Strategic supplier partnership (6.63), collaborative distribution (6.59), distribution flexibility (6.58) are ranked third, fourth, and fifth, respectively. It is concluded that these five dimensions are considered mostly used in the supply chain management.

TABLE 5.3 Friedman Test.

N	250
Chi-square	26.462
Df	11
P	0.006

The ranking result from 250 sample respondents shows the difference in the ranking for each factor is significant. The calculated Chi-Square value is 26.462

for the degree of freedom 11 is more than expected level. The value of probability is 0.006. It shows that the ranks given by the respondents are significant.

5.10 DISCUSSION

In summary, the effectiveness of organizations in SCM is crucial for optimizing performance, minimizing costs, and delivering high-quality products and services to customers (Parung et al., 2004). By prioritizing collaboration, integration, continuous improvement, and risk management, organizations can achieve optimal supply chain performance and maintain a competitive edge in the marketplace Strategic relationships with several suppliers chosen purely on cost will allow businesses to more effectively connect with suppliers (Sukati et al., 2006). The best component may be chosen to help in a more precise evaluation of the design, and the cost of those components can be reduced if suppliers are brought in early (Makena and Mike, 2014). Thus, strategic collaborations with suppliers are useful for both local and international suppliers. Strategic supplier relationships, on the other hand, entail more than just buying something from suppliers; they also involve shaping the suppliers' internal infrastructure and operations in ways that impact. In a partnership, suppliers are incentivized to aid in the success of the organization's performance through collaborative problem-solving, information sharing, and continuous quality improvement efforts. In this context, agreements with key suppliers are viewed as an indicator of future success (Bengtsson et al., 2010). Supply chain management techniques affect manufacturing businesses' productivity, the study found. The study found that supply chain managers must communicate with suppliers and ensure their goals match the company's. If a manufacturing business wants to improve customer satisfaction, it must set customer acquisition and retention goals and include them in staff performance appraisals. SCM adoption, deployment, and improvement will assist manufacturing organizations, according to the research (Bengtsson et al., 2010). If factories want to maintain working with their suppliers, they should keep communication lines open, according to studies. High-quality raw materials or production-ready components will improve production flow and speed up customer delivery. Future studies may employ regression, correlation, or a mix of quantitative and qualitative methodologies to evaluate manufacturing organizations (Rao, 2006). The data show that supply chain management techniques affect manufacturing enterprises' productivity. Structural equation modeling (Path Analysis) was used to examine data and test hypotheses for the study. Most studies had similar results. In support of Null Hypothesis 2, we find that customer satisfaction is directly connected to strategic supplier relationships. Mohammad et al. (2019) discovered that supplier connections improved long-term performance. Rodriguez and Boyer (2020) have hypothesized that CRM improves consumer encounters when cooperation mediates the discourse. Sharing information has no impact on company outcomes, supporting the third hypothesis. The study indicated that integrating information systems across business activities in the organizations evaluated did not increase output productivity (Spohrer, 2006). A manufacturer's production efficiency and financial outcomes depend on inventory management and control. Lean manufacturing improves innovation performance, disproving. Firms used all lean product components from the survey (Parung et al., 2004). All the organizations evaluated have a culture of continuous development and match output to client's demand. Lean manufacturing is essential for profitable companies. To sustain such routines and improve organizational performance, many strategies and relevant approaches must be used. These tactics have been found to minimize costs in manufacturing, supervision, cycle durations, customer response, investment, sales, and profitability. Lokpriya et al. (2020) discovered that lean manufacturing improves performance. It has been proposed that we monitor resource allocation over time to avoid stalling this phase.

5.10.1 THE IMPACT OF SUPPLY CHAIN MANAGEMENT ON OUTPUT

One of the most important aspects of SCM is customer relations, which include tasks like evaluating customer complaints, enhancing customer support, following up on customer feedback, predicting key factors affecting customer relationships, gauging customer expectations, interacting with customers to establish standards, and gauging customer satisfaction. Mentzer et al. (2000) pointed out that the knowledge about customers that flows through the data about logistics operations may be of different types. Logistics, customer orders, forecasts, schedules, the market, and other issues were the main focus of the information exchanged. Information sharing also includes access to confidential data so that business partners may monitor the supply chain system's handling of the goods and the order's development (Parung et al., 2004). To succeed in today's global economy, businesses must integrate supply chain management practices into their corporate culture. It is important that they have a balanced set of methods, as the sum of their effects will be greater than the sum of any one of them (Sukati et al., 2006).

5.11 CONCLUSION

The global market is extremely competitive; therefore, businesses need to maximize their use of all available resources. In an effort to better coordinate the whole business process along the value chain, some companies are adopting new management paradigms that extend beyond the bounds of the traditional organization (Bengtsson et al., 2010). Companies in the modern era of supply chain management need a fully functional infrastructure that can efficiently distribute products and services in order to adapt to the ever-changing nature of the global market. If they want to thrive in a market where the competitive landscape is always evolving, businesses need to become experts in SCM (Akyuz et al., 2010). A company's unique selling proposition (USP) is the product of deliberate strategic management decisions and comprises the qualities that set it apart from other businesses (Goyal, 2008). The findings indicate that many factors contribute to a company's sales success, including its strong relationships with its customers, keep adequate levels of safety stock on hand, work with a diverse set of suppliers, outsource tasks, develop a comprehensive strategic plan, and employ subcontractors (Parung et al., 2004).

KEYWORDS

- **organizational performance**
- **manufacturing industries**
- **supply chain performance management**
- **value chain**
- **logistics**

REFERENCES

Abdallah, A. B.; Obeidat, B. Y.; Aqqad, N. O. The Impact of Supply Chain Management Practices on Supply Chain Performance in Jordan: The Moderating Effect of Competitive Intensity. *Int. Bus. Res.* **2014,** *7* (3), 13–27.

Akyuz Arzu, G.; Erman Erkan, T. Supply Chain Performance Measurement: A Literature Review. *Int. J. Prod. Res.* **2010,** *48* (17), 5137–5155.

Aruna Kumari, C. P.; Vijaya Kumar, Y. An Effective Way To Optimize Key Performance Factors Of Supply Chain Management. *Int. J. Manag.* **2013,** *4* (3), 11–20.

Bengtsson, M.; Eriksson, J.; Wincent, J. Co-opetition Dynamics – An Outline for Further Inquiry. *Compet. Rev. Int. Bus. J. Incorp. J. Global Compet.* **2010,** *20* (2), 194–214.
Bititci, U. S.; Martinez, V.; Albores, P.; Parung, J. Creating and Managing Value in Collaborative Networks. *Int. J. Phys. Distrib. Logist. Manag.* **2004,** *34* (3/4), 251–268.
Brandy Berry, A.; Rai, A.; White, G. P. Intermediate Performance Impacts of Advanced Manufacturing Technology Systems: An Empirical Investigation. *Decis. Sci.* **1999,** *30* (4), 993–1020.
Byrd, T. A.; Davidson, N. W. Examining Possible Antecedents of IT Impact on the Supply Chain and its Effect on Firm Performance. *Inf. Manag.* **2003,** *41* (2), 243–255.
Christopher, M. Logistics and Supply Chain Management: Strategies for Reducing Costs and Improving Services. Financial Times, 1992.
Chopra, S.; Meindl, P. In *Supply Chain Management: Strategy, Planning and Operation*, 3rd Ed.; Prentice-Hall. Inc: New Jersey, 2007,
Christopher, M.; Peck, H.; Towill, D. R. A Taxonomy for Selecting Global Supply Chain Strategies. *Int. J. Logist.* **2006,** *17* (2), 277–287.
Cooper, M. C.; Ellram, L. M. 'Characteristics of Supply Chain Management and the Implications for Purchasing and Logistics Strategy. *Int. J. Logist. Manag.* **1993,** *4* (1), 13–24.
Ellram, L. M.; Tate, W. L.; Billington, C. Understanding and Managing the Service Supply Chain. *J. Supply Chain Manag.* **2004,** *40* (4), 17–32.
Feciková, I. An Index Method for Measurement of Customer Satisfaction. *TQM Mag.* **2004,** *16* (1), 57–66.
Goyal, P. Supply Chain Management Integration Performance Measurement and Evaluation. *Int. J. Res. Manag. Eco. Comm.* **2008,** *2* (1), 100–113.
Green, K. Jr.; Zelbst, P.; Meacham, J.; et al. Green Supply Chain Management Practices: Impact on Performance. *Suppl. Chain Manag. Int. J.* **2012,** *17* (3), 290–305.
Gunasekaran, A.; Mc Gaughey, R. E. TQM is Supply Chain Management. *TQM Mag.* **2003,** *15* (6), 361–363.
Heydari, J.; Baradaran Kazemzadeh, R.; Chaharsooghi, S. K. A Study of Lead Time Variation Impact on Supply Chain Performance. *Int. J. Adv. Manuf. Technol.* **2009,** *40* (11-12), 1206–1215.
Jain, V.; Wadhwa, S.; Deshmukh, S. G. Revisiting Information Systems to Support a Dynamic Supply Chain: Issues and Perspectives. *Prod. Plan. Control* **2009,** *20* (1), 17–29.
Jelti, F.; Allouhi, A.; Buker, M.; Saadani, R.; Jamil. Renewable Power Generation: A Supply Chain Perspective. Sustainability, 2021, 13,1271.
Jie, F.; Parton, K. A.; Cox, R. J. Linking Supply Chain Practices to Competitive Advantage: An Example from Australian Agribusiness. *Brit. Food J.* **2013,** *115* (7), 1003–1024.
Lambert, D. M.; Cooper, M. C.; Pagh, J. D. 'Supply Chain Management Implementation Issues and Research Opportunities. *Int. J. Logist. Manag.* **1998,** *9* (2), 1–19.
Li, S.; Ragu-Nathan, B.; Ragu-Nathan, T. S.; Rao, S. S. The Impact of Supply Chain Management Practices on Competitive Advantage and Organizational Performance. *OMEGA* **2006,** *34* (2), 107–124.
Luo, X.; Slotegraaf, R.; Pan, X. Cross-Functional "Coopetition": The Simultaneous Role of Cooperation and Competition Within Firms. *J. Mark.* **2006,** *70*, 67–80.
Lydeka, Z.; Adomavicius, B. Cooperation among the Competitors in International Cargo Transportation Sector: Key Factors to Success. *Eng. Econ.* **2007,** *1* (51), 80–90.

Maglio, P. P.; Srinivasan, S.; Kreulen, J. T.; Spohrer, J. Service Systems, Service Scientists, SSME, and Innovation. *Commun. ACM* **2006,** *49* (7), 81–86.

Mahamani, A.; Rao, K. P. Development of a Spreadsheet Based Vendor Inventory Model for a Single Echelon Supply Chain: A Case Study. *Serbian J. Manag.* **2010,** *5* (2), 199–2011.

Qrunfleh, S. M. Alignment of Information Systems with Supply Chains: Impacts on Supply Chain Performance and Organizational Performance. *J. Univ. Toledo* **2010,** *3* (6), 23–39.

Karimi, E.; Rafiee, M. Analyzing the Impact of Supply Chain Management Practices on Organizational Performance through Competitive Priorities (Case Study: Iran Pumps Company). *Int. J. Acad. Res. Acc.* **2014,** *4* (1), 1–15.

Kroes, J. R.; Ghosh, S. Outsourcing Congruence with Competitive Priorities: Impact on Supply Chain and Firm Performance. *J. Operat. Manag.* **2010,** *28* (2), 124–143.

Lam, L. W. Impact of Competitiveness on Salespeople's Commitment and Performance. *J. Bus. Res.* **2012,** *65*, 1328–1334.

Lewis, M. Lean Production and Sustainable Competitive Advantage. *Int. J. Operat. Prod. Manag.* **2000,** *20* (6), 959–976.

Makena, N. M.; Mike, I. Impact of Supply Chain Management Practices on Organizational Performance: A Case Study of Haco Industries Limited (Kenya). *J. Bus. Manag.* **2014,** *16* (4), 62–64.

Mentzer, J. T.; Flint, D. J.; Hult, G. T. M. Logistics Service Quality as a Segment Customized Process. *J. Market.* **2001,** *65* (4), 82–104.

Saini, R.; Osorio-Gonzalez, C.S.; Hegde, K.; Brar, S.K.; Magdouli, S.; Vezina, P.; Avalos-Ramirez, A. Lignocellulosic biomass-based biorefinery: an insight into commercialization and economic standout. *Current Sustainable/Renewable Energy Reports*. **2020,** *7*, 122–36.

Sukati, I.; Hamid, A. B.; Baharun, R.; Yusoff, R. M. The Study of Supply Chain Management Strategy and Practices on Supply Chain Performance. *Soc. Behav. Sci.* **2006,** 225–233.

Sukati, I.; Hamid, A. B.; Baharun, R.; Yusoff, R. The Study of Supply Chain Management Strategy and Practices on Supply Chain Performance. *Soc. Behav. Sci. Int. J. Bus. Mark.* **2012,** *1* (6), 56–62.

Vickery, S. K.; Jayaram, J.; Droge, C.; Calantone, R. The Effects of an Integrative Supply Chain Strategy on Customer Service and Financial Performance: An Analysis of Direct Versus Indirect Relationships. *J. Operat. Manag.* **2003,** *21* (5), 523–539.

CHAPTER 6

The Influence of Transportation System on Manufacturing Firm's Performance in Ghana: A Case Study of Ghana Nuts Company Limited in Techiman

MOHAMMED MAJEED[1], DAVID INUSAH OFFEI[2], and SUMAILA SEIDU SALAAM[3]

[1]*Marketing Department, Tamale Technical University, Tamale, Ghana*

[2]*Tamale Technical University, Tamale, Ghana*

[3]*Automotive Engineering Department, Tamale Technical University, Tamale, Ghana*

ABSTRACT

The aim of this research is to analyze how the implementation of supply chain management techniques impacts the overall effectiveness of an organization. The study employed a quantitative research methodology, with questionnaires as the primary data collection instrument. A total of 204 individuals from various sectors of the supply chain, including suppliers, manufacturers, and distributors, were surveyed to gather the necessary data. The data analysis for Ghana Nuts Company Limited in Techiman involved the utilization of factor analysis and hypothesis testing using SPSS-Amos software. The results of the study indicate that in order to enhance organizational efficiency, it is imperative for enterprises to develop a keen interest in transportation services. The study's theoretical implications contribute to a deeper comprehension of the factors that impact organizational performance, while its practical implications facilitate the adoption of practises

Essentials of Supply Chain Management: Strategy, Planning and Operations.
Mohammed Majeed, Abdul-Rasheed Akeji Alhassan Alolo, Seidu Alhassan, and S. Sekar (Eds.)

that can effectively influence organizational performance. It is recommended for companies to incorporate transportation oversight into their operational protocols. This involves putting in place efficient management of their vehicle fleet, arranging vehicle timetables, strategizing routes, and upkeeping the vehicles. By taking these steps, organizations can guarantee the seamless sourcing of resources and the effective distribution of goods. This amalgamation ultimately results in improved cost-effectiveness, a larger portion of the market, and shorter lead times, all of which provide favorable contributions to the company.

6.1 GENERAL INTRODUCTION

6.1.1 BACKGROUND OF THE STUDY

Transportation is still very important to the success of Ghana Nut Company Limited (GNCL), since most of its actions involve moving goods. Kenyon and Meixell (2011) say that transportation is the process of moving raw materials or finished goods from suppliers to factories, warehouses, and sales sites. Bowersox et al. (2010) assert that transportation administration involves strategizing, overseeing, and decision-making within the realm of logistics for the relocation and distribution of inventory to various locations. Transportation has always gotten a lot of attention from managers because of how important it is and how much it costs. Almost every business, big and small, had a transportation manager (Bowersox et al., 2010).

Because transportation expenses make up a significant portion of total logistics costs, the effectiveness of the logistics system is greatly influenced by transportation management (Bowersox et al., 2010). Throughout the production process, transportation is essential, spanning from manufacturing to distribution, reaching end consumers, and handling returns. Effective coordination and collaboration among all components are essential for maximizing the advantages of logistics. A well-executed transportation management strategy holds the potential to enhance logistics efficiency, minimize operational expenses, and elevate the quality of service provided by enterprises (Bowersox et al., 2010). The success of transportation within the logistical framework hinges on three key factors: cost, speed, and reliability (Bowersox et al., 2010). The cost of transportation encompasses both shipping charges between different geographical points and the expenses associated with maintaining inventory during transit. Employing transportation within logistics strategies serves the purpose of reducing the overall system cost (Bowersox et al., 2010).

Bowersox et al. (2010) mentioned that the velocity of transportation encompassed the duration needed to execute a specific task. There existed a connection between the expense and pace of transportation in a pair of manners. First of all, companies that could get packages to their customers faster were usually paid more for their services. Second, the quicker the transportation service, the shorter the time inventory was in transit and the higher the costs (Bowersox et al., 2010). In order to choose the best means of transportation for a business, it is important to find a good balance between speed and cost.

Product distribution is a difficult part of the delivery process, and manufacturers are moving toward a more convenient method, which is to skip the distribution routes and go straight to direct marketing. Traditional distributors have reacted to this situation in a number of different ways, as has been seen. Some were interested in leaving because they thought they could get better service and build better relationships elsewhere (Bowersox, 2016). Some individuals express their grievances, objections, or frustration driven by a sense of loyalty, aiming to stimulate enhancements in service quality. The effectiveness of distribution channel roles is notably eroded, especially in the context of exports. The distribution channel plays essential roles, which encompass categorization, movement/shipment, warehousing, manipulation, and information exchange (Bowersox, 2016).

6.1.2 PROBLEM STATEMENT

The fragmented and diverse nature of the oil manufacturing industrial chain, as well as the fact that small and micro businesses predominate, add to the chain's complexity. This has led to the integration of sustainability into the supply chains for the oil manufacturing industry by several textile and oil manufacturing enterprises (Shen et al., 2017). Product delivery is a challenging issue, and companies are moving away from distribution networks in favor of direct marketing as a more practical strategy. As mentioned before, it has been seen that traditional distributors have addressed this issue in a variety of ways. Many staff have shown interest in leaving because they thought they could find better relationships and a greater level of service elsewhere (Bowersox, 2016). Some people are compelled by a sense of loyalty to voice their displeasure, criticism, or outrage in an effort to enhance the level of service. Distribution channel functions are devalued, particularly by enterprises focused on exports. Among the main tasks carried out by the distribution channel are assortment, transfer/transportation, storage, handling, and communication (Bowersox, 2016). Numerous research have been conducted locally to look into the variables that affect the success of manufacturing enterprises across a range of industries: Finance (Seghete, 2016), Government entities (Weeks and Namusonge, 2016; Kanda and Iravo, 2015; Karimi and Namusonge, 2014), and Production sector (Obura, Ombok; Barasa et al., 2015; Wabwile and Namusonge, 2015; Waithaka et al., 2012).

Additionally, it has been noted that following supply chain practises can result in outputs that are in accordance with organizational goals and performance while also lowering operational costs (Muma et al., 2014; Osuga et al., 2015). Additional support for the importance of supply chain management techniques is provided by Kimotho (2014), who contends that an organization's profitability, supplies, quality, and competitiveness are all directly impacted by satisfactory performance. Hence, it is undeniable that employing suitable methods for the transportation system will continue to be the answer to the challenges encountered by the oil production sector in Ghana. Nevertheless, due to the insufficient exploration of the oil manufacturing field, the present investigation sought to pinpoint the transport variables that could most accurately predict business outcomes in this vital sector.

Despite the numerous research endeavors carried out within the Ghanaian setting, the analysis unearthed that none of these studies were dedicated to exploring the impact of supply chain factors on the operational effectiveness of oil production firms. This topic is of paramount importance in realizing Ghana's 2030 vision. The attainment of success in oil manufacturing businesses hinges on recognizing pivotal elements of the supply chain and implementing optimal managerial approaches for their oversight.

6.1.3 OBJECTIVES OF THE STUDY

The main objective of this research is to evaluate how the transportation system impacts the operational effectiveness of manufacturing companies in Ghana.

6.1.3.1 SPECIFIC OBJECTIVES

1. To examine the importance of transportation system in distribution of products at Ghana Nuts Company Limited.
2. To examine the efficiency of the distribution channel of Ghana Nuts Company Limited.
3. To analyze the challenges of transportation system on Ghana Nuts Company Limited performance.

6.1.4 SIGNIFICANCE OF THE STUDY

The government of Ghana has always wanted to create a mixed economy with both state and private businesses (RoK, 2007). As a result of policy changes made by the government, the public is much less involved in manufacturing than in the private sector, and this trend is still going down. Now, the focus is on privatizing the industrial sector. Because of this, the government has to work hard to improve travel services if it wants to make Ghanaian businesses more productive. The study could help the government learn more about how transport management and the efficiency of the production sector are linked. This will help come up with policies and rules that can help make the manufacturing sector more efficient and effective. A better manufacturing sector could boost the national GDP and, in turn, create more jobs. Better transportation management could lead to more trade and lower costs for exports, which would mean more money from exports, cheaper goods and services, and a more stable supply chain.

The study may be helpful to manufacturing organizations since it will help them better understand the underlying transportation elements that affect their performance and better prepare them to cope with challenges that stand in the way of effective transportation management. The growth of industrial companies, improved productivity, cheaper production costs, better distribution, higher-quality products, and more customer satisfaction would all be supported by effective and efficient transportation. These conclusions offer some potential approaches for improving Ghanaian transport so that it is more competitive with international best practices.

The transportation domain in Ghana involves a range of participants, such as those offering transportation services, carriers, those managing warehouse services, individuals in the distribution sector, and any other contributor to guaranteeing the punctual availability of goods and services to customers from suppliers. The findings of this study have the capacity to serve as a robust indicator for the various parties involved in transportation, underscoring the significance of information systems in the realm of transportation and the benefits associated with efficiently organized transportation methods. These advantages encompass heightened effectiveness in customs clearance procedures, improved infrastructure quality for trade and transportation, simplified processes for economical shipments, upgraded transportation services, and the ability to track shipments (World Bank, 2012).

Furthermore, this research possesses the potential to assist academics by contributing to the expanding body of transportation literature. It lays the groundwork for future research by introducing a framework outlining different aspects of transportation management. Since there has been little research on transportation in the developing world to date, researchers in the field, especially those in Ghana, may be interested in reviewing the results of this project. Rooted in a case study from Ghana, this research is poised to drive theoretical and practical advancements in the adoption, implementation, and enhancement of transportation practices across diverse cultural and business contexts.

6.2 LITERATURE REVIEW

6.2.1 THEORETICAL REVIEW

6.2.1.1 GAME THEORY

Inventory management and transportation management continue to be major obstacles in supplier management decisions. It has been shown that using game theory, and the cooperative game in particular, to manage centralized inventory systems and transportation can result in significant cost savings and an increase in customer satisfaction (Fiestras-Janeiro et al., 2011). The selection process based on game theory was adjusted so that it could provide solutions for both inventory and transportation management. According to Xu et al. (2013), the "official study of conflict and cooperation between players" is game theory. It is also known as the "formal study of decision-making in which many players are required to make choices that may have an impact on the interests of opposing players." In scenarios characterized by interconnected behaviors among numerous entities, the principles of game theory find relevance (Dai and Chen, 2012). Agents can encompass individuals, groups, corporations, or any conceivable combination thereof. Utilizing game theory concepts, such as those pertinent to inventory management, enables the formulation, assessment, and comprehension of strategic scenarios (Dai and Chen, 2012).

Two fundamental approaches within game theory are noncooperative and cooperative game theories, as outlined by Xu et al. (2013). In noncooperative game theory, players engage in competitive interactions. When players may gain more as a group by working together than they can by doing it alone, cooperative game theory comes into play (Xu et al., 2013). Cooperative games, as proposed by Mateo and Aghezzaf (2013), bring together a group of players with the goal of maximizing the good for everybody.

Managers of different supply chain sales points may reduce their stock holdings by working together in a game that mimics the distribution route (Mateo and Aghezzaf, 2013). They might work together to negotiate a fair price for the item's exchange. According to game theory, under these circumstances, cooperative groups of sales stations, reasonable exchange prices, and allowable inventories must all be adapted to suit particular supply chains. Game theory was chosen with regard for its potential utility in transportation management in mind as well.

Due to its potential to analyze and resolve situations wherein the decisions of competing players influence each other's rewards, Slimani and Achchab (2014) suggest that game theory offers a means to enhance the study of transportation and inventory scenarios. Game theory serves as a framework for collaborative endeavors, such as those within supply chains, where entities like retailers and raw material suppliers cooperate to manage transportation operations, among other instances. Extensive research has delved into cooperative game theory, particularly concerning issues related to sharing gains. As a result, cooperative game theory emerges as the most suitable model for examining transportation and inventory dynamics within companies. The growing significance of cooperation in global transportation systems is underscored as a means to enhance overall performance (Drechsel and Kimms, 2010).

Horizontal cooperation in transport has been found to be effective in game theory studies (Pan et al., 2012) to lower global costs and increase performance. However, despite these benefits, horizontal collaboration is still underutilized in the transportation sector, according to research by Muir (2010). This study utilized a cooperative-game-theoretic methodology to facilitate decision-making in assessing the efficiency of transport and the impact of company performance on transport. In the field of cooperative game theory, scholars have developed many methodologies for equitable profit distribution and the establishment of stable coalitions. These aspects are considered fundamental components within the framework of cooperative models. The field of cooperative game theory has aimed to analyze the dynamics of player interactions within cooperative relationships (Dror et al., 2012). This form of collaboration happened among enterprises operating at a similar market level, necessitating the exchange of secret information and resources within the transportation industry (Drechsel and Kimms, 2010). The objective of the study conducted by Cruijssen et al. (2007) was to optimize transportation expenses while simultaneously mitigating the environmental consequences associated with transportation operations.

The objective was to enhance the efficacy of transport systems, such as reducing transport expenses (Pan et al., 2011). The primary focus of the hypothesis revolved around the cost associated with transportation. The research has provided evidence that effective implementation of horizontal cooperation in transport can lead to a reduction of at least 10% in transport costs (Groothedd et al., 2005; Ergun et al., 2007; Pan et al., 2011). Given its size, Ghana's industrial sector has received a substantial amount of investment. To better understand how transportation management affects the success of manufacturing companies, this research heavily relied on concepts from game theory. The theory's value comes from the savings in transport costs it predicts would result from its implementation. Because of this, we decided to use this idea in our investigation.

6.3 GHANA NUTS COMPANY LIMITED (GNCL)

Established in 2001, Ghana Nuts Limited is a prominent agro-processing company in Ghana. GNCL, a prominent company in the industry, engages in the production and global distribution of a diverse assortment of edible oils. Shea oil, soybean oil, and animal feed meals are all included in this category of oils (GNCL, 2021). Located in Techiman, Brong-Ahafo Region, The Ghana Nuts Company Ltd has been going strong since its inception in 2001.

Having a present yearly crushing ability of approximately 90,000 metric tons, the corporation stands as a significant participant in the shea nuts sector. Its entire yearly yield of unrefined shea butter is sent abroad. Ghana Nuts owns a manufacturing facility with an annual processing potential of 35,000 tons for handling soya beans, in addition to a refining facility with the capability to process 70 tons each day. The company presently maintains a direct labor force of 350 individuals and an indirect workforce of 1000 individuals for the shea nuts and soya bean value chains. The variety of high-quality items offered by GNCL is produced with the most superior raw materials that are currently available. GNCL was established as a leading commodity trader specializing in the trading of various agricultural products such as soya, groundnuts, cashew, shea nuts, and sesame seeds. The corporation maintains a substantial amount of overseas trade, each year dispatching over 30,000 tons of these goods to Europe, the UK, India, and Japan (GNCL, 2021). The growth of Ghana's Nuts Company, serving as the main industrial establishment in Techiman, has continuously generated employment prospects for a labor force comprising more than 250 workers. According to

MDP (2014), GNCL was selected as the ideal candidate for this study due to their remarkable capacity to transition from a vertically integrated company and adopt the novel concept of conducting transportation logistics services internally. The firm's adoption of an in-house transport strategy, as opposed to outsourcing, allowed for a clear distinction between transport strategy and the vertical integrated technique. As a result, this firm serves as an exemplary case study for scientifically confirming the advantages of conducting transport logistics activities in-house, yielding world-class outcomes.

6.3.1 TRANSPORTATION MANAGEMENT

Transport management refers to the strategic process of planning, controlling, and decision-making within the operational realm of transportation systems, which facilitate the movement and placement of inventories within certain regions (Musau et al., 2017). Transportation has historically received significant managerial focus owing to its essential nature and perceived costliness, leading to the presence of transportation managers in virtually all types of enterprises, regardless of size (Musau, et al., 2017). The impact of transportation management on the performance of the system is important, as transportation expenditures make up a substantial portion, ranging from one-third to two-thirds, of the total transportation costs (Musau et al., 2017). Transportation plays a key role in facilitating the many stages of the production process, encompassing manufacture, distribution, reaching the end users, and managing returns. The optimization of transport benefits necessitates effective management and coordination among all constituent elements. According to Ristovska et al. (2017), the implementation of a robust transportation management system has the potential to enhance transportation efficiency, reduce operational expenses, and enhance the quality of service provided by businesses. According to Ristovske et al. (2017), the transportation system's performance was influenced by three key factors: cost, speed, and consistency.

An investigation carried out by Muchori (2015) analyzed the impacts of traffic gridlock on the effectiveness of cargo conveyance, particularly at the Mombasa harbor. The study employed a method of detailed examination and included a subset of 150 participants from a potential pool of 10,450 workers. The choice of participants was influenced by the noticeable issues with infrastructure along the Nairobi–Mombasa route, which have consistently influenced transportation operations at the port. The correlation information indicates that there is a favorable connection between traffic congestion and the costs related to transportation. As a result, the existence of traffic congestion has negatively affected the efficiency of freight transportation. The research carried out by Mukolwe and Wanyoike in 2015 investigated how the utilization of transportation management systems influenced the operational effectiveness of Mumias Sugar Company. By employing descriptive and inferential statistics, the research findings revealed that the use of transportation management and physical distribution strategies is closely associated with an economically efficient movement of raw materials and goods, hence positively influencing operational efficiency.

The cost of transportation includes both the cost of moving goods from one place to another and the cost of keeping goods safe while they are in transit. Transportation systems used ways to get around that cut down on the cost of the system as a whole (Ristovske et al., 2017). Bowersox et al. (2010) said that the speed of transportation was the amount of time it took to do a certain action. Cost and speed of transportation were tied in two ways. First of all, companies that could send things faster usually charged more for their services. Second, the rates were higher and the time goods spent in transit was shorter when the service was faster (Ristovske et al., 2017). In order for a business to choose the best mode of transportation, it is important to find a good balance between speed and cost.

6.3.2 THE IMPORTANCE OF TRANSPORTATION SYSTEM

You cannot say enough about how important transportation is to the supply line of a business. As companies move their supply chains from the local to the global level, transportation becomes more and more important to their total performance. According to Gupta et al. (2013), the demand for transport services has skyrocketed due to developments in technology, an increase in the global need for resources, and an increase in international commerce. Supply chain efficiency, according to Moller and Torronen (2013), is synonymous with delivery efficiency. If a company cares about its supply chain's performance, it should consider how efficient its supply networks currently are.

According to Gupta et al. (2013), supply chain management encompasses all of an organization's efforts to coordinate its logistics, transportation, and distribution processes. This demonstrates how transportation management is crucial to a company's supply chain. However, according to Coyle et al.

(2011), transportation's effectiveness in the supply chain is crucial to the overall efficiency of a company's supply chain. Reason being, transporting products is the primary means through which a company communicates with its suppliers and consumers. Mixing up different kinds of transportation makes it possible for new ideas like intermodal and mixed transportation systems to come about.

An intermodal transportation system refers to a logistical approach that incorporates many modes of transportation to facilitate the movement of goods from their source to their final destination. This transportation technique ensures that all stakeholders in the transportation process are held responsible for their respective roles in the travel that falls within their jurisdiction. The financial burden of the damage is assumed by the transporter responsible for that specific segment of the journey. According to Möller and Törrönen (2013), the term "multimodal transport" refers to the practise of using more than one mode of transportation to move commodities from one location to another. In this scenario, the multimodal carrier is responsible for monitoring the shipment at every stage of its travel (Tawiah, 2019).

6.3.3 THE EFFICIENCY OF THE DISTRIBUTION CHANNEL

Distribution channels are the routes through which products and services move from their starting point to their final destination. This includes the process from the creator or maker to different middlemen in the marketing process, like wholesalers, distributors, and retailers. These intermediaries help deliver the end products to consumers, thus adding value as the supply chain progresses. The movement can involve either physically transporting the items or simply transferring ownership of the product. The concept of "distribution channel" encompasses several terminologies such as "distribution channel," "distribution pipeline," "supply chain," "marketing channel," "market channel," and "trade channel" (Ostrow, 2009). In order to achieve effective supply chain management, it is important to possess a comprehensive comprehension of the unique requirements and preferences of individual clients and market segments, alongside the identification and implementation of the most efficient strategies to effectively cater to their needs (Ayers and Odegaard, 2008).

The efficiency of a distribution system can be seen as its ability to effectively accomplish predetermined goals, such as enhancing market share, profitability, or competitive advantage (Szelg-Sikora and Rorat, 2016).

Financial indicators such as revenue, net profit, turnover, and logistical expenses are widely employed for the assessment of a distribution channel's success. Nevertheless, in light of the global competitive landscape, nonfinancial indicators, such as the degree of customer service or enhanced customer value, are gaining significance. The measurement of channel efficiency can be determined by the capacity of each company within the channel to effectively reduce costs related to the execution of essential channel operations, including distribution and sales (American Marketing Association, n.d.; Fayaz and Azizinia, 2016).

The timeliness of product delivery is a key determinant of distribution channel effectiveness. The performance of this indicator is directly influenced by the quantity and configuration of distribution channels. The primary objective of all stakeholders involved in the distribution channel is to minimize the duration required for product delivery to clients. When evaluating the efficiency of distribution methods, it is crucial to consider not just the delivery duration, but also the extra costs linked with the distribution procedure. These supplementary expenditures encompass various elements like storage costs, shipping costs, stock costs, equipment costs, and more (Andreji and Kilibarda, 2015).

6.3.4 THE CHALLENGES OF TRANSPORTATION SYSTEM

According to Davids (2012), there is a prevalent presence of inadequately built and inadequately maintained road networks throughout the transportation infrastructure of numerous affluent nations. The limited progress of the transport sector can be attributed to this particular issue. In addition to the suboptimal condition of infrastructure development, there exists a dearth of institutional protocols for overseeing the transport business, particularly in developing nations. This deficiency has impeded the efficacy of the transport sector in these countries. In developing countries, the transport sector has witnessed the adoption of several regulations and conventions aimed at ensuring its efficiency. However, the implementation of these measures has generally been inadequate, leading to unsatisfactory outcomes in the practical execution of these policies and conventions (Davids, 2012; Tawiah, 2016).

According to Lewis (as referenced by Tawiah (2016)), the transport industry in most developing nations exhibits a prevalent culture of poor maintenance. This observation is made in an attempt to further support the thesis. A significant proportion of transport vehicles in developing nations exhibit inadequate maintenance practises, leading to frequent occurrences of vehicle breakdowns and traffic accidents. The absence of cargo security in relation to transportation management in impoverished nations has been ascribed to the substandard quality of transport vehicles utilized within those regions. The transport management sector in developing countries has significantly trailed behind its counterparts in affluent nations due to the substantial level of uncertainty associated with it (Tawiah, 2016; Weisbrod et al., 2016). According to Lewis (2014), the economic volatility seen in many emerging nations has led to a significant capital requirement for enterprises, making it challenging to attain profitability. In the majority of developing nations, the financial resources necessary to establish a transport enterprise are of such magnitude that only a limited subset of enterprises and individuals possess the capability to undertake such an endeavor. As a result, the lack of rivalry in the transportation industry gives rise to widespread inefficiencies in delivering transportation services (Tawiah, 2016). The financial load linked to hiring specialized professionals in the upkeep culture of the transportation sector has become a noteworthy worry in contemporary times. To alleviate maintenance expenditures, there is a tendency to use vehicles with insufficient upkeep that are prone to frequent breakdowns and damage to cargo. The shortage of transportation experts and the resulting elevated labor costs have significantly impacted transportation administration in developing countries such as Ghana (Weisbrod et al., 2003). The source cited is from the year 2013. Rodrigue et al. (2009) argue that the process of urbanization has led to a notable surge in the global demand for transport services. Hence, with the ongoing process of urbanization and the consequent rise in demand for transportation services, it becomes imperative to consistently enhance the capacity of the transportation sector to align with the escalating demand. Failure to do so would have adverse effects on urbanization and its corresponding economic progress (Taweeh, 2016).

As outlined in the study conducted by Harriet et al. (2013), the availability and pricing of a product within a given market are frequently influenced by the existing circumstances of transportation operations within the companies responsible for vending the commodities. Inadequately administered transportation operations, along with the associated challenges, give rise to consequences such as a scarcity of goods in the market and an escalation in product prices. Ensuring the proficient and successful management of transport is imperative in order to facilitate socioeconomic advancement (Harriet et al., 2013).

6.3.5 ORGANIZATIONAL PERFORMANCE

Organizational performance is still a recurrent theme in contemporary writing. Academics continue to discuss several factors that affect success in a variety of organizations. Awino (2015) analyzes whether organizational structure contributes to the success of significant businesses in Ghana's industrial sector. Her study demonstrates that success in major manufacturing businesses can be influenced by factors beyond finances, such as customer satisfaction, internal company processes, and corporate reputation. This conclusion is drawn from a cross-sectional examination of significant manufacturing entities. Shisia et al. (2014) propose that introducing strategic innovation holds potential for improving the operational efficiency of public universities in Ghana. The research carried out by Shisia et al. (2014) discovered that incorporating strategic innovation offers potential for boosting the overall performance of public establishments in Ghana. Furthermore, investigations have been conducted into the impact of human capital on the performance of organizations.

In a 2015 analysis, Odhon'g and Omolo explored the effects of a pharmaceutical company's investments in human capital on organizational effectiveness. Utilizing inferential assessments of connection, the investigation demonstrated that organizational performance was linked to enhancements in the caliber, applicability, and dependability of human capital. In a research effort conducted by Kinyua-Njuguna et al. (2014), it was identified that an organization's internal operational atmosphere significantly shapes its significance, efficacy, and proficiency. The study specifically delved into the internal organizational milieu within community-based entities addressing concerns pertaining to HIV and AIDS.

Moreover, while considering corporate governance, the importance of pinpointing the many factors that shape an organization's performance has grown in recent years. The study conducted by Mbalwa et al. (2014) revealed a positive correlation between corporate governance and the success of sugar-producing companies. A correlation analysis was conducted on a sample of industrial enterprises from Western Ghana to demonstrate a positive association between corporate governance practises and organizational performance. More focus is placed in this part on the roles of the board of directors, the executive team, and the communication with stakeholders.

The effective performance of nonprofit enterprises is influenced by key factors in strategic leadership, including human resources, ethical conduct, and strategic orientation, as indicated in the research of Kitonga et al. (2016). To address this, Kariuki and Murimi (2015) explored the connection between enhancing employee authority and the overall achievement of an organization. Enhancing the capabilities of staff through education and sharing of knowledge had a minor impact on the operational effectiveness, as evidenced by investigations carried out on Tata Chemicals in Magadi, Ghana.

Although several metrics may be used to analyze procurement performance (Chimwani et al., 2014), it is believed that the success of the evaluation depends mostly on a small number of indicators that may be examined using a balanced score card. The procurement objectives are taken into account by the balanced scorecard, which usually combines internal metrics for resource utilization management and total quality metrics demanded by customers. Additionally, it has been noted that following supply chain best practices can result in outputs that are in accordance with organizational goals while also lowering operational costs (Muma et al., 2014; Osuga et al., 2015). Achievable procurement performance, according to Kimotho (2014), also directly affects the profitability, supplies, quality, and competitiveness of an organization. Additional support for the significance of supply chain operations is provided by Kimotho (2014). There is minimal uncertainty regarding the efficacy of implementing appropriate supply chain strategies as a means to address the challenges encountered by the oil manufacturing industry in Ghana. However, due to the limited availability of research pertaining to the oil manufacturing business, the present study aimed to identify supply chain elements that could serve as predictive indicators of organizational success within this crucial sector.

6.3.6 TRANSPORTATION AND FIRM'S PERFORMANCE

The research carried out by Mukolwe and Wanyoike (2015) sought to analyze how logistics management methods affect the operational effectiveness of Mumias Sugar Company. Using both descriptive and inferential data analysis techniques, the study discovered a connection between transportation oversight and the execution of physical distribution tasks. This connection results in a cost-effective flow of raw materials and goods, subsequently enhancing operational efficiency. According to Yung-Yu et al. (2005), transportation systems play a crucial role in facilitating the movement of commodities and products, ensuring their timely delivery and regional impact, all while promoting value-added benefits. The impact of transportation on logistics operations, development, and sales has been extensively studied by Hesse and Rodrigue (2000). Moreover, Yung-Yu et al. (2005) argued that transportation serves as the fundamental basis for enhancing performance in logistics management. They further said that an efficient transportation system not only enhances the quality of services but also contributes to the growth of sales inside an organization. Additionally, the authors Geraldine and Bagshaw (2019) noted that the escalation of transportation expenses resulting from inadequate road conditions and the high costs of vehicles and replacement parts present a significant challenge in terms of effectively covering territories and ensuring timely delivery of a company's merchandise.

Given that items are rarely produced and consumed within the same geographical area, transportation plays a significant role in logistics operations and has a direct impact on a firm's success, particularly in terms of its sales volume. In addition, the implementation of transport initiatives that ensure timely and intact delivery of goods to customers contributes to fostering client loyalty and confers a competitive edge upon the organization (Cooper et al., 2013). Moreover, the role of transportation within the logistics system is inherently more intricate than the mere act of conveying commodities for commercial purposes. The efficient management of a transportation system enables the timely and accurate delivery of goods to their designated destinations, hence facilitating the fulfilment of customer requests. According to Yung-Yu et al. (2005), the utilization of this approach enhances efficacy, establishes a link between manufacturers and consumers, and exerts an impact on the distribution of products.

The optimal utilization of a robust logistics strategy necessitates the integration of transportation systems. According to Bagshaw (2019), the escalating expenses associated with transportation, such as inadequate road conditions and the high costs of vehicles and spare parts, provide a significant challenge to effectively covering territories and ensuring timely delivery of a company's goods. In order to achieve punctual delivery targets, firms must possess a dependable transportation infrastructure that facilitates the unimpeded movement of their merchandise. Furthermore, the implementation of effective transportation management practises contributes to a company's sustainability objectives by guaranteeing the timely delivery of goods to clients. Furthermore, it is crucial to note that enhancing the rate at which organizations manufacture goods enables them to effectively cater to the needs of their clientele (Jack, 2006).

6.4 RESEARCH METHODOLOGY

6.4.1 RESEARCH DESIGN

Correlational, experimental, or quasi-experimental research designs are three options for quantitative studies (Khaldi, 2017; Saunders et al., 2016). In this paper, the research issue was addressed and the data were evaluated using the correlation analysis idea. When a scientist seeks to establish if a connection exists between factors, the most suitable method is correlational design (Khaldi, 2017). As stated by Khandi (2017) and Leedy and Ormrod (2015), correlational design represents a quantitative approach in research, investigating linear associations amid self-reliant and reliant variables. To evaluate whether the viewpoints of frontline managers' direct home healthcare staff concerning the five transition leadership subcategories distinctly projected the likelihood of departing their positions, the employment of correlational design was apt for this examination.

6.4.2 RESEARCH DESIGN

The study did not find experimental and quasi-experimental approaches to be the most suitable. When examining causality, researchers often opt for experimental and quasi-experimental methodologies, as outlined by Khaldi (2017). Causal connections are not solely established through correlation techniques, as demonstrated by Hair et al. (2015). Given the complexities of manipulating or controlling variables in field research, those who frequently employ experimental designs tend to manage independent variables (Khaldi, 2017). The right choice of study designs furnishes a response to the research query, as indicated by Hair et al. (2015) and Khaldi (2017). However, this study did not aim to determine causality degree as its research focus. Consequently, I refrained from utilizing experimental or quasi-experimental models to amass data and address the research query.

6.4.3 RESEARCH STRATEGY

The research employed a quantitative methodology. The method of quantitative research involved gathering significant volumes of data to explore the connection between different factors. This was accomplished by applying standardized techniques, structured analyses, testing theoretical hypotheses, and prioritizing statistical information over subjective analysis (McCusker and Gunaydin, 2015). The researcher opted for quantitative analysis as an appropriate approach for this study due to its utilization of numerical variables or measures to test the transformational leadership hypothesis and assess statistical data in order to ascertain the explanatory or predictive capabilities of the theory in relation to the phenomenon under investigation. Once more, the study employed a systematic approach by formulating and testing a hypothesis, as well as collecting and analyzing data or surveys in a controlled manner.

The process of quantifying or determining the dimensions, extent, or quantity of an object or according to Goertzen (2017), the principal objective of employing a quantitative methodology is to utilize proven and pertinent information for the purpose of data evaluation.

I chose to utilize the quantitative approach to employ reliable tools for evaluating whether a linear blend of logistic employees' viewpoints on the five subdivisions of their frontline supervisors' logistic tasks could predict organizational effectiveness. In a longitudinal investigation carried out by McCall (2016), thorough and reliable techniques were utilized to create and conduct a questionnaire. Moreover, statistical examination was utilized to assess the potential connection between logistic management's function subcategories and organizational performance. The survey was designed and implemented utilizing precise and pertinent methodologies, incorporating statistical analysis for data measurement, and offering participants a means to respond to survey inquiries. The study employed a quantitative approach and utilized a correlational design, employing valid and reliable instruments. This methodology facilitated the execution of a regression analysis, enabling the investigation of the hypotheses and the resolution of the research issue. I refrained from engaging in a pilot study due to the availability of established instruments employed by previous researchers, which provided substantiation for the accuracy and validity of the procedures. According to Larson-Hall and Plonsky (2015), scholars employing quantitative methodologies construct surveys to assess structures utilizing precise and suitable questionnaires. Additionally, they employ regression analysis to either corroborate or refute the hypotheses under investigation.

6.4.4 POPULATION

The populace denotes the entire group of people for whom the survey results are meant to be extrapolated. The components of this populace, also referred to as basic elements, indicate the individual constituents within the populace whose characteristics are meant to be evaluated (Hakim, 2016). When conducting a survey, it is crucial to have a comprehensive understanding of both the target population and the sample population. This study focused on manufacturing enterprises as the population of interest, constituting an unlimited population. The study's population consists of 350 individuals engaged in direct labor (GNCL, 2021).

6.4.5 *SAMPLING AND SAMPLE SIZE*

The method used to collect data is called Sapling. A census is the process of gathering information from each entity within a limited population (Hakim, 2016). However, it is challenging to conduct a census for an infinite population. Due to the restricted resources, time and money play a vital role in determining the sample size. Sampling only provides a partial picture of the population. According to scholars like (Hussey, 2017), a meaningful factor analysis needs a larger sample size. The GNCL provided 204 respondents for this study.

6.4.5.1 SAMPLING METHOD AND TECHNIQUE

This pertains to the title or alternative label of the approach employed for recognizing the sampled subjects. The utilization of sampling methodologies for the investigation relies on the effective choice of the sample framework from the population's sample size (Johnson and Clark, 2015). Samples could be chosen through a random process (probabilistic sample) or a nonrandom process (nonprobabilistic sample).

6.4.5.2 PROBABILITY SAMPLING

This approach relies solely on random outcomes and disregards individual preferences. Each element within the population possesses an equal probability of being selected as a sample.

6.4.5.3 NON-PROBABILITY SAMPLE

This method chooses entities based on individual preference rather than mathematical chance. This typically occurred when the inclusion and exclusion entities in the sample were under control. Judgment, convenience, and quota samples are examples of nonrandom samples. In order to be representative of the population, nonrandom samples are chosen.

6.4.5.4 JUSTIFICATION FOR THE SELECTED SAMPLING TECHNIQUE

This study employed convenience sampling as the chosen strategy for data collection in order to facilitate subsequent analyses. This sampling approach is classified as non-probability and involves selecting individuals from a readily accessible or conveniently reachable population. The utilization of this sampling method is justified by its cost-effectiveness and expeditious nature.

6.4.6 INSTRUMENT

Instruments encompass a variety of technologies utilized for the purpose of gathering data, including questionnaires, tests, planned interview schedules, and checklists. According to Kothari (2015), a questionnaire is a research tool used to collect data from respondents regarding their attitudes, knowledge, beliefs, and feelings. A survey instrument was developed with the purpose of collecting data pertaining to the six distinct functional domains within the field of logistics. The questionnaire design was customized to effectively address all pertinent research inquiries.

The structure of the study was derived from the research questions. The study was conducted with a focus on maintaining validity and reliability. Validity is the extent to which an instrument accurately measures the intended construct, whereas reliability pertains to the level of consistency with which an instrument assesses a certain feature it is designed to assess (Kothari, 2015). In order to accomplish this objective, the questionnaire was presented to the study supervisor for feedback and revisions, followed by a phase of pretesting. A subset of 10 personnel was chosen to participate in a preliminary exercise in order to assess the suitability of the data collected for meeting the study's objectives, as well as to evaluate the quality of the questionnaire's questions to ensure they were clear and relevant. This exercise was conducted prior to the final administration of the questionnaire to the intended respondents. The efficacy of the instrument employed resided in its capacity to collect pertinent data pertaining to the objective of the investigation. Nevertheless, a notable limitation of the study was the utilization of a closed-ended questionnaire, which restricted the ability to capture a comprehensive range of perspectives from the participants.

6.4.7 DATA COLLECTION PROCEDURES

This means figuring out the steps and ways to collect the data that needs to be analyzed to solve the study problem. Before making important decisions or coming to the right conclusion from a survey, it is important to have enough knowledge. To avoid bias and sampling mistakes, it is important to think about how the data will be collected. How data is collected and analyzed relies on a lot of things, such as the situation, the issue that needs to be watched, the reason for collecting the data, and the type and size of

TABLE 6.1 Respondents' Information.

Variable	Category	Count	% of n
Gender	Male	78	38.2
	Female	126	61.8
	Total	**204**	**100.0**
Age (years)	18–30	102	50.0
	31–40	71	34.8
	41–50	20	9.8
	Above 50	11	5.4
	Total	**204**	**100.0**
Education level	MSLC/JHS	-	-
	SSSCE	20	9.8
	Diploma	71	34.8
	Degree	72	35.3
	Post graduate	30	14.7
	Other (specify)	11	5.4
	Total	**204**	**100.0**
Marital	Single	95	46.6
	Married	70	34.3
	Divorced	39	19.1
	Total	**204**	**100.0**
Staff category	Senior manager	100	49
	Middle level manager	29	14
	Supervisor	75	37
	Total	**204**	**100.0**

Source: Field study (2021).

the organization from which the information is taken. For this study, the staff were asked for the necessary details over the course of about 2 weeks. Branch managers and other important leaders were asked for permission. They were told why the study was being done, and those on duty who were not as busy were asked to take part. Others also filled out the form on their own. Due to limited time and money, the researcher hired other trained research assistants to help with this project. Using the convenience sampling method, we talked about earlier and with the permission and consent of the people being studied, they were able to reach 204 respondents.

6.4.8 DATA ANALYSIS

Data analysis includes putting together, choosing, and entering data into computer files. The data is then checked for mistakes and tabulations, and other statistical tests are run to get the right results for the study. SPSS version 24 was used to analyze the data, which was shown in charts, graphs, and tables. This software is used to look at info about numbers. It is first used to code the questionnaires, and then the analyses toolbar is used to do the appropriate analysis. For any kind of study problem, it is important to use the right statistical method. In this study, summary statistics (like the mean and standard deviation) and estimates of proportional values were used and put into tables.

6.5 DATA ANALYSIS AND RESULTS

6.5.1 RESPONDENTS INFORMATION

During the survey, information about the respondents' gender, age, marital status, and level of schooling was collected. Based on the data gathered about gender, 61.8% (126) of the total study respondents were women, while 38.2% (78) of the respondents were men. This fits with the general observation that there are more women working in industry than men. When it comes to how old the interviewees are, most of them are between the ages of 18 and 30 and between 31 and 40, which is 50% (102) and 34.8% (71), respectively. This means that Ghana has a young manufacturing population. Furthermore, the survey included a question on the marital status of the participants. The results revealed that a significant proportion of the respondents, namely 46.6% (95 individuals), identified themselves as single, while 34.3% (70 individuals) reported being married.

The greatest level of education reported by the respondents was certificates, diplomas, postbasic education, bachelor's degrees, and master's degrees, with proportions of 34.8%, 35.3%, and 14.7% correspondingly. Lastly, with regards to the respondents' job positions, the majority of them (100), accounting for 49%, were senior managers. This was followed by 29 individuals (14%) who held middle-level managerial positions, and 75 individuals (37%) who were supervisors.

6.5.2 DESCRIPTIVE STATISTICS

Using statistical metrics like the mean, standard deviation, mode, and median, descriptive statistics summarize survey data in a concise manner. The data for this research was gathered by administering a 5-point Likert scale to the participants, which was used to assess all the factors under investigation. The survey results are shown in Table 6.2.

TABLE 6.2 Importance of Transportation Management.

Importance of transportation management	Mean	SD
Materials delivered on time	4.52	0.646
Decreasing transport costs	4.79	0.413
Reduced Departmental complaints	4.66	0.596
Overall	**4.32**	**0.615**

Source: Field study (2021).

The three most crucial aspects of timely delivery of materials, reduced transport, and decreased departmental complaints were identified by the researcher as the three most significant aspects of transportation management. Based on the available data, it can be seen that the delivery of products was consistently punctual, with a mean score of 4.52 and a standard deviation of 0.646. Additionally, there was a noticeable downward trend in transport expenses, as shown by a mean score of 4.79 and a standard deviation of 0.413. Furthermore, there was a decline in departmental complaints, with a mean score of 4.66 and a standard deviation of 0.596.

To examine employee survey responses, means and standard deviations were used. Eight different elements in all were utilized to examine how the personnel of the procurement department perceive the methods for managing transport. Table 6.3 lists the outcomes of this investigation. When asked about the transport management systems employed by Techiman's oil manufacturing companies, employees' total mean response scores were 4.28. This result falls between the ranges of 3.5 and 4.5, indicating that employees may have expressed agreement with the usage of different transportation management techniques inside the companies. Additionally, the respondents' overall agreement was consistent, as seen by the standard deviation (SD = 0.641) being rather low overall.

Employees tended to concur that the organizations used the following transport management strategies, in particular. Businesses have a fleet management system (M = 4.30 and SD = 0.634), a fleet management system (M = 4.30 and SD = 0.634), a tracking system (M = 4.25 and SD = 0.619), a thorough route planning system (M = 4.25 and SD = 0.619), a defined disposal policy (M = 4.34 and SD = 0.659), and a transportation department (M = 4.23 and SD = 0.670). Additionally, respondents believed that

TABLE 6.3 Transport Management Aspects.

Transport management	Mean	SD
GNCL has improved vehicle scheduling	4.40	0.611
GNCL has a department for transportation	4.23	0.670
GNCL conducts thorough route planning	4.25	0.619
GNCL does preventive vehicle maintenance	4.12	0.645
GNCL has installed Tracking	4.26	0.633
GNCL has a system for managing its fleet	4.30	0.634
GNCL has a clear Disposal policy	4.34	0.659
Put in place vehicle inspection schedules	4.34	0.659
Overall	**4.28**	**0.641**

Source: Field study (2021).

oil-producing companies carry out preventative maintenance (M = 4.26 and SD = 0.633) and have established timetables for vehicle inspections (M = 4.34 and SD = 0.659). These findings suggest that companies producing oil in the Techiman region are aware of the critical role that efficient transport management plays in boosting supply networks' operational efficiency. As a result, the majority of those businesses have implemented a number of methods to guarantee that the supply chain procedures include proper transport management. These findings, which highlight the importance of transport management to Techiman's oil-manufacturing companies, are consistent with other studies that have found that doing so can centralize production operations to regions with lower costs without sacrificing levels of customer service by enabling end-to-end network visibility. Visibility across the entire network is the first step in creating a responsive transport network (Mukolwe and Wanyoike, 2015). Furthermore, the results of the survey of the employees back up earlier arguments regarding the value of transport management in supply chain operations. Among these roles are those that affect the performance of logistics companies (Kithiia, 2015), have a negative effect on the effectiveness of freight logistics (Muchori, 2015), promote operational efficiency (Mukolwe and Wanyoike, 2015), and predict performance (Mwangangi, 2016).

6.5.3 CHALLENGES ASSOCIATED WITH TRANSPORT MANAGEMENT AT GNCL

The study's second purpose aimed to investigate the difficulties related to transportation management inside manufacturing organizations.

When computing the means, a scale ranging from 1 to 5 was utilized. In this scale, a score of 1 corresponds to a significant disagreement, while a score of 5 indicates a strong agreement. The midpoint of the scale is represented by a score of 3. Regarding the difficulties encountered by GNCL in overseeing their transportation operations, the participants expressed a clear consensus that the vehicles employed for cargo transportation are inadequately maintained (mean = 4.15, standard deviation = 0.612). The findings of this study corroborate those of Eddington (2016), who similarly cited inadequate vehicle maintenance, particularly in developing countries, as a contributing cause to transportation management challenges.

The study findings once again indicate a lack of effective deployment of ICT in the transport management system at GNCL. The shortcoming in question had a mean score of 4.26, accompanied by a standard deviation of 0.633. This observation suggests that research organizations have not placed sufficient focus on the integration of ICT in transportation management. Additionally, based on the obtained mean score of 4.10 and standard deviation of 0.615, the participants expressed a significant consensus regarding the existence of a widespread deficiency in transport management professionals capable of efficiently strategizing and overseeing the transportation of goods throughout market centres. This discovery aligns with the research conducted by Fawcett (2010), which observed that a deficiency in expertise had a negative impact on transportation management within organizations. Sheingold and Hadley (as mentioned in Odoom et al. (2016)) emphasize the significance of employing information and communication technologies (ICTs) in achieving organizational objectives. Furthermore, the participants expressed a high level of agreement with the ineffectiveness of GNCL's transport management strategies, with a mean score of 3.90 and a standard deviation of 1.065. This finding aligns with the research conducted by Davids (2012), which revealed that inadequate transport management policies have a

TABLE 6.4 Organizational Performance.

Organizational performance	Mean	SD
Profitability	4.09	0.612
Reliability	4.12	0.645
Responsiveness	4.26	0.633
Flexibility	3.99	1.052
Overall	**4.10**	**0.625**

Source: Field study (2021).

significant impact on transport management within organizations. Moreover, according to the mean score of 4.09 (SD = 0.612), it can be concluded that the respondents exhibited a high agreement toward the notion that the institutional processes pertaining to transport operations in GNCL are generally inadequate. This makes it harder for businesses to handle the transportation of their goods in an efficient way. The present study backs up what Rodingue et al. (2009) found. The research conducted by the authors highlights poor institutional policies and infrastructure as significant elements that have an impact on transport management inside organizations. However, the participants expressed a strong consensus about the significant impact of the elevated transportation expenses (M = 3.99, SD = 1.052) resulting from the escalating fuel prices on the management of transportation inside organizations. The findings of this study support the conclusions drawn by Lewis (2016) and other researchers, who have previously noted that elevated transportation expenses impede the efficacy of transportation management inside organizations. According to the mean score rankings of the responses, it can be concluded that the general lack of experts in transport management, followed by the high cost of transportation operations, and poor planning and management of transportation operations, are the three biggest challenges facing GNCL's transportation management. Furthermore, the results from the interviews with the chosen employees at GNCL regarding the difficulties facing transport management are comparable to those from the quantitative data. The key informants generally stated that GNCL's transport management is a very difficult endeavor as a result of a number of problems. The absence of skilled employees to manage transit in GNCL is one issue raised. "Most frequently, transport owners are either people with low levels of education or lack the necessary technical know-how to effectively manage the fleet as well as the cargos in their care," one manager said. Even though there are numerous employees at GNCL who work in the transportation industry, very few of them have any expertise of the industry. Many of the operators lack the necessary management abilities. The interviewees also mentioned that inadequate vehicle upkeep and the high cost of delivering goods to and from market centers were other issues. According to one of the informants, "Effective transport management is hampered by the high cost of moving goods in the market centres." Another manager remarked that the expense of vehicle maintenance makes it a major challenge. Additionally, it was believed that a lackluster institutional framework made it difficult to handle transit in market centers effectively. Poor roads were once again determined to be a significant barrier for the companies. The interviewees in this case all agreed that previous administrations had neglected to make significant investments in the expansion of the road network, particularly in the rural areas of market centers. All of these difficulties contribute to make it more difficult to successfully manage transport for the benefit of GNCL. In contrast to the quantitative findings, the qualitative findings revealed that the primary obstacle to achieving efficient transport management at GNCL was identified as inadequate road infrastructure. Several scholars, such as Davids (2012) and Rodingue et al. (2009), have identified inadequate road infrastructure as a significant obstacle that hinders effective transport management, particularly in developing countries.

6.5.4 SUMMARY OF FINDINGS

While logistics and other supply chain tasks demand attention and resources, organizational managers prioritize enhancing organizational efficiency. Managers are primarily focused on enhancing marketing efficiency with the objective of increasing revenue and expanding market share. The augmentation of revenue figures can be attributed to the positive impact of market share and sales growth on financial outcomes. GNCL's management has adopted initiatives aimed at establishing efficient processes for the management of supply and goods transportation. The primary objective of this effort is to enhance the overall efficacy of the supply chain system, hence leading to an enhancement in the overall performance of the company. The implementation of vehicle scheduling, route planning, fleet management, and vehicle tracking has been undertaken in order to optimize overall operational efficiency.

The favorable impact of customer satisfaction, as assessed through marketing success, on financial performance, as evaluated through return on investment, has been seen. In their study, Green et al. (2006) performed a survey among factory sales managers and identified a significant association between marketing activities and financial efficiency. The enhancement of organizational procedures pertaining to transportation can contribute to the enhancement of the competitive position of the supply chain, hence leading to improved efficiency among the individual partners within the supply chain. Although there is currently no empirically proven metric for assessing supply chain efficiency, firms prioritize their performance by emphasizing the manufacturer/customer relationship beyond the production function. As stated by Bowersox et al. (2000), a firm's performance is indicative of its dominance within the supply chain. The prevailing viewpoint suggests that fostering firms' interest in transport operations is crucial for enhancing corporate efficiency.

6.6 CONCLUSION

This study explores how the management of transportation impacts the operational effectiveness of organizations. The investigation involved analyzing data obtained from a group of 204 members associated with the GNCL. As per the study's outcomes, the administration of transportation has a noteworthy influence on a company's overall achievement and triumph. The management of transportation holds a crucial role within the logistics domain, as it is accountable for the movement of goods and resources across the entire supply chain. Thus, it is imperative for enterprises to place considerable emphasis on this facet to attain success within the realm of transportation. The study's findings underscore that the management of transportation holds a favorable and statistically notable effect on the comprehensive performance of textile production firms located in Ghana. In view of this, GNCL's management has taken steps to introduce appropriate protocols aimed at addressing the transportation of resources and merchandise, with the aim of augmenting the general operational efficiency. They have instituted procedures for coordinating vehicles, plotting routes, overseeing vehicle fleets, and maintaining real-time vehicle tracking, all geared toward amplifying productivity and streamlining operations. It is essential to uphold the current significant transportation-linked systems while incorporating fresh tactics that possess the potential to enhance transportation management. The study's discoveries suggest that manufacturing enterprises in Ghana could enhance their performance by prioritizing the assurance of their organizations' profitability, dependability, cost efficiency, responsiveness, and adaptability, in addition to effective asset management.

6.7 RECOMMENDATIONS

The inclusion of transportation management inside an organization's operations is crucial. This encompasses several aspects such as effective fleet management, efficient vehicle scheduling, strategic route planning, and regular vehicle maintenance. This will facilitate the efficient transportation of raw materials and products to their intended destinations, so enhancing cost-effectiveness, expanding market share, and reducing lead time, all of which contribute positively to the organization's financial performance. Furthermore, enhancing the maintenance of the cars is vital as it has the potential to significantly enhance the productivity of the company. The consideration of expertise in the transportation domain should be seen as a crucial factor for manufacturing companies when formulating business strategies, as it enables the effective allocation and utilization of organizational resources. The implementation of transport management techniques is crucial for enhancing stock levels in storage, improving productivity, minimizing waste through just-in-time procurement, reducing inventory expenses, and optimizing holding costs and ordering costs through the utilization of the economic order quantity (EOQ). Lastly, managers have the ability to provide employees with precise information pertaining to transportation. Implementing this strategy will effectively mitigate any misunderstandings, hence minimizing any potential complications that may arise in fulfilling client requirements. The implementation of information technology devices and information systems for the purpose of storing, transferring, and sharing data among managers in manufacturing operations has the potential to enhance product quality, reduce transportation expenses, improve worker efficiency, and significantly impact the sustained development of present and future generations.

The report further proposes the establishment of information technology infrastructure capable of facilitating automated inventory management, order processing, and seamless information flow for manufacturing companies, regardless of their location in urban or rural areas, at a reduced expenditure. Additionally, the enhancement of transportation, inventory management, the order process, and information flow would have a significant impact on the expansion of manufacturing enterprises in Ghana. The research has contributed to the government's enhanced comprehension of logistical management and operational efficiency in the manufacturing industry. This might potentially enable the formulation of rules and regulations with the objective of improving efficiency and effectiveness within the industrial sector. As a result, this might potentially result in enhanced regional commerce, lowered production expenses, inducements for international capital inflows, diminished pricing for commodities and services, and the creation of a reliable supply chain that is appealing to multinational corporations. Moreover, it has the potential to facilitate an increase in market penetration for our merchandise.

KEYWORDS

- **transportation**
- **manufacturing**
- **performance**
- **vehicle scheduling**
- **route planning**
- **vehicle maintenance**

REFERENCES

American Marketing Association. [Online] (n.d.). Retrieved March 18, 2019 from www.marketingpower.com

Andrejić, M.; Kilibarda, M. Distribution Channels Selection Using PCA-DEA Approach. *Int. J. Traff. Transp. Eng.* **2015,** *5* (1), 74–81. http://dx.doi.org/10.7708/ijtte.2015.5(1).09

Atnafu, D.; Balda, A. The Impact of Inventory Management Practice on Firms' Competitiveness and Organizational Performance: Empirical Evidence from Micro and Small Enterprises in Ethiopia. Taylor & Francis: Abingdon. *Cogent Bus. Manag.* **2018,** *5.* ISSN 2331-1975. http://dx.doi.org/10.1080/23311975.2018.1503219

Awino, Z. B. Organizational Structure and Performance of Large Manufacturing Firms in Ghana: An Empirical Investigation. *J. Bus. Eco.* **2015,** *6* (11), 1883–1891.

Ayers, J. B.; Odegaard, M. A. In *Retail Supply Chain Management*; Auerbach Publications, Taylor & Francis Group: New York, London, 2008.

Aziz, A.; Memon, J. A.; Ali, S. Logistics Capability, Logistics Outsourcing and Firm Performance in Manufacturing Companies in Pakistan. *J. Asian Fin. Eco. Bus.* **2020,** *7* (8), 435–444.

Bagshaw, K. B. Logistics Management from Firms' Performance Perspective. *Eur. J. Logist. Purch. Supply Chain Manag.* **2019,** *7* (1), 12–28.

Barasa, C. A.; Namusonge, G. S.; Iravo, M. Determinants of Financial Risk of Listed Companies on Nairobi Securities Exchange in Ghana. Unpublished PhD Thesis, Juja: JKUAT, 2015.

Barney, J. Firm Resources and Sustained Competitive Advantage. *J. Manag.* **1991,** *17* (1), 99–120.

Busby, J. S. The Co-evolution of Competition and Parasitism in the Resource-Based View: A Risk Model of Product Counterfeiting. *Eur. J. Operat. Res.* **2019,** *276* (1), 300–313. https://doi.org/10.1016/j.ejor.2018.12.039

Cooper, M. C.; Lambert, D. M.; Pagh, J. D. Supply Chain Management: More than a New Name for Logistics. *Int. J. Logist. Manag.* **2013,** *8* (1), 57–69.

Cruz, A. M.; Haugan, G. L. Determinants of Maintenance Performance: A Resource-Based View and Agency Theory Approach. *J. Eng. Technol. Manag.* **2019,** *51*, 33–47. https://doi.org/10.1016/j.jengtecman.2019.03.001

Eddington, M. Traffic Congestion and Trucking Managers' use of Automated Routing and Scheduling. *Transp. Res. E Logist. Transp. Rev.* **2016,** *39* (1), 61–78.

Fayaz, R.; Azizinia, M. Current Challenges in Distribution Channels of Cultural Goods and Services. *Mark. Brand. Res.* **2016,** *3*, 75–85. https://doi.org/10.19237/MBR.2016.01.07

Fawcett, P. In *Managing Passenger Logistics: The Comprehensive Guide to People and Transport*; Kogan Limited: London, 2010.

Fawcett, S. E.; Ogden, J. A.; Magnan, G. M.; Bixby Cooper, M. Organization Commitment and Governance for Supply Chain Success. *Int. J. Phys. Distrib. Logist. Manag.* **2006,** *36,* 22–35. DOI: 10.1108/ 09600030610642913

Fugate, B. S.; Mentzer, J. T.; Stank, T. P. Logistics Performance: Efficiency, Effectiveness, and Differentiation. *J. Bus. Logist.* **2010,** *31* (1), 43–62.

Geraldine, N. O.; Chikwendu, D. U. Correlational Analysis of Distribution Cost and Freight Characteristics of Manufactured Goods (Case Study of Unilever Nigeria plc). *J. Logist. Manag.* **2013,** *2* (1), 26–34.

Harriet, T.; et al. In *Visions for City Logistics*, Proceedings 3rd International Conference on City Logistics, Institute for City Logistics, 2013; pp 3–17.

Hesse, M.; Rodrigue, J. P. Evolution of Logistical Integration. *Transp. Geogr.* **2000,** 383–397.

Jack, N. Distribution: The Key to Success Overseas. *Manag. Rev.* **2006,** 40–57.

Kimotho, H. K. Assessment of Insurance Uptake and Penetration in Ghana (A Case of Nakuru County), 2014. http://ir-library.ku.ac.ke/handle/123456789/10087

Kinyua-Njuguna, J. W.; Munyoki, J.; Kibera, F. Influence of Internal Organizational Environment on Performance of Community-Based HIV and AIDS Organizations. *Eur. Sci. J.* 2014, *10* (1), 405–426.

Kwateng K. O.; Nkrumah, K.; Manso J. F.; Osei-Mensah R. Outbound Logistics Management in Manufacturing Companies in Ghana. *Rev. Bus. Fin. Stud.* **2014,** *5* (1), 83–92.

Mentzer, J. T.; Min, S.; Bobbitt, M. L. Toward a Unified Theory of Logistics. *Int. J. Phys. Distrib. Logist. Manag.* **2004,** *34* (8), 606–627.

Möller, T.; Törrönen, S. The Private and Social Cost Efficiency of Port Hinterland Container Distribution through a Regional Logistics System. *Transp. Res. Policy Pract.* **2013,** *46* (9), 1424–1448.

Musau, G. E.; Namusonge, P.; Makokha, D. N.; Ngeno, D. Supply Chain Determinants of Organizational Performance among Textile Manufacturing Firms in Ghana. The *Moderating Effect of Background Characteristics,* 2017.

Naliaka, V. W.; Namusonge, G. S. Role of Inventory Management on CompetitiveAdvantage among Manufacturing Firms in Ghana: A Case Study of Unga Group Limited. *Int. J. Acad. Res. Bus. Soc. Sci.* **2015,** *5* (5), 87–104.

Nzuza, Z. W. Factors Affecting the Success of Inventory Control in the Stores Division of the Thekwini Municipality Durban: A Case Study. Durban University of Technology, Durban, South Africa, 2015.

Odhiambo, H.; Onyango, R.; Kibet Y.; Kimutahi, G. Effect of Logistics Activities on Performance of Agro Processing Firms in Uasin Gishu County, Ghana. *IOSR J. Bus. Manag.* **2017,** *12* (4), 21–28.

Odhon'g, E. A.; Omolo, J. Effect of Human Capital Investment on Organizational Performance of Pharmaceutical Companies in Ghana. *Global J. Hum. Resour. Manag.* **2015,** *3* (6), 1–29.

Odoom, D.; Opoku, E.; Ayipah-Ntiakoh, D. Staff Development Needs at the Colleges of Education in Ghana: Evidence from the Agogo College. *Int. J. Innovat. Res. Dev.* **2016,** *5* (1), 127–137.

Odoom, D.; Opoku, E.; Ayipah-Ntiakoh, D. Exploring the Staff Development Challenges and Strategies at Agogo College of Education, Ghana. *Int. J. Innovat. Res. Dev.* **2017,** *6* (2), 78–92.

Ostrow, R. In *The Fairchild Dictionary of Retailing*, Second Edition, Fairchild Books, Inc.: New York, 2009.

Ristovska, N.; Kozuharov, S.; Petkovski, V. The Impact of Logistics Management Practices on Company's Performance. *Int. J. Acad. Res. Acc. Fin. Manag. Sci.* **2017,** *7* (1), 245–252.

Rodrigue, T.; Comtois, Y.; Slack, H. Comparison of the Use of Third-Party Logistics Service by Large American Manufacturers. *J. Bus. Logist.* **2009,** *17* (1), 305–320.

Sila, I. E. Quality in Supply Chain: An Empirical Analysis. *SCM Int. J.* **2006,** *11,* 491–502.

Szeląg-Sikora, A.; Rorat, J. M. Performance of Distribution Channels Shown on the Example of Company Specialising in Meat Processing. *Logist. Transp.* **2016,** *29* (1), 19–24.

Tawiah, S. Examining the Transportation Management Challenges in Ghana: A Study of Three Selected Companies in Sekondi-Takoradi Metropolis. An unpublished MBA Dissertation, Coventry University/GTUC, 2019.

Weisbrod, B.; Vary, N.; Treyz, L. Theoretical Perspectives on the Outsourcing of Information Systems. *J. Inf. Technol.* **2013,** *10* (4), 209–219.

CHAPTER 7

A Study of the Factors that Affect the Performance of the Supply Chain with Reference to SME in Chennai City

R. PRADEEP KUMAR PATNAIK[1], K. SOUNDARAPANDIYAN[2], VISHALKUMAR JAGDISHCHANDRA MALI[3], and T. RAJAMANICKAM[4]

[1]*K L Business School, Koneru Lakshmaiah Education Foundation, Vaddeswarm, India*

[2]*Department of Commerce, BS Abdur Rahman Crescent Institute of Science and Technology, Vandalur, Chennai, India*

[3]*Department of Commerce (CA), Naran Lala School of Industrial Management &Computer Science, Navasari, India*

[4]*PG Department Commerce, Naran Lala School of Industrial Management &Computer Science, Navasari, India*

ABSTRACT

Purpose: The major objective of this chapter is to examine what aspects of supply chain management (SCM) are influenced by what external influences, and how much of an impact those external elements had. The purpose of this research is to show how small and medium-sized enterprises (SMEs) may improve supply chain performance. They might operate as buyers, sellers, wholesalers, or retailers. This study compares and contrasts the strategic and operational choices made by SMEs.

Design/methodology/approach: By using a simple random sampling method, 250 of Chennai's SME manufacturing firms were chosen. Researchers in this study used Friedman and Garret rankings to analyze the impact of different variables on SCM efficiency.

Essentials of Supply Chain Management: Strategy, Planning and Operations.
Mohammed Majeed, Abdul-Rasheed Akeji Alhassan Alolo, Seidu Alhassan, and S. Sekar (Eds.)

Findings: The study's findings and concerns focus on how the factors were identified in this investigation of SCM industry. Factors such as customer demand and SCM are identified as important aspects that affect the actualization of a supply chain.

Research limitations/implications: Outlined growth strategies for SMEs show a wide variety of patterns. Given the vast number of SMEs that make up the world's economy and the crucial roles they play as suppliers, component manufacturers, service providers, and distributors, identifying trends in their expansion over a relatively brief period of time may prove challenging. This study has important managerial implications, such as the possibility for SME executives to conduct a self-assessment of their company's strengths and weaknesses and formulate a long-term strategy for growth and change in response to shifting market conditions by strengthening their operational capabilities and chain relationship positions. The paper's road map could be used as a reference when evaluating existing practices and preparing for changes in the future. This allows the management of SMEs to take actionable actions toward implementing ideal growth paths by employing sound management practices that make good use of the resources available inside and across their organizations.

7.1 INTRODUCTION

Supply chain management (SCM) is an integral part of running a successful organization. Logistics is the study and practice of organizing and managing the delivery of products, services, and data from a provider to an end user (Bottani and Montanari, 2010). Good SCM guarantees that the correct products and services are supplied to the right customers at the right times. It's useful for cutting expenses, working more effectively, and making customers happier (Shepherd and Günter, 2006). To efficiently manage their supply chain (SC), small and medium-sized businesses (SMEs) typically encounter several obstacles. In this short note, we'll talk about the SC's performance in light of the difficulties faced by SMEs. Having reliable suppliers may help a SME weather tough times. Adaptability is crucial to the success of any SC (Yin, 2003). Improvements in SCM are being more recognized as crucial by enterprises of all sizes. Several scholars point to SC flexibility as a key factor in the industry's success and a major megatrend in the field as a way to gain and maintain a competitive edge (Rogers, 2001). To define an SC, one must consider the flow of goods, information, and money among a set of involved parties (Dominguez et al., 2015). The quantity and placement of intermediary facilities might affect the supply structure. The demands of the downstream facility are satisfied by the upstream plant. The upstream facility represents the route followed by products and services before they reach the final consumer, whereas the flowing facility depicts the route taken by these same products and services after they have been purchased by the final customer. Customers collect their orders at the final distribution facility at the conclusion of the distribution process. A company's financial viability may be gauged by its profit margins. There has been a shift away from gauging the success of a project by its stage-by-stage profits and toward looking at the overall profitability of the venture (Meehan and Muir, 2008). The competitive strategy lays out the variety of client requirements that the business intends to meet with its products and services. The potential and capabilities of the SC in terms of effectiveness and responsiveness may determine the nature of a company's strategic alliance. To conclude, creating strategic cohesiveness requires striking a balance between productivity and flexibility. The performance bar continues rising despite the best efforts of today's enterprises. In response to the development of reasonably priced alternatives to their present suppliers, consumers are becoming more demanding (Chaharsooghi and

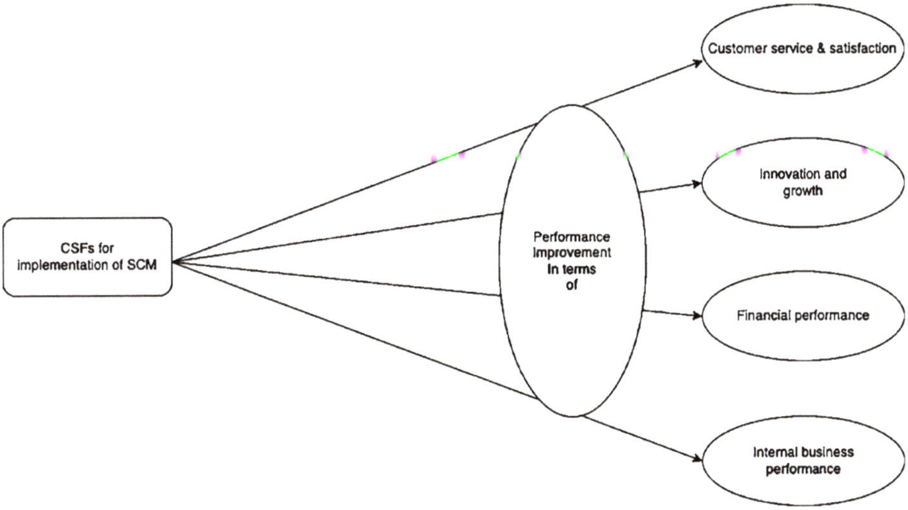

FIGURE 7.1 CSFs for implementation of SCM.

Heydari, 2010). The achievement of these goals and the maintenance of a sustainable competitive advantage need a highly functional and adaptable SC. With SCM, a business may better focus on core competencies. If there is a link in the chain that is more competent in a particular area, it will take on that responsibility. An integrated SC is a competitive team in which all relevant linkages are maintained tight and cooperative in order to attain specified objectives.

7.2 SCM SUCCESS FACTORS: UNDERLYING THEORY

The study aims to investigate how SME resilience affects their production. Every day, SC managers use their knowledge, connections, routines, and structures to ensure the success of SMEs. That's why we're going with the dynamic capacity hypothesis. The term "SC resilience" describes an organization's ability to recover quickly from disruptions and resume normal operations. The ability of a company to recover rapidly from a supply network shock is one example of its resilience. When faced with SC interruptions, organizations with high SC resilience are able to continue operations and even thrive. The theoretical framework of dynamic capabilities may be used for this study (Dominguez et al., 2015). There has been widespread uptake of the framework because of its usefulness in describing the dynamics of company performance. Companies may use the model's unified framework of concepts and techniques to ride out economic storms. Increased productivity and competitive advantages result from using the dynamic capacity theory in this manner. Business "dynamic capabilities" are the innovative processes and procedures that provide a company a leg up in a crowded industry. The capacity viewpoint examined how businesses may foster the growth of long-term human competencies in the workplace by building or encompassing corporate resources to expand the firm's capacities. SMEs are defined in a variety of ways across regions and continents. The disparities in production methods and output capability among, for example, the industrial, retail, and service sectors mean that each has its unique definition. Economists rely on several different measures of economic activity's scale, including earnings, sales volume, balance sheet total, invested capital, and profit. However, the number of workers and annual sales are the two key factors that are typically used to classify a business's size (Loecher, 2000).

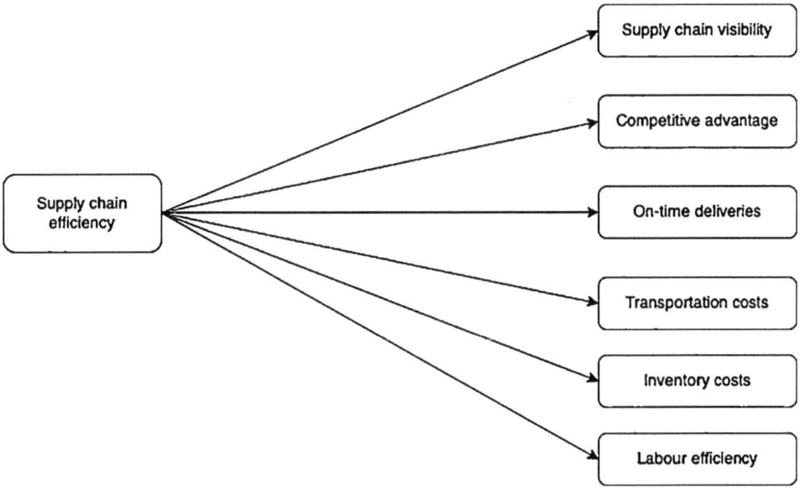

FIGURE 7.2 Supply chain efficiency.

Businesses in the wholesale and retail sectors, which by their very nature see larger turnover rates than manufacturers, should not use turnover as the only justification for allocating financial resources. Because of how commonplace SMEs are, we may all feel the effects of their actions. The European Union's 20 million SMEs account for 99% of the bloc's enterprises and are vital to the region's economic and social progress. There have been several studies conducted by various international organizations highlighting the significance of SMEs and the necessity of providing assistance to them so that they can reach their full potential. In order to promote economic growth, employment, and poverty reduction, the World Bank has identified the development of the SME sector as a fundamental aspect of its strategy. SCM aims to meet the needs of customers by meeting their demands for products in terms of price, availability, quality, and quantity (Stewart, 1995). While maximizing efficiency in the short term is a primary goal of SCM, the long-term goal is to maximize revenues by expanding market share and improving service to existing customers (Rogers, 2001). This research was conducted with the goals of (1) identifying, from the available literature, the most important aspects that may affect the SC's performance, and (2) developing a standardized model based on these variables. The essential elements or drivers that affect SC production are identified for Saudi SMEs. We also provide a modeling framework based on ISM for determining and summarizing the interplay of the many elements that come together to form a given problem or challenge.

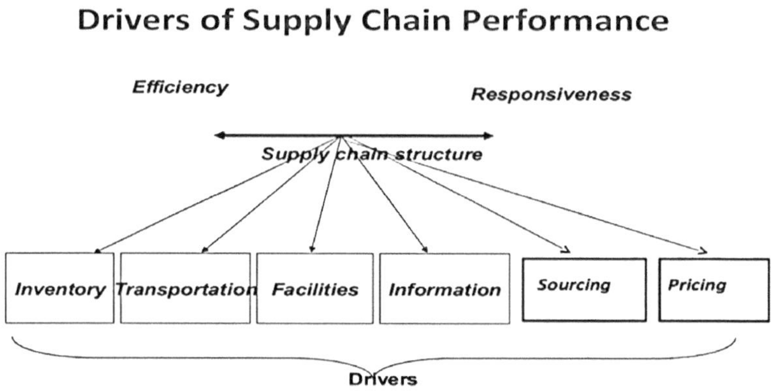

FIGURE 7.3 Drivers of supply chain performance.

Source: Courtesy ujjmishra. https://www.slideshare.net/slideshow/supply-chain-drivers-metrics/29011207

SMEs face several challenges in managing their SC effectively. The following are the challenges faced by SMEs in managing their SC:

1. Limited resources: SMEs often have limited resources in terms of finance, manpower, and technology.
2. Lack of bargaining power: SMEs often have less bargaining power with suppliers and customers due to their small size. This makes it difficult for them to negotiate better prices and terms.
3. Poor infrastructure: SMEs often operate in areas with poor infrastructure, such as inadequate transportation facilities and poor communication networks. This can cause delays in the delivery of goods and services.
4. Inadequate information: SMEs often lack access to timely and accurate information about demand, supply, and inventory levels. This can result in stock outs or excess inventory.
5. Lack of expertise: SMEs often lack the expertise to manage complex SC operations. This can lead to inefficiencies and increased costs.
6. Increased efficiency: Effective SCM can help SMEs improve their efficiency by reducing wastage, optimizing production processes, and improving communication and coordination.
7. Increased competitiveness: A well-managed SC can help SMEs increase their competitiveness by improving their ability to respond to changes in demand and supply, and by providing a better customer experience.

There are several strategies that SMEs can adopt to improve their SC performance. Some of these strategies are:

1. Use of technology: SMEs can leverage technology to manage their SC more effectively. They can use tools such as inventory management software, transport management systems, and customer relationship management systems to improve their SC operations.
2. Collaboration: SMEs can collaborate with other businesses in the SC to share resources, costs, and improve efficiency. SMEs can collaborate with logistics service providers to optimize transportation costs.
3. Outsourcing: SMEs can outsource non-core SC activities such as transportation and warehousing to third-party logistics providers.
4. Lean management: SMEs can adopt lean management practices to reduce wastage, optimize production processes, and improve efficiency.
5. Continuous improvement: SMEs can continuously monitor and improve their SC operations to ensure that they remain competitive and efficient.
6. Build strong supplier relationships: SMEs should focus on building strong relationships with their suppliers. This can help to ensure timely deliveries, reduce costs, and improve the overall quality of the products or services being provided.
7. Implement SC visibility tools: SMEs can implement SC visibility tools such as enterprise resource planning (ERP) systems, which can help to improve the tracking and monitoring of inventory levels, production schedules, and delivery times.
8. Adopt lean manufacturing practices: SMEs can adopt lean manufacturing practices to improve the efficiency of their SC. This can involve reducing waste, improving production processes, and optimizing inventory levels.
9. Embrace technology: SMEs can leverage technology to improve their SC performance. For instance, they can use automated systems for order processing, inventory management, and logistics to reduce costs and improve accuracy.
10. Invest in staff training: SMEs should invest in staff training to ensure that their employees have the necessary skills to manage the SC effectively. This can include training in areas such as logistics, inventory management, and procurement.

11. Monitor performance: SMEs should regularly monitor their SC performance to identify areas for improvement. This can involve tracking metrics such as delivery times, inventory levels, and production efficiency.

7.3 SCM PRACTICES: THE OPPORTUNISTIC BEHAVIOR OF ORGANIZATIONS

From the available literature, it is clear that the SCM has the ability to catapult a company to new heights. The roads to achieving world-class performance are paved by an organization's capacity to detect and overcome obstacles in the application of SCM techniques. Meehan and Muir's (2008) study of British SMEs (Shepherd and Günter, 2006). The lack of knowledge and experience with performance development programs, computerized business, and skilled personnel are examples of personal obstacles. Relationship obstacles include being unable to influence other SC participants, having limited trust in one's partners, and lacking the drive of other participants to pursue the activities required for SC development. Organizational challenges might include things such as a lack of confidence in the benefits of SCM or a lack of confidence in where customers and suppliers are located. So, in order to profit from SCM, both LEs and SMEs must get beyond these challenges (Chaharsooghi and Heydari, 2010). The United Nations Industrial Development Organization suggests that the clustering technique might be a useful tactic for SMEs in navigating the many challenges they encounter on the road to sustainable long-term growth. When businesses are located in close proximity to one another, they may work together to take advantage of economies of size and scope that would be impossible for any individual business to achieve on its own (Rogers, 2001). Overall, SMEs can improve their SC performance by focusing on building strong relationships with suppliers, implementing SC visibility tools, adopting lean manufacturing practices, embracing technology, investing in staff training, and monitoring performance. By taking a strategic approach to SCM, SMEs can improve their competitiveness and achieve sustainable growth (Meehan and Muir, 2008).

SCM practices involve managing the flow of goods and services from suppliers to customers, with the aim of achieving efficiency and effectiveness in the process. However, organizations may engage in opportunistic behavior that can negatively affect the performance of the SC. Opportunistic

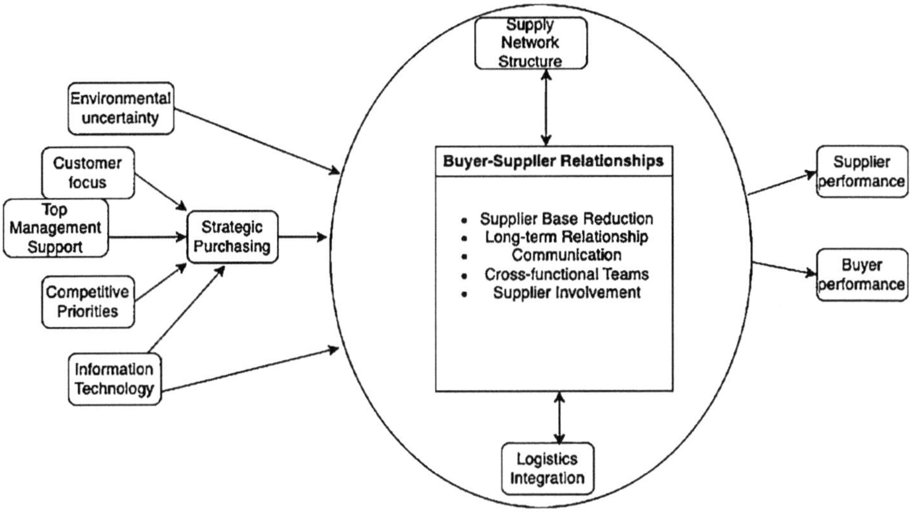

FIGURE 7.4 Supply chain management (SCM) practices.

behavior refers to actions taken by organizations to maximize their own interests at the expense of other SC partners. For instance, a supplier may demand higher prices from a buyer in a situation where the buyer has no alternative suppliers, or a buyer may demand longer payment terms from a supplier who is desperate for business. Such opportunistic behavior can lead to SC disruptions, lower quality products, increased costs, and reduced trust among SC partners. Therefore, it is important for organizations to avoid such behavior and instead promote cooperation and collaboration within the SC (Steckel et al., 2004). One way to reduce opportunistic behavior is to establish long-term relationships with SC partners based on trust and mutual benefit. This can involve regular communication, joint planning, and sharing of information and resources. Additionally, organizations can use contracts and other formal agreements to establish clear expectations and prevent opportunistic behavior. Another approach is to use performance-based incentives to encourage SC partners to act in the best interests of the SC as a whole (Stewart, 1995). This can involve linking rewards to metrics such as on-time delivery, quality, and cost savings, rather than just individual performance. In summary, SCM practices aim to achieve efficiency and effectiveness in the SC. However, opportunistic behavior by organizations can undermine these efforts. By promoting cooperation, collaboration, and mutual benefit, organizations can reduce opportunistic behavior and improve the performance of the SC.

7.4 FACTORS AFFECTING SC PERFORMANCE: AN OVERVIEW

SC performance systems are not worth the effort required to set them up and keep them running. Getting a handle on SC metrics and measuring methods is the primary objective of this literature study. Planning, sourcing, production/assembly, and distribution/customer service are all processes in the SC that are analogized. The essential for tools managing integrated supply networks was enhanced by the foundation (Shepherd and Günter, 2006). Effective measurement methods may stimulate ongoing process improvement; therefore, managers should be permitted to zero in on the causes of process variance. Insights gathered from employee evaluations may be used to assist businesses either prevent or swiftly address problems. Real-time process analysis and tracking is at the heart of process monitoring. As problems develop during process execution, administrators and managers can utilize monitoring data to adjust how processes behave (Shepherd and Gunter, 2006). An organization's responsiveness to customer complaints can be enhanced by means of process monitoring. The focus of operational SC administration is on analyzing the efficiency of the current SC. Managers are better able to detect changes in material or monetary flow patterns and departures from previously agreed-upon process routes when they conduct research using a formal process description. In business, controlling resources and maximizing their worth across the SC is referred to as SCM.

The most effective SCs may be around for quite some time. The efficiency of the SC is affected by both internal and external factors. The workforce landscape will appear very different in ten years. Scientists predicted that developing nations would see rapid expansion while developed nations would witness more modest growth (Steckel et al., 2004). Leaders in the SC must account for this change in the availability of labor when designing global supply networks. Talent planning in the SC will be significantly affected by this ongoing trend. It is crucial to have a plan in place for acquiring and maintaining A-list employees. Every future SC worker will need the capacity to multitask digitally (Stewart, 1995). The capacity to swiftly adapt to new technologies and the willingness to use complicated data and artificial intelligence (AI) in making decisions will be vital in a future where automation is advancing. Humans will still be needed in the futuristic manufacturing facility to oversee daily operations, troubleshoot breakdowns, and run the machines. Those in charge of a business must be ready to experiment with new approaches if they want to steer the organization in the right path.

Elmuti and Kathawala (1997) stated that the people that make up the benchmarking team need to be selected with care. Members of the team should come from across the company, and they should know it well. As a rule, SMEs are on a tight budget and have limited resources, therefore it is important to have an idea of how much time and money would be needed to complete the benchmarking process before diving in. The business owners might use this information to plan ahead for their financial responsibilities. The point of benchmarking is to use comparable data to go above and beyond, which is why it is so popular. Planning the research, gathering data, assessing the performance disparity, implementing fixes, and keeping tabs on the results are the five steps that make up the benchmarking process.

1. **Lead time:** A long lead time can result in delays in the delivery of goods and services, which can impact customer satisfaction and profitability. To minimize lead time, businesses need to have efficient transportation and logistics systems, effective inventory management, and streamlined production processes.

2. **Inventory management:** Inventory management is a critical aspect of SCM. Too much inventory can result in increased holding costs and reduced cash flow, while too little inventory can result in stock outs and lost sales. To optimize inventory levels, businesses need to have an effective inventory management system that uses advanced forecasting techniques and real-time data analysis. If suppliers fail to deliver goods and services on time or provide substandard quality, it can result in delays, increased costs, and reduced customer satisfaction. To manage supplier performance, businesses need to have a robust supplier management system that includes regular performance evaluations, supplier development programs, and contingency plans.

3. **Transportation:** Transportation is a critical aspect of SCM. Efficient transportation systems can help businesses reduce lead time, minimize transportation costs, and enhance customer satisfaction. To optimize transportation, businesses need to have a well-designed transportation network that includes multiple transportation modes, efficient routing, and real-time tracking.

4. **Information technology:** It enables businesses to collect and analyze real-time data, monitor inventory levels, and track shipments. To leverage information technology effectively, businesses need to have a robust information technology infrastructure that

includes advanced software systems, data analytics tools, and secure communication networks.

5. **Demand variability:** If the demand for a product or service is unpredictable, it can lead to several problems in the SC, such as stock outs or excess inventory. This can result in increased costs, reduced customer satisfaction, and decreased profitability. To manage demand variability, businesses need to have a robust forecasting system and agile SCM.

7.5 CONCEPTUAL FRAMEWORK AND HYPOTHESIS DEVELOPMENT

Collaboration is the act of making decisions together by people who are dependent on one another. Participation in making decisions and taking credit for outcomes together. Three crucial factors include interdepartmental breadth, a collaborative spirit, and a common goal or thread collaboration across internal processes have a significant impact on the performance of logistical services, they should be fostered by firms aiming to improve their logistical efficiency. Surprisingly, there is no evidence linking external collaboration with improved service performance, showing that customer and supplier relationships do not boost efficiency. Collaboration with international SC firms also increases internal cooperation and therefore, logistical service (Stewart, 1995). Working together is essential both within and outside of a company. The advantages add up over time. When businesses work together and share information, they are able to put more human and financial resources into their operations. Hence, it's easier to make educated decisions and lessen danger (Fawcett et al., 2008b). When two entities operate together in the SC, they are said to be partners. Having a long-term connection with one another is the key to success in this type of communication, as it facilitates joint problem-solving and strategic planning. Developing a rapport with your suppliers will help you secure better pricing and expedite the sourcing process. When it comes to fostering and fortifying alliances, it's vital to take into account the factors that must be taken into account throughout analysis. The success of supplier partnerships may be gauged, for instance, by looking at how well suppliers work together to address common problems. By using these standards to evaluate potential collaborations, win–win associations may be formed, leading to improved SC efficiency and visibility (Shepherd and Günter, 2006).

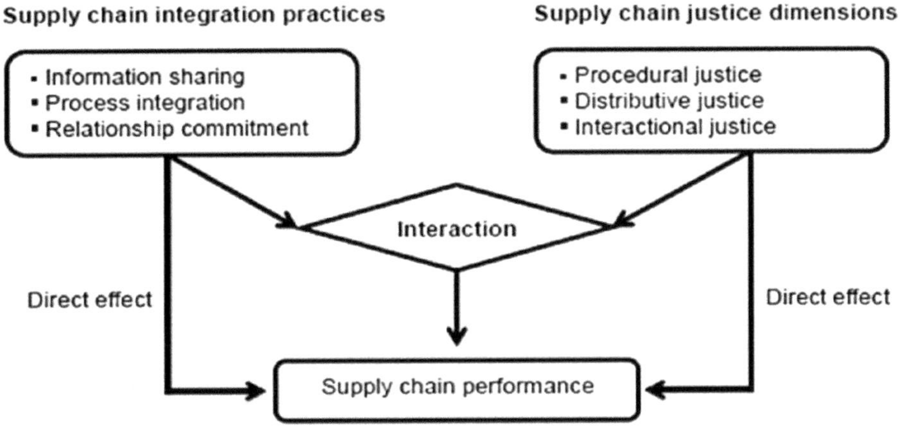

FIGURE 7.5 Complementarities and main effects.

The study's goals are:

1. To investigate variables that influence SCM
2. To quantify the elements' effects on SCM
3. To study the awareness level toward the SC performance with reference to SME

7.6 RESEARCH METHODOLOGY

As theoretical explanations of SCM phenomena are limited, an empirical investigation was deemed necessary. Research in Chennai was conducted using a sample size of 250 from the city. Empirical testing is important to the research strategy. The study's construct domain is developed by a literature analysis and in-depth interviews with industry leaders and academic specialists. All of the questionnaire's components were evaluated by respondents using a five-point Likert scale to measure their relative importance (Gunasekaran, 2004). As positivism is the overarching philosophy of this enquiry, we may anticipate that only evidence obtained via scientific means will be regarded as credible and devoid of prejudice. Positivists argue that future events may be predicted and controlled by establishing a connection between present and future conditions based on established causal patterns and regularities (Stewart, 1995).

7.7 ANALYSIS, FINDINGS, AND DISCUSSION

7.7.1 *FACTORS AFFECTING THE PERFORMANCE OF THE SCM*

SCM is impacted by a number of elements, many of which are explained by expert opinion and theory. The duration of the review period, the manner of demand forecasting, lead times, and review periods. The responses to these questions are ranked based on the respondents' opinions using the Kendall's Coefficient of Concordance.

TABLE 7.1 Factors Affecting the Performance of the SCM.

Factors	Mean	Std. deviation	Mean rank
Customer demand	3.17	1.305	4.17
Forecasting method	2.28	1.456	2.75
Information sharing	3.15	1.327	3.08
Inventory control policy	2.87	1.424	4.80
Lead time	3.21	1.470	3.13
Review period length	3.14	1.418	4.92
Supply chain structure	3.06	1.234	4.14

According to Table 7.1, review period duration (4.92) is one of the most important parameters affecting SCM success. The majority of respondents have also thought about the SC system's inventory management policy (4.80). The survey respondents also take into account customer demand (4.17). Fourth and fifth on the list are lead time (3.13), and the SC structure (4.14). The importance of the rankings is tested as follows.

TABLE 7.2 Kendall's Coefficient of Concordance.

N	250
Kendall's W	0.006
Chi-Square	8.792
df	6
Asymp. Sig.	0.179

The calculated Chi-Square value (8.792) for the degree of freedom 6 is not significant. The p value is 0.179 which is not significant at 5% level. The result shows that the ranks given for the Factors affecting the performance of the SCM is not significantly varying.

7.7.2 ELEMENTS: INFLUENCING THE PERFORMANCE OF SUPPLY CHAIN

SCM is crucial to the success of any firm. It entails organizing and controlling the flow of products. The profitability, customer happiness, and competitiveness of the company can all be impacted by the operation of the SC. In this succinct note, we'll go over the elements that have an impact on SC performance. For find the most preferred brand, Garret ranking technique is applied. The result is given in the Table 7.3.

TABLE 7.3 Elements Influencing *Performance of Supply Chain*: Garret Ranking.

Factors	**Rank**	**1**	**2**	**3**	**4**	**5**	**6**	**7**	**Score**	**Rank**
	GV	**79**	**66**	**58**	**50**	**43**	**35**	**22**		
Company environment	f	79	66	58	50	43	35	22	15,398	I
	fx	124	15	14	38	20	14	25		
Suppliers and competition	f	9796	990	812	1900	860	490	550	15,234	II
	fx	27	145	26	12	11	24	5		
Quality	f	2133	9570	1508	600	473	840	110	13,703	III
	fx	24	32	151	5	17	10	11		
Customer satisfaction	f	1896	2112	8758	250	731	350	242	12,853	IV
	fx	23	12	11	162	26	8	8		
Innovation	f	1817	792	638	8100	1118	280	176	11,909	V
	fx	13	12	30	14	147	25	9		
Flexibility	f	1027	792	1740	700	6321	875	198	10,465	VI
	fx	14	25	11	9	18	157	16		
Production system	f	1106	1650	638	450	774	5495	352	8204	VII
	fx	25	9	7	10	11	12	176		

The result shows that the respondents mostly consider the company environment (15,392), followed by suppliers and competition (15,284) which is ranked second as most preferred factor, followed by quality (17,303).

TABLE 7.4 Awareness Toward the Supply Chain.

Awareness	**Mean**	**Std. deviation**	**Mean rank**	**Rank**
Communication tools	2.85	1.034	3.22	I
Planning tools	2.68	1.011	2.89	IV
Process strategy	2.59	1.065	2.83	V
Marketing strategy	2.69	1.137	2.90	III
Environmental uncertainty	2.82	1.149	3.15	II

Table 7.4 shows that the respondents are highly aware of the SCM. As ranked by the respondents, they are also highly aware of the following— first, the communication tools (3.22), followed by environmental uncertainty (3.15, second), marketing strategy (2.90, third), planning tools (2.89, fourth), process strategy (2.83, fifth). The hypothesis to test the significant difference in the awareness level about the various dimensions is checked with Friedman test (Table 7.5).

TABLE 7.5 Friedman Test.

N	250
Chi-Square	15.723
df	4
Asymp. Sig.	0.004

The calculated chi-Square value (15.273) in the Friedman test for the degree of freedom 4 is significant at 1% level. The significance is 0.004 (<0.01). Hence, the hypothesis is not accepted. It is found that the respondents' awareness of the communication tools, environmental uncertainty, and marketing strategy are extremely high.

7.8 DISCUSSION AND CONCLUSION

The recommendations should allow for the integration of SC aspects relevant to performance. In addition to the concepts covered in detail elsewhere in this work, this part focuses on some additional factors influencing SC efficiency. The organization and the community as a whole will benefit from the incorporation of past and present study findings. This research has supplied hard data to support claims about the similarities and differences in SMEs. Based on the results of the research, it is clear that LEs and SMEs share the same SC goals and practices (Shepherd and Günter, 2006). The results also show that both industries share a commitment to building partnerships based on mutual trust, but that SMEs are lagging on both the relationship-building and skill-building fronts with their suppliers. It is discovered that SMEs and LEs see the obstacles to implementing SCM methods, the company culture, and benchmarking processes differently. SMEs share similar views on the most important prerequisites for adopting benchmarking activity. SMEs often look to their rivals for benchmarking partners. It appears like a solid approach for SMEs, as it affords both employees and owners the chance to gain knowledge. It has been noted that compared to large corporations, SMEs devote fewer resources to continuous benchmarking activity. Belief on the efficacy of benchmarking, or significant expenses and time required. SME owners and managers need to stop being so cautious of benchmarking initiatives, as they may help identify areas for improvement and help reorganize such areas to become competitive advantages. As a result of the encouragement of "out of the box" thinking that benchmarking provides, both employees and managers are better equipped to come up with novel approaches to boosting productivity. There are no signs that the global slump will end soon. An important goal of this program is to support small and medium-sized businesses in their expansion and viability. The federal government is also evaluating the regulations' guiding principles in an effort to simplify and more amenable to SMEs. The key finding of the research is that, for SME owners and managers to prosper in the face of fierce competition from bigger businesses at every point of LEs' SCs, they must undergo a cultural revolution. SMEs would benefit if they focused more on strategic planning and management of their business than only on economic factors (Shepherd and Günter, 2006). In conclusion, a number of elements, such as demand fluctuation, lead time, inventory management, supplier performance, transportation, and information technology, have an impact on how well the SC functions (Yin, 2003). These variables must be recognized by businesses in order to create methods for managing them successfully. Businesses may boost their profitability, increase customer happiness, and become more competitive in the market by improving SC performance.

7.9 PRACTICAL CONSEQUENCES

The research's conclusions are anticipated to have application in the SC managed by SMEs. In this regard, the study discovered that although it is crucial for a firm to be able to endure and survive market upheaval, it should do so at affordable prices. The researchers believe that SC managers will understand that robustness increases the cost of marketing and sales. SMEs are adaptable and nimble enough to adjust when confronted with SC disruptions (Bottani and Montanari, 2010). These SMEs are fast to adapt their marketing, sales, and manufacturing strategies to the demands of the market. In the recent COVID-19 pandemic lockdowns, it was noted that many of these SMEs had no presence online (Fawcett et al., 2008b). As the pandemic-related disruptions hit, these Businesses swiftly recovered by learning how to create an internet presence and become very visible to their target market and beyond (Meehan and Muir, 2008). The research presents important implications for SMEs' practical response to obstacles while boosting their performance by examining how firms may enhance their performance by overcoming adversity and workplace issues Lambert et al. (1996). For instance, the research provides SMEs with a mechanism to resume operations while retaining high performance during times of global pandemics like COVID-19 that interrupt the global SC. One effective strategy to show SC resilience is to reduce distribution costs and increase delivery speed and dependability (Shepherd and Günter, 2006).

7.10 LIMITS AND FUTURE RESEARCH

Although this study helps to address a research vacuum on the impact of resilience on performance, further research is needed in this area (Fawcett et al., 2008b). These restrictions also leave room for new areas of study (Lambert et al., 1996). While this study is quantitative, future research should employ mixed approaches to better capture nuanced facts and perspectives (Dominguez et al., 2015). To learn more about how firms cope with turbulence and how resilience aids them, the researcher advises doing a mixed-method study that includes interviews with management. Gunasekaran (2004), also, given the scope of the current study is restricted to SMEs, future studies should gather empirical data from a wider range of organizations and industries to ascertain whether or not the results hold true in other settings Yin (2003). In conclusion, the performance of the SC is critical to the success of SMEs. Effective SCM can help SMEs reduce costs, improve efficiency, and enhance customer satisfaction (Meehan and Muir, 2008). The study's primary goal is to examine the relationships between the many elements that affect SCM deployment and to develop a hierarchy of SCM variables that would enable decision-makers to take these aspects into consideration Ab Rahman et al., 2008). The absence of autonomous components in this study suggests that each of the variables has a significant impact on the adoption of SCM. For the effective deployment of SCM, the decision-makers should thus pay closer attention to all the relevant aspects (Chaharsooghi and Heydari, 2010).

KEYWORDS

- **effects of key variables on supply chain efficiency**
- **supply chain performance**

REFERENCES

Ab Rahman, M. N.; Ismail, A. R.; Md Dero, B.; Rosli, M. E. Barriers to SCM Implementing. *J. Achiev. Mater. Manuf. Eng.* **2008,** *31* (2), 718–724.

Bordonaba-Juste, V.; Cambra-Fierro, J. J. Managing Supply Chain in the Context of SMEs: A Collaborative and Customized Partnership with the Suppliers as the key for Success. *Supply Chain Manag. Int. J.* **2009,** *14* (5), 393–402.

Bottani, E.; Montanari, R. Supply Chain Design and Cost Analysis Through Simulation. *Int. J. Prod. Res.* **2010,** *48* (10), 2859–2886.

Cachon, G. P.; Fisher, M. Supply Chain Inventory Management and the Value of Shared Information. *Manage. Sci.* **2000,** *46* (8), 1032–1048.

Cannella, S.; Ciancimino, E. On the Bullwhip Avoidance Phase: Supply Chain Collaboration and Order Smoothing. *Int. J. Prod. Res.* **2010,** *48* (22), 6739–6776.

Chaharsooghi, S. K.; Heydari, J. LT Variance or LT Mean Reduction in Supply Chain Management: Which one has a Higher Impact on SC performance? *Int. J. Prod. Econ.* **2010,** *124* (2), 475–481.

Chan, F. T. S.; Chan, H. K. Simulation Modeling for Comparative Evaluation of Supply Chain Management Strategies. *Int. J. Adv. Manuf. Technol.* **2005,** *25* (9–10), 998–1006.

Christopher. *Logistics and Supply Chain Management*, 3rd ed.; Prentice Hall, 2005; pp 9–11.

Cooper, M. C.; Lambert, D. M.; Pagh, J. D. Supply Chain Management: More Than a New Name for Logistics. *Int. J. Logist. Manag.* **1997,** *8* (1), 1–15.

Dominguez, S. C.; Framinan, J. M. The Impact of the Supply Chain Structure on Bullwhip Effect. *Appl. Math. Model.* **2015,** *39* (23–24), 7309–7325.

Elmuti, D.; Kathawala, Y. An Overview of Benchmarking Process: A Tool for Continuous Improvement and Competitive Advantage. *Benchmark. Qual. Manag. Technol.* **1997,** *4* (4), 229–243.

Fawcett, S. E.; Magnan, G. M.; McCarter, M. W. Benefits, Barriers, and Bridges to Effective Supply Chain Management. *Supply Chain Manag. Int. J.* **2008b,** *13* (1), 35–48.

Gunasekaran A framework for Supply Chain Performance Measurement. *Int. J. Prod. Econ.* **2004,** *87,* 333–347.

Gunasekaran A Framework for Supply Chain Performance Measurement. *J. Prod. Econ.* **2004,** *87,* 333–347.

Holten, R. et al.; In *Enabling Technologies for Supply Chain Process Management*, Proceedings of the IRMA 2002 Conference, Seattle. pp 5–7, 2002.

Kelepouris, P. M.; Pramatari, K. The Impact of Replenishment Parameters and Information Sharing on the Bullwhip Effect: A Computational Study. *Comput. Oper. Res.* **2008,** *35* (11), 3657–3670.

Khosroshahi, H.; Husseini, S. M. M; Marjani, M. R. The Bullwhip Effect in a 3-stage Supply Chain Considering Multiple Retailers Using a Moving Average Method for Demand Forecasting. *J. Appl. Math. Model* **2016,** *40* (21), 8934–8951.

Lambert, D. M.; Emmelhainz, M. A.; Gardner, J. T. Developing and Implementing Supply Chain Partnerships. *Int. J. Logist. Manag.* **1996,** *7* (2), 1–17.

Lee, H. L.; Padmanabhan, V.; Whang, S. Information Distortion in a Supply Chain: The Bullwhip Effect. *Manag. Sci.* **2004,** *50* (12), 1875–1886.

Meehan, J.; Muir, L. SCM in Merseyside SMEs: Benefits and Barriers. *TQM J.* **2008,** *20* (3), 223–232.

Mentzer Defining Supply Chain Management. *J. Bus. Logist.* **2001,** *22* (2).

Mentzer et al. Defining Supply Chain Management. *J. Bus. Logist.* **2001,** *22* (2), 3–9.
Pillai, M.; Talari, P. C.; Elluri, P. V. Performance Analysis of Some Supply Chain Replenishment Strategies. *Int. J. Logist. Res. Appl. 17* (5), 357–376.
Rogers. The Supply Chain Management Processes. *Int. J. Logist. Manag.* **2001,** *12* (2), 13–36.
Sezen, S.; Kitapci, H. Spreadsheet Simulation for the Supply Chain Inventory Problem. *Prod. Plan. Control* **2007,** *18* (1), 9–15.
Shepherd, C.; Günter, H. Measuring Supply Chain Performance: Current Research and Future Directions. *Int. J. Prod. Perform. Manag.* **2006,** *55* (3–4), 242–258.
Simchi-Levi. *Designing and Managing the Supply Chain: Concepts, Strategies and Case Studies*, 3rd ed.; Tata McGraw-Hill: New Delhi, 2008; pp 1–3.
Stank. Supply chain Collaboration and Logistical Service Performance. *J. Bus. Logist.* **2001,** *22* (1), 29–49.
Stank, T. P.; Emmelhainz, M. A.; Daugherty, P. J. The Impact of Information on Supplier Performance. *J. Mark. Theory Pract.* **1996,** *4* (4), 94–106.
Steckel, J. H.; Gupta, S.; Banerji, A. Supply Chain Decision Making: will Shorter Cycle Times and Shared Point-of-sale Information Necessarily Help? *Manage. Sci.* **2004,** *50* (4), 458–464.
Stewart, G. Supply Chain Performance Benchmarking Study Reveals Keys to Supply Chain Excellence. *Logist. Inform. Manag.* **1995,** *8* (2), 38–44.
Tan, K. C.; Kannan, V. R.; Handfield, R. B.; Ghosh, S. Supply Chain Management: Empirical Study of Its Impact on Performance. *Int. J. Operat. Prod. Manag.* **1999,** *19* (10), 1034–1052.
Yin, R. K. Case Study Research, Design and Methods, 3rd ed.; Sage Publications, Inc.: Thousand Oaks, 2003; pp 3–5.
Zinkhan. Two Contributions from Sociology to Marketing Thought: A Qualitative and a Quantitative Perspective. *J. Mark. Res.* **1994,** *31,* 312–314.

CHAPTER 8

A Study on Food Supply Chain Management, System Implementation, and Future Research

S. V. PRADEEPA[1], PURVI DIPEN DERASHRI[2], ARUP ROY CHOWDHURY[3], and MANO ASHISH TRIPATHI[4]

[1]*School of Management, Ajeenkya D Y Patil University, Lohegaon, Pune, India*

[2]*Faculty of Management studies, Parul Institute of Management and Research, Parul University, Vadodara, Gujarat, India*

[3]*School of HRM, XIM University, Harirajpur, Bhubaneswar, Odisha, India*

[4]*Department of Humanities and Social Sciences, Motilal Nehru National Institute of Technology, Prayagraj, Uttar Pradesh, India*

ABSTRACT

Purpose: Food supply chain management (FSCM) involves the planning, execution, and control of the movement of food goods and associated data from the starting point to the site of consumption. It involves a variety of tasks, including manufacturing, processing, moving, storing, distributing, and selling. Integration of diverse stakeholders, distributors, retailers, and consumers is necessary for effective FSCM. The food supply chain (FSC) is intricate and faces several difficulties that have an impact on its effectiveness and efficiency.

Research methodology: In this chapter, a framework for reviewing the relevant literature is proposed that is both systematic and hierarchical. To organize this paper, several categorizations and classifications have been identified.

Essentials of Supply Chain Management: Strategy, Planning and Operations.
Mohammed Majeed, Abdul-Rasheed Akeji Alhassan Alolo, Seidu Alhassan, and S. Sekar (Eds.)

Research limitations/implications: A small subset of highly cited or prominently published papers were chosen for inclusion in this work. The concepts presented in this study might likely be applied to various contexts, providing participants with fresh ideas with which to enhance the FSCM. Practitioners may benefit from future deployments of IT-based solutions for FSCM.

Findings: More and more FSCM tools are becoming digital, which means more and more information will be utilized to make decisions. The forthcoming of a more environmentally friendly FSC lies in data-driven FSCM systems.

Originality/value: This research is the first effort at reviewing FSCM in depth from the perspective of information IT systems.

8.1 INTRODUCTION

India's agriculture industry is the second largest in the world behind China's and may become the largest if given the chance. One of the most significant segments of India's processed food industry is the baking sector. According to King and Phumpi (1996), more than 82% of all bakery items produced in the nation are bread and biscuits, which together make up the majority of baked foods. Scale economies, negotiating strength, and vertical integration are some of the economic considerations in favor of companies engaging in group marketing (Garnett, 2011). Small-scale farmers may be motivated to take collective action by political and social concerns (Accorsi et al., 2014). Poor, small-scale producers have few opportunities for successful group marketing activities. The management of the whole chain of production, distribution, and consumption of food and its associated information is known as food supply chain management (FSCM) (Agustina et al., 2014). Organizations may increase productivity, save expenses, and better satisfy consumer needs by using an FSCM system (MacCarthy et al., 2016). Businesses may increase their responsiveness and ability to compete by automating and simplifying a variety of procedures. System implementation in FSCM involves the adoption of technology solutions to automate and streamline various processes, including inventory management, logistics, traceability, and quality control (Cooper and Ellram, 1993). The following are the key steps involved in system implementation in FSCM:

1. Needs assessment: The first step in system implementation is to assess the organization's current processes, identify the pain points, and determine the requirements for the new system.

2. System selection: The second step involves selecting the appropriate system that meets the organization's requirements. Factors to consider include cost, scalability, ease of use, and compatibility with existing systems.
3. System configuration: The third step involves configuring the system to meet the organization's specific needs. This includes setting up workflows, data fields, and user roles.
4. Data migration: The fourth step involves migrating data from the old system to the new system. This includes data on suppliers, products, inventory, and customers.
5. User training: The fifth step involves training users on how to use the new system. This includes providing training manuals, conducting online or in-person training sessions, and offering ongoing support.
6. System testing: The sixth step involves testing the system to ensure that it functions as expected. This includes testing workflows, data validation, and user interface.
7. Go-live: The final step involves launching the new system and ensuring that it is integrated with other systems and processes.

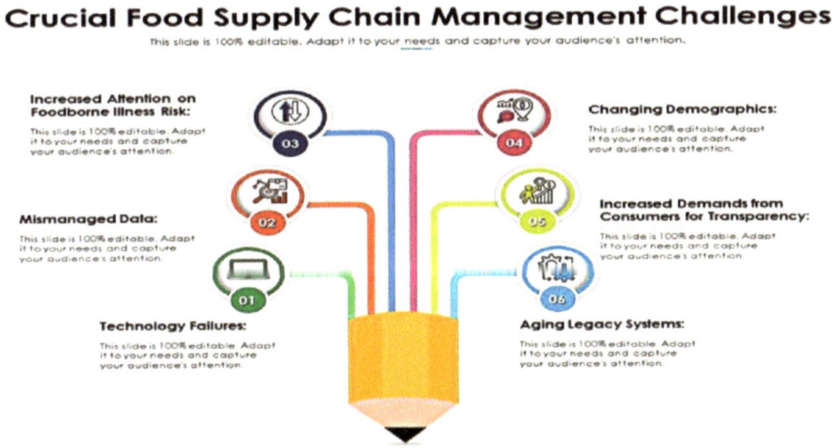

FIGURE 8.1 Challenges faced in FSCM.

Source: Slide Team. https://www.slideteam.net/crucial-food-supply-chain-management-challenges.html

8.2 CHALLENGES FACED IN FSCM

The term "FSCM" is used to describe the process of organizing and coordinating the flow of food items and associated data from production through final consumption (Dubey et al., 2017). It includes several processes, such as manufacturing, packaging, shipping, warehousing, and retailing. Farmers, manufacturers, wholesalers, merchants, and consumers must all be brought into the fold for FSCM to work well.

1. Quality control: Maintaining high standards for food safety (FS) and quality across the whole supply chain. This requires implementing effective quality control measures, including regular testing and inspections, to minimize the risk of contamination or spoilage.
2. Inventory management: Managing inventory levels is crucial for ensuring that food products are delivered to customers in a timely manner. This requires implementing effective inventory management systems that enable stakeholders to track inventory levels and optimize replenishment.
3. Logistics: The food supply chain are complex, involving transportation, storage, and distribution. Managing logistics requires implementing effective transportation and storage systems that minimize the risk of spoilage or damage to food products.
4. Sustainability: Ensuring the sustainability of the FSC is becoming increasingly important, given the growing concern about the environmental consumption. This requires implementing sustainable practices, including reducing waste, using renewable energy, and minimizing the use of harmful chemicals.
5. For food products to be supplied to customers on time, cheaply, and sustainably, good FSCM is essential. By implementing best practices and leveraging technology solutions, organizations can improve their efficiency, reduce costs, and enhance their ability to meet customer demands.

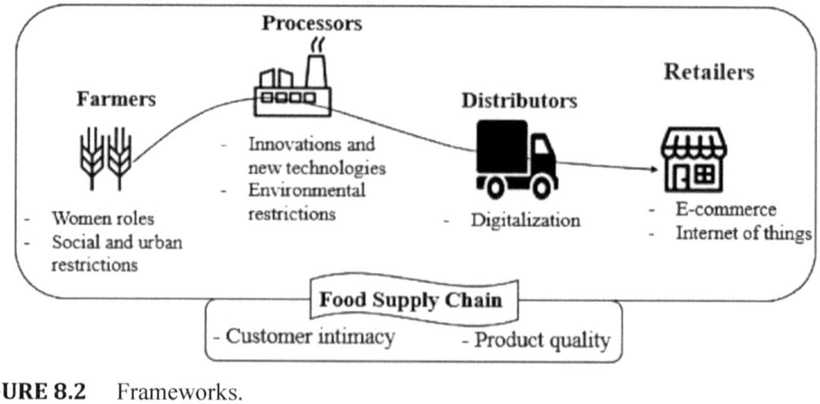

FIGURE 8.2 Frameworks.

8.3 FRAMEWORKS

With the use of an FSCM framework, major industries such as forestry, agriculture, finishing, and so on, may provide their raw materials and semifinished goods to manufacturers for further processing and transformation (MacCarthy et al., 2016). For the objective of identifying item-to-item relationships, we employed interpretive structural modeling (ISM) to build a tree-like structure. Users of this paradigm may get an understanding of the interplay between the many participants in a FSC. An ISM-enabled framework assisted in risk management by identifying and making sense of interconnections between hazards throughout the various stages (Cooper and Ellram, 1993). Using a methodical approach across several stages of production, this framework proved useful in organizing risks in FSCM (Garnett, 2011). The addition of information considerably improves the effectiveness of FSCM. By combining graph theory (used for quantifying information risks) and ISM (used for understanding FSCM's interdependencies), this study offers a framework for evaluating IRM (Agustina et al., 2014, 2014). As the global FSCM develops through international cooperation, the number of actors involved has grown beyond what can be described by the ISM-enabled architecture in terms of either causal or transitive linkages. Later, an entirely ISM was developed to examine the factors that promote and counteract FSCM. Ten promoters and eight detractors of FSCM during a period of rapid globalization are dissected using two distinct frameworks in this research. Chains are highly regarded in the FSCM sector as they enhance both production and consumption. Pirog (2008) proposed a chain architecture for partnerships between farmers, processors, and distributors to increase the overall value of the FSC. The framework analyzes the economic performance of a food supply chain based on its general structure, organization, and processes. The last few decades have seen a rise in the importance of food traceability in several different arenas. Nevertheless, suggestions of widespread implementation frameworks are uncommon. Karlsen et al. found that using a unified framework increases the likelihood that food traceability would be consistent and that implementation strategies will be goal-oriented and efficient (2013). By offering a complete framework and experimental data, Regattieri et al. (2007) analyzed the legal and administrative issues of food tracking. They developed a robust foundation for a tracking system based on the study of alphanumeric codes, barcodes, and radio frequency identification (RFID). Cheesemakers and buyers alike will profit from the framework's incorporation of alphanumeric codes and RFID technology. It is now more important than ever to have a well-coordinated food supply chain that effortlessly moves food from farm to table. Hobbs and Young (2000) demonstrate how contractual ideas have been applied to the agri-food supply chain to further increase vertical collaboration in FSCM. Since this strategy enhances vertical coordination, it has profound effects on the economics of transaction costs. Folkerts and Koehorst's (1997) approach to vertical coordination in the global FSC is created. For optimal performance at every stage of the food supply chain, its framework requires the employment of an analytical service tailored to benchmarking initiatives across the board. When confronted with a global FSCM, it is essential to make strategic decisions so that the overall profitability of the chain can be maximized through the coordinated efforts of an effective framework. Users will be able to make educated decisions about infrastructure components such as network architecture, stock policy, SCM integration, outsourcing, and procurement within this framework. Despite the many obstacles that stand in the way of cooperation between businesses in the food sector around the world, collaboration is increasingly seen as a need. Doukidis et al. (2007) created a framework for assessing supply chain collaboration to study a seminal idea in the agri-food industry. This paradigm emphasizes the need of a coordinated supply chain and the specific difficulties and constraints experienced by the agri-food industry.

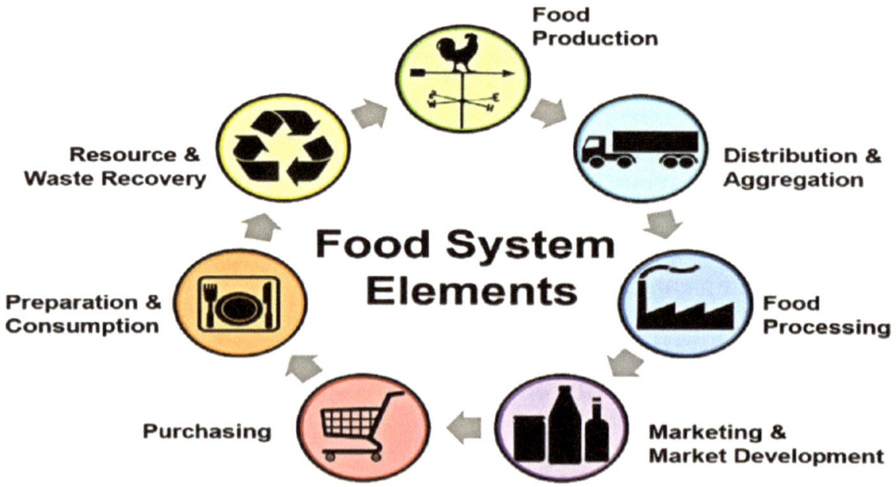

FIGURE 8.3 Models for FSCM.

Source: Reprinted with permission from Kaufman, 2020. Copyright © 2020, Springer Nature Switzerland AG

8.4 MODELS FOR FSCM

These models will use some sophisticated methods, such as deep machine learning, to allow for the definition of several goals simultaneously. After training, learning, and calculating, they may choose relevant data for a variety of objective purposes. Future decision models can intelligently collaborate in the present, thanks to smart decision-making (Dubey et al., 2017). Several models will be developed to make insightful judgments in real time using the big data's intelligent learning capabilities.

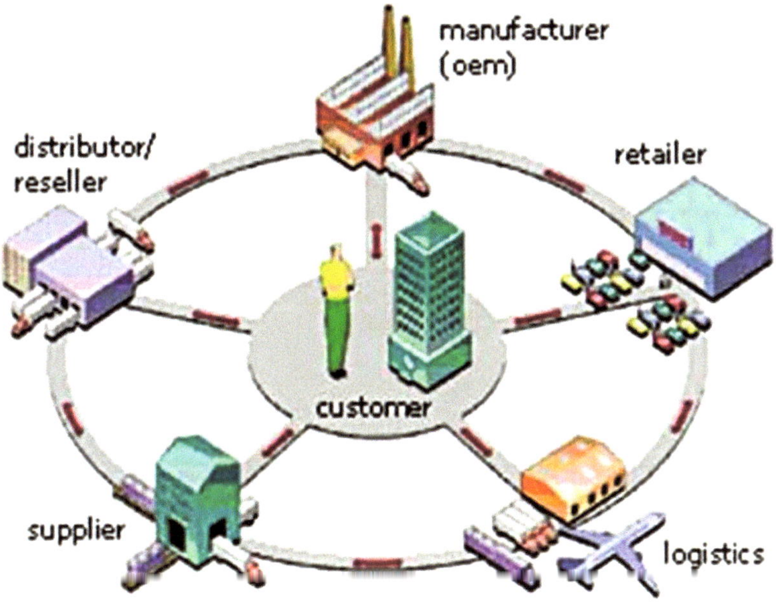

FIGURE 8.4 Data management of FSCM.

Source: Analytikus education. https://www.analytikus.com/post/2016/12/30/21-data-science-systems-used-by-amazon-to-operate-its-business

Data may be gathered in a variety of environments, including those where, for example, the temperature must be kept constant to preserve wines or other perishable goods. Hence, they are wearable or flexible in construction, so they may be quickly deployed and operated. Each collector is equipped with a unique set of skills that may be learned, and they are all monitored and controlled by a single supercomputer that acts as the collective brain for a sizable army of collectors.

1. Adaptive robots: These data collectors are built to do many tasks at once by combining robotics and smart sensors. Advanced technologies allow an adaptable smart robot to mimic human performance. Real-time data from environmental fluctuations may be collected, and the system can then make choices based on this information in an adaptable manner.
2. Systems for making choices: More information is being generated throughout the food supply chain, and this information is needed by decision-making models in order to arrive at effective and systematic solutions. Challenges posed by big data cannot be overcome using the conventional methods that are prepackaged or built in decision-making frameworks. To begin, there are many different types of data that may be used in FSCM decision-making models, each of which can help optimize planning and scheduling, cut down on waste, etc. Unfortunately, because to the massive amount of data used in these models, the calculation time will be quite lengthy. In the age of big data, these methods may no longer be applicable. Finally, existing models address only the issues experienced by one firm or one food distribution system. Seldom do we hear about models that serve many purposes.

8.5 CHALLENGES AND FUTURE PERSPECTIVES—SUPPLY CHAIN NETWORK STRUCTURE

An effective and efficient supply chain network structure is crucial to maintaining high standards of food quality. The present food system is struggling to meet the growing worldwide demand for high-quality, wholesome fare. Initially, a warehouse management system (WMS) is the central focus of attention throughout the planning and creation of a network structure for a food supply chain. Proper locations and distribution network topologies are often suggested using mixed-integer linear programming models. There must be a complete and worldwide framework. And second, in a network architecture, optimizations are always taken into account. Nonetheless, time, money, and profit are always taken into account. There is no mention of environmental effects or sustainable performance. In light of rising resource demands, it is essential to redesign the current supply chain to minimize waste and carbon emissions. Finally, as sophisticated technologies such as the Internet of Things (IoT) continue to grow, conventional network architectures are becoming inadequate for supporting the operations of today's food supply chains, which include an abundance of digital devices, sensors, and robots. Thus, FSCM need a fresh, transparent framework. In order to satisfy future needs and handle existing difficulties, the food supply chain's future structure (Blandon et al., 2009). The ultimate goal of this internationally coordinated architecture is to provide efficient closed-loop monitoring and control of the global food supply by bringing together all the essential partners. There needs to be greater study of the development in order to reach this objective. Future sustainability in the food supply chain may be achieved by measures such as lowering environmental impact, increasing food waste recycling, and increasing facility sharing Ghosh 2016). Sustainable development necessitates innovative approaches and coordinated expansion with other areas such as industry and the economy. With the use of encapsulation, interfaces, and protocols, the FSCM PI achieves operational interconnection. The FSCM sector might benefit from using the PI principle in order to enhance the methods in which food is transported, stored, and distributed on a global scale (Dubey et al., 2017).

8.6 RESEARCH PROBLEM

There is growing expectation that the food business would streamline its supply chain. The implementation of technology solutions, such as inventory management systems, traceability systems, and logistics management systems. However, implementing these systems can be challenging, and many organizations struggle with system implementation and adoption (Cooper and Ellram, 1993). Therefore, a research problem related to FSCM system implementation could be: What are the key factors that influence the successful implementation and adoption of technology solutions in FSCM? (Chen et al., 2014). This research problem could be further refined by focusing on specific technology solutions, such as traceability systems or inventory management systems, and specific stakeholders in the food supply chain, such as farmers or retailers (Dubey et al., 2017). The research examined the impact of cultural and organizational factors, such as resistance to change and lack of technology expertise, on the implementation and adoption of technology solutions. The findings of this research could help organizations to better understand the challenges and opportunities associated with system implementation in FSCM and develop strategies to improve implementation and adoption (Ghosh, 2016).

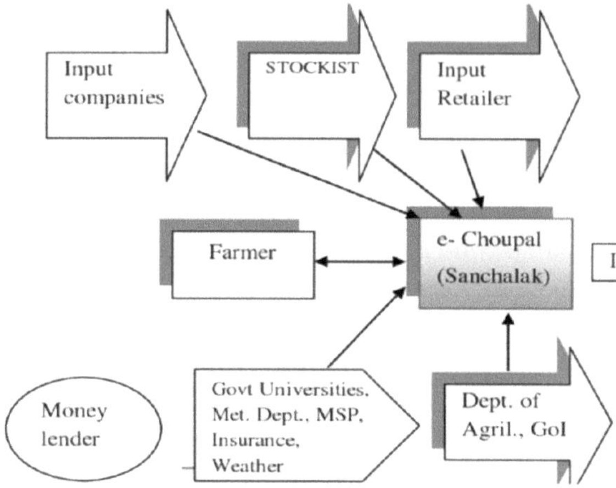

FIGURE 8.5 Implementation in FSCM.

Source: Reprinted from Parwez, 2013. https://creativecommons.org/licenses/by/4.0/

8.7 NEED FOR THE STUDY

The food supply chain is a complex network of interconnected actors involved in the production, processing, distribution, and consumption of food products (Ghosh, 2016). As such, there is a need for the study of FSCM to address several important issues, including:

1. The food supply chain has significant environmental impacts, including greenhouse gas emissions, water consumption, and waste generation. Managing the food supply chain can help reduce these impacts and promote sustainable practices.
2. Managing the food supply chain can help identify areas for cost savings, such as reducing waste, improving inventory management, and optimizing transportation.
3. The food supply chain is becoming increasingly global, with food products being sourced from all over the world. Managing the food supply chain can help ensure that food products are produced and transported in a socially responsible and environmentally sustainable manner. Overall, the study of FSCM is crucial to ensure the safety, quality, and sustainability of food products, as well as to promote cost efficiency and social responsibility within the food industry.

8.8 SIGNIFICANCE OF THE STUDY

The significance of studying FSCM and system implementation lies in the crucial role that the food industry plays in our society. FSCM involves the coordination and management of all the activities involved in the production, processing, storage, and distribution of food products from the farm to the table. Effective FSCM can help to ensure that food products are delivered to consumers in a timely and efficient manner, while also maintaining their quality and safety. It can also help to reduce waste, minimize costs, and improve the profitability of food companies. Implementing a FSCM system can bring numerous benefits to food companies. It can help to improve the accuracy and efficiency of inventory management, enhance supply chain visibility, reduce lead times, and improve customer satisfaction. It can also help to ensure compliance with regulatory requirements, such as FS regulations. Furthermore, the COVID-19 pandemic has highlighted the importance of resilient and sustainable food supply chains. As a result, there is an increasing need for food companies to implement robust supply chain management systems that can cope with disruptions and ensure the continuity of food supply. Therefore, the study of FSCM and system implementation is significant in providing insights and recommendations for the improvement of the food industry. It can help to identify best practices, challenges, and opportunities for food companies to optimize their supply chains and increase their competitiveness in the market.

8.9 PURPOSE AND SCOPE

The purpose of the article is to identify and analyze the most significant determinants of food supply chain efficiency in relation to food quality schemes and the domestic market (Jacxsens et al., 2010). Research in the field and an examination of relevant statutes led to the identification of the fundamental elements (Blandon et al., 2009). FSCM is the process of organizing, implementing, and overseeing the movement of food products and related data from the point of production to the point of consumption. It entails several activities, including producing, processing, transferring, storing, and selling. Integration of diverse stakeholders, distributors, retailers, and consumers is necessary for effective FSCM (Choi et al., 2016).

8.10 RESEARCH METHODOLOGY

Many obstacles persist, limiting the scope of data-driven decision-making, despite the widespread use of data-collecting technologies employed throughout the food supply chain. Inaccurate and partial information is common when using these methods (Hen, 2014). As a consequence, conclusions drawn from such information cannot be trusted. In addition, the data formats used by sensors, smartphones, and GPS units, among other data-gathering devices, tend to be unstructured and varied (Cooper and Ellram, 1993). Sharing and integrating this information throughout the food supply chain is challenging. Last, the existing data-collecting technology is not equipped to handle the simultaneous capture of a large amount of data (Choi et al., 2016). In the future, smart and intelligent gadgets will be utilized to gather data along the following aspects of the food supply chain (Ghosh, 2016). One hundred samples were collected from the respondents in the study area through a questionnaire (Google Form).

8.11 ANALYSES, FINDINGS, DISCUSSION, AND CONCLUSION

8.11.1 FACTORS THAT INFLUENCE THE FSCM

Many industrial, technological, economic, social, and political elements all have a role in shaping the food market and food business. They are crucial to the food industry because they determine supply, variety, and distribution channels (Garnett, 2011). Coordination in the agri-food supply chain is crucial for ensuring that people have easy access to healthy, safe food, so studies focusing on this topic have garnered a lot of attention. The FSC is the system of businesses, institutions, and people engaged in the production, storage, transportation, sale, preparation, and consumption of food and associated goods. Golan et al. (2004a), the globe, the environment, and the surrounds are ever-evolving. Performance indicators and the efficiency of supply chains need to be reevaluated in light of technological advancements, new business models, globalization, and population shifts (Akhtar et al., 2016). New processing and transportation innovations enable global product distribution, while improved management techniques and the proliferation of information and communication technology enable businesses to meet the increasingly nuanced needs of their customers (Blandon et al., 2009). In turn, the ability to recreate the process by which a product goes from raw material to finished goods to end users is inextricably tied to product safety (Chen et al., 2014). The aforementioned difficulties in food units are compared to different industry classifications. The ANOVA test is used to assess every variable in every group of the food processing plant.

TABLE 8.1 Factors that Influence the Food Supply Chain Management.

Variables	Mean	SD	F	P
Environmental uncertainty	21.3820	2.73327	0.299	0.925
Efficient inventory management	18.6400	2.20746		
Electronic data capture	21.3629	2.45912		
Leveraging technology	20.8494	2.32428		
Inventory optimization	20.4258	2.21213		
Leveraging technology	21.1125	2.42942		

Table 8.1 shows that environmental uncertainty is found more influencing factor (21.3820), followed by leveraging technology (20.8494). The F value (0.299) shows that the difference is insignificant. It is concluded that the factors do not differ much according to the SCM. All types of food processing units are incurring more on environmental uncertainty.

8.12 DISCUSSION

1. **Efficient inventory management:** Now that global marketplaces exist, information may be entered at any point in the production process. The information available to those making choices is vast. Proper inventory management requires making the most of such information. For an SCM to be developed, inventory control has been a crucial first step. Machine learning, artificial intelligence, and big data have all contributed to greater productivity in recent years. Storage facility management, expiration loss, over- or under-ordering, and transportation logistics all fall under the purview of the inventory manager's responsibilities. Some aspects of efficient inventory management include the following.
2. **Environmental uncertainty:** Uncertainty is defined as any event that modifies or compels a change in supply chain management. Supply chain performance can be impacted by environmental uncertainties, which are unanticipated events outside of the organization. Supply chain efficacy can be diminished if a company fails to anticipate and adapt to changes in the external environment, such as those

brought on by shifting client tastes, new technologies, fluctuations in demand or supply, and so on. Organizations need to respond rapidly and appropriately to these kinds of shifts. The quality of the product, the behavior of competitors, and the dependability of suppliers are all potential sources of uncertainty across the supply chain. To combat these unknowns, businesses are developing management solutions to adapt to shifting environments and boost supply chain efficiency. The ability to adapt quickly to new circumstances is essential for businesses.

3. **Inventory optimization:** Finding a happy medium between under- and over-ordering is essential when it comes to stockpiling goods. Optimal inventory levels and adaptability are achieved through transparency in the supply chain, which is determined by the raw materials used and the sales made.
4. **Warehouse management:** Keeping an eye on what customers want can aid in the creation of storage, distribution, and order fulfillment systems. Warehouse management improves stock visibility and cuts down on theft. By strategically placing warehouses and prioritizing customer satisfaction, delivery times can be cut.
5. **Transportation management:** It connects storage facilities to delivery hubs. Customers are increasingly interested in same-day and on-time delivery options, therefore couriers would do well to take the initiative. The ability to follow the movement of commodities thanks to supply chain transparency is invaluable in times of uncertainty. It is possible to improve inventory management with the help of forecasting models based on market research, prediction, safety stock, etc.
6. **Electronic data capture:** Electronic data capture refers to the process of capturing and storing information digitally for later use and exchange. Such a language allows for the electronic coordination of company operations. Supply chain security, visibility, and traceability are all improved by electronic data recording. It connects parties so they may monitor each other's actions, which saves money and improves productivity, efficiency, flow, accuracy, and safety.
7. **Supply chain relationships:** All supply chain participants must be in agreement and on good terms for the SCM's development to proceed smoothly. Stakeholder relationships are crucial to the

growth and success of a company. Increased openness and support for new ideas and expansion are two benefits of working together. The supplier is regarded as the central figure in the supply chain because they are the ones responsible for driving new developments and innovations. Managing the people within an organization is just as crucial as managing the connections with external parties. Partnerships like these would aid in supply chain optimization by improving things such as transparency, trust, planning, forecasting, and product restocking.

Leveraging technology: Improvements in technology have been made in many areas of supply chain management, including quality control software, cash flow management, inventory management, security, and distribution. Blockchain's capacity to streamline operations while also offering traceability and security throughout the supply chain has become increasingly well known as the amount and variety of international trades they include has grown. Data is recorded in a distributed, secure, consensual, unchangeable, and time-stamped digital ledger called a blockchain. It helps to strengthen the supply chain from the very beginning to the very end. All supply chain participants have access to a complete record of all transactions. Blandon et al. (2009), a digital identity for the product is established due to the time stamped transactions and the immutability of the data. The result is increased trust in the product. A QR code can show the consumer the entire production chain, from farm to table. Consumers' expectations for sustainably produced food are met by well-managed food supply chains. The environmental and societal benefits must also be considered. It is a compilation of several elements that affect the supply chain and the decisions that lead to the success or failure of a company, including the five factors shown above. Food supply chain systems are built with traceability in mind from the ground up. Blockchain technology has enabled traceability solutions to combat not just FS issues but also sustainability and legitimacy of product claims.

8.13 CONCLUSION AND IMPLICATIONS

FSCM refers to the coordination and management of all the activities involved in the production, processing, storage, and distribution of food products from the farm to the table. The food supply chain is a complex system that involves many stakeholders, including farmers, processors, manufacturers, distributors, retailers, and consumers. The main objective of FSCM is to ensure that food products are delivered to consumers in a timely and efficient manner, while also maintaining their quality and safety. Effective FSCM can help to reduce waste, minimize costs, and improve the profitability of food companies. Some of the challenges in the food supply chain may be mitigated with the use of state-of-the-art technology, which are the basis for FSCM deployments in real-world businesses. Golan et al. (2004b), Literature case studies often focus on proving a theory or demonstrating an improvement after implementing an IT solution. Cooper and Ellram (1993), several studies have focused on distilling the core of FSCM by highlighting the inherent features of the food supply chain or general challenges aggregated from a group of firms. Consider the case of food waste; every year, the United States throws away almost 40% of the food it produces, costing the country around $165 billion (Choi et al., 2016). The decay of all that discarded food has a substantial impact on the environment, both in the form of water pollution and an increase in greenhouse gas emissions (Ghosh, 2016). First, isolated areas have been brought together with little investment, thanks to cloud computing. King and Phumpi (1996), with a cloud-enabled solution, even a small team working from home with just a computer and an internet connection may share files and work together effectively. Second, the industrial and aerospace industries have seen extensive adoption of IoT technology such as auto-ID and smart sensors. Government agencies are essential to the implementations since they are the ones who will create the long-term plans for assisting companies (Accorsi et al., 2014). So, future implementation could be beneficial for all users. Planning, organizing, and regulating the movement of items, data, and other resources associated with food production, distribution, and service, from farm to fork, is the essence of FSCM. Food quality and safety first—protecting consumer health and keeping a positive brand image necessitates paying close attention to food product quality and safety. To do this, it is necessary to comply with applicable regulations and put into place efficient quality control and traceability systems.

1. Managing stock is essential for keeping food waste to a minimum and providing prompt service to clients. For this reason, efficient inventory management systems must be put in place so that all involved parties can monitor stock and determine when and how much to reorder.
2. Transportation and storage are also important links in the food supply chain's logistical web. Implementing efficient transportation and storage solutions that reduce food spoilage and damage is an important part of managing logistics. There are a plethora of difficulties and promising prospects to discuss across a wide range of

disciplines. As a result of global warming, glaciers are melting and weather extremes are becoming more commonplace. To lessen the effects of climate change, it is necessary to cut down on emissions of greenhouse gases and embrace more environmentally friendly behaviors

3. As AI develops further, it will be important to make sure it is responsible, transparent, and ethical. The long-term goal is to make the most of its capabilities to spur economic expansion. The COVID-19 pandemic has emphasized the need to enhance health systems worldwide, making it more difficult to guarantee everyone has access to medical care and provide vaccinations for new illnesses.
4. Cybersecurity: As cyber threats grow, it becomes more difficult to keep sensitive data and vital infrastructure safe. The long-term goal is to use cutting-edge tools such as blockchain to build systems that are both more secure and more resistant to failure.
5. Education: The worldwide epidemic has wreaked havoc on classrooms throughout the world, underlining the need of adjusting to different instructional contexts. The difficulty is in creating innovative approaches to education that equip all pupils for the future. These are only some of the pressing issues and potential future outcomes that call for global participation from people, groups, and governments.

KEYWORDS

- **problems**
- **marketing**
- **customer and food products**
- **sustainable food value chains**

REFERENCES

Accorsi, R.; Cascini, A.; Cholette, S.; Manzini, R.; Mora, C. Economic and Environmental Assessment of Reusable Plastic Containers: A Food Catering Supply Chain Case study. *Int. J. Prod. Econ.* **2014,** *152,* 88–101.

Agustina, D.; Lee, C.; Piplani, R. Vehicle Scheduling and Routing at a Cross Docking Center for Food Supply Chains. *Int. J. Prod. Econ.* **2014,** *152,* 29–41.

Ahearn, M. C.; Armbruster, W.; Young, R. Big data's Potential to Improve food Supply Chain Environmental Sustainability and Food Safety. *Int. Food Agribus. Manag. Rev.* **2016,** *19* (A), 155–172.

Ahn, Y. Y.; Ahnert, S. E.; Bagrow, J. P.; Barabási, A. L. Flavor Network and the Principles of Food Pairing. *Sci. Rep.* **2011,** *1,* 1–7.

Ahumada, O.; Villalobos, J. R. Application of Planning Models in the Agri-food Supply Chain: A Review. *Eur. J. Operat. Res.* **2009,** *196* (1), 1–20.

Akhtar, P.; Tse, Y. K.; Khan, Z.; Rao-Nicholson, R. Data-driven and Adaptive Leadership Contributing to Sustainability: Global Agri-Food Supply Chains Connected with Emerging Markets. *Int. J. Prod. Econ.* **2016,** *181* (Part B), 392–401.

Baker, S.; Bender, A.; Abbass, H. and Sarker, R. A Scenario-based Evolutionary Scheduling Approach for Assessing Future Supply Chain Fleet Capabilities. In *Evolutionary Scheduling*; Dahal, K. P., Tan, K. C., Cowling, P. I., Eds.; Springer: Berlin, Heidelberg and New York, NY, 2007; pp 485–511.

Balaji, M.; Arshinder, K. Modeling the Causes of Food Wastage in Indian Perishable Food Supply Chain. *Resour. Conserv. Recycl.* **2016,** *114,* 153–167.

Banasik, A.; Kanellopoulos, A.; Claassen, G.; Bloemhof-Ruwaard, J. M.; Vorst, J. G. V. D. Closing Loops in Agricultural Supply Chains Using Multi-objective Optimization: A Case Study of an Industrial Mushroom Supply Chain. *Int. J. Prod. Econ.* **2017,** *183* (B), 409–420.

Bertolini, M.; Bevilacqua, M.; Massini, R. FMECA Approach to Product Traceability in the Food Industry. *Food Control* **2006,** *17* (2), 137–145.

Beulens, A. J.; Broens, D. F.; Folstar, P.; Hofstede, G. J. Food Safety and Transparency in Food Chains and Networks Relationships and Challenges. *Food Control* **2005,** *16* (6), 481–486.

Bevilacqua, M.; Ciarapica, F.; Giacchetta, G. Business Process Reengineering of a Supply Chain and a Traceability System: A Case Study. *J. Food Eng.* **2009,** *93* (1), 13–22.

Blandon, J.; Henson, S.; Cranfield, J. Small-scale Farmer Participation in new Agri-food Supply Chains: Case of the Supermarket Supply Chain for Fruit and Vegetables in Honduras. *J. Int. Dev.* **2009,** *21* (7), 971–984.

Chen, C.; Zhang, J.; Delaurentis, T. Quality Control in Food Supply Chain Management: An Analytical Model and Case Study of The Adulterated Milk Incident in China. *Int. J. Prod. Econ.* **2014,** *152,* 188–199.

Chiou, T. Y.; Chan, H. K.; Lettice, F.; Chung, S. H. The Influence of Greening the Suppliers and Green Innovation on Environmental Performance and Competitive Advantage in Taiwan. *Transp. Res. E: Logist. Transp. Rev.* **2011,** *47* (6), 822–836.

Choe, Y. C.; Park, J.; Chung, M.; Moon, J. Effect of the Food Traceability System for Building Trust: Price Premium and Buying Behavior. *Inform. Syst. Front.* **2009,** *11* (2), 167–179.

Choi, T. M.; Chiu, C. H.; Chan, H. K. Risk Management of Logistics Systems. *Transp. Res. E: Logist. Transp. Rev.* **2016,** *90,* 1–6.

Colin, J.; Estampe, D.; Pfohl, H. C.; Gallus, P.; Thomas, D. Interpretive Structural Modeling of Supply Chain Risks. *Int. J. Phys. Distribut. Logist. Manag.* **2011,** *41* (9), 839–859.

Cooper, M. C.; Ellram, L. M. Characteristics of Supply Chain Management and the Implications for Purchasing and Logistics Strategy. *Int. J. Logist. Manag.* **1993,** *4* (2), 13–24.

Doukidis, G. I.; Matopoulos, A.; Vlachopoulou, M.; Manthou, V.; Manos, B. A Conceptual Framework for Supply Chain Collaboration: Empirical Evidence from the Agri-Food Industry. *Supply Chain Manag.: An Int. J.* **2007,** *12* (3), 177–186.

Dubey, R.; Gunasekaran, A.; Papadopoulos, T.; Childe, S. J.; Shibin, K.; Wamba, S. F. Sustainable Supply Chain Management: Framework and Further Research Directions. *J. Clean. Prod.* **2017,** *142* (2), 1119–1130.

Friel, S.; Barosh, L. J.; Lawrence, M. Towards Healthy and Sustainable Food Consumption: an Australian Case Study. *Public Health Nutrit.* **2014,** *17* (5), 1156–1166.

Garnett, T. Where are the Best Opportunities for Reducing Greenhouse Gas Emissions in the Food System (Including the Food Chain)? *Food Policy* **2011,** *36,* S23-S32.

Genovese, A.; Acquaye, A. A.; Figueroa, A.; Koh, S. L. Sustainable Supply Chain Management and the Transition Towards a Circular Economy: Evidence and Some Applications. *Omega* **2017,** *66* (B), 344–357.

Georgiadis, P.; Vlachos, D.; Iakovou, E. A System Dynamics Modeling Framework for the Strategic Supply Chain Management of Food Chains. *J. Food Eng.* **2005,** *70* (3), 351–364.

Ghosh, D. Food Safety Regulations in Australia and New Zealand Food Standards. *J. Sci. Food Agric.* **2016,** *96* (9), 3274–3275.

Gianni, M.; Gotzamani, K.; Linden, I. How a BI-wise Responsible Integrated Management System may Support Food Traceability. *Int. J. Decis. Support Syst. Technol.* **2016,** *8* (2), 1–17.

Global Strategy United States of America food and Beverage Market Study. Global Strategy, Inc. International Business Development: Oviedo, FL, 2013; pp 1–55.

Golan, E.; Krissoff, B.; Kuchler, F. Food Traceability. Amber Waves **2004a,** *2* (2), 14–21.

Golan, E.; Krissoff, B.; Kuchler, F.; Calvin, L.; Nelson, K.; Price, G. Traceability in the US Food Supply: Economic Theory and Industry Studies. *Agric. Econ. Rep.* **2004b,** *830* (3), 183–185.

Gorris, L. G. Food Safety Objective: An Integral part of Food Chain Management. *Food Control* **2005,** *16* (9), 801–809.

Hasuike, T.; Kashima, T.; Matsumoto, S. Data-driven Food Supply Chain Optimization Under Uncertain Crop Productions and Consumers' Demands. *Innov. Supply Chain Manag.* **2014,** *8* (4), 150–156.

Hemert, P. V.; Iske, P. L. Framing Knowledge-based Urban Development and Absorptive Capacity of Urban Regions: A Case-study of Limburg, the Netherlands. *Int. J. Knowledge-Based Dev.* **2015,** *6* (4), 314–349.

Hemphill, T. A.; Banerjee, S. Genetically Modified Organisms and the US Retail Food Labeling Controversy: Consumer Perceptions, Regulation, and Public Policy. *Bus. Soc. Rev.* **2015,** *120* (3), 435–464.

Henson, S.; Reardon, T. Private Agri-food Standards: Implications for Food Policy and the Agri-food System. *Food Policy* **2005,** *30* (3), 241–253.

Hsu, Y. C.; Chen, A. P.; Wang, C. H. In *A RFID-enabled Traceability System for the Supply Chain of Live Fish,* Proceeding of IEEE International Conference on Automation and Logistics, IEEE, Qingdao, September1–3, pp. 81–86, 2008.

Hu, J.; Zhang, X.; Moga, L. M.; Neculita, M. Modeling and Implementation of the Vegetable Supply Chain Traceability System. *Food Control* **2013,** *30* (1), 341–353.

Jacxsens, L.; Luning, P.; Vorst, J. V. D.; Devlieghere, F.; Leemans, R.; Uyttendaele, M. Simulation Modelling and Risk Assessment as Tools to Identify the Impact of Climate Change on Microbiological Food Safety – the Case Study of Fresh Produce Supply Chain. *Food Res. Int.* **2010,** *43* (7), 1925–1935.

Jacxsens, L.; Uyttendaele, M.; Devlieghere, F.; Rovira, J.; Gomez, S. O.; Luning, P. Food Safety Performance Indicators to Benchmark Food Safety Output of Food Safety Management Systems. *Int. J. Food Microbiol.* **2010,** *141,* S180-S187.

Kannan, D.; Khodaverdi, R.; Olfat, L.; Jafarian, A.; Diabat, A. Integrated Fuzzy Multi Criteria Decision Making Method and Multi-objective Programming Approach for Supplier Selection and Order Allocation in a Green Supply Chain. *J. Clean. Prod.* **2013,** *47,* 355–367.

Karaman, A. D.; Cobanoglu, F.; Tunalioglu, R.; Ova, G. Barriers and Benefits of the Implementation of Food Safety Management Systems Among the Turkish Dairy Industry: A Case Study. *Food Control* **2012,** *25* (2), 732–739.

Karlsen, K. M.; Dreyer, B.; Olsen, P.; Elvevoll, E. O. Literature Review: Does a Common Theoretical Framework to Implement Food Traceability Exist? *Food Control* **2013,** *32* (2), 409–417.

Kelepouris, T.; Pramatari, K.; Doukidis, G. RFID-enabled Traceability in the Food Supply Chain. *Industrial Manag. Data Syst.* **2007,** *107* (2), 183–200.

Kilger, C.; Reuter, B.; Stadtler, H. Collaborative Planning. In *Supply Chain Management and Advanced Planning*; Hartmut, S., Christoph, K., Herbert, M., Eds.; Springer: Berlin and Heidelberg, 2015; pp 257–277.

Kim, J. K.; Oh, B. R.; Chun, Y. N.; Kim, S. W. Effects of Temperature and Hydraulic Retention Time on Anaerobic Digestion of Food Waste. *J. Biosc. Bioeng.* **2006,** *102* (4), 328–332.

King, R. P.; Phumpiu, P. F. Reengineering the Food Supply Chain: The ECR Initiative in the Grocery Industry. *Am. J. Agric. Econ.* **1996,** *78* (5), 1181–1186.

Knemeyer, A. M.; Naylor, R. W. Using Behavioral Experiments to Expand Our Horizons and Deepen Our Understanding of Logistics and Supply Chain Decision Making. *J. Bus. Logist.* **2011,** *32* (4), 296–302.

Low, S. A.; Vogel, S. J. Direct and Intermediated Marketing of Local Foods in the United States. *USDA-ERS Econ. Res. Rep.* **2011,** *128,* 1–38.

MacCarthy, B. L.; Blome, C.; Olhager, J.; Srai, J. S.; Zhao, X. Supply Chain Evolution – Theory, Concepts and Science. *Int. J. Operat. Prod. Manag.* **2016,** *36* (12), 1696–1718.

Parwez, S. Food supply chain management in Indian Agriculture: Issues. *Opportunities and Further Res.* **2014,** *8*, 572–581.

CHAPTER 9

Components of SC Management in the Hospitality Sector

MUSTAPHA ABDUL-AZIZ

Department of Logistics and Procurement Management, Tamale Technical University, Tamale, Ghana

ABSTRACT

The hospitality industry is highly competitive. This is driving managers of hotels and related businesses to adopt practices that can give them a competitive advantage. This makes supply chain management (SCM) an increasingly important area for hotels to focus on. By employing SCM, which increases efficiency and enables collaboration among the establishments that make up the hotel chain as a whole, hotels may better meet the demands of each individual guest. Hence, the purpose of this chapter is to look at the specific components of SCM and the benefits and challenges of SCM in the hospitality industry. Experienced SC managers ensure that all suppliers adhere to predetermined standards, such as on-time delivery, affordable prices, and high quality products and services. The ultimate objective of SCM is to provide the best items at the best time at the best prices, and they accomplish this by providing a vast array of products and services, which are the most pressing issues in hotel SC management. Unpredictable demand in the hospitality industry is one of the greatest obstacles, making it difficult to standardize SCM procedures. Cancellations and other uncontrollable events only exacerbate the situation. Keeping track of products throughout their lifecycles is one of the greatest obstacles that lead to excess waste. New competitors and expanding markets may disrupt the established SC. Beneficial and adverse consequences of automation have contributed to the

Essentials of Supply Chain Management: Strategy, Planning and Operations.
Mohammed Majeed, Abdul-Rasheed Akeji Alhassan Alolo, Seidu Alhassan, and S. Sekar (Eds.)

dynamic character of the logistics and SC ecosystem. Constraints in accessibility and other areas of logistics pose an ongoing risk to the hotel industry.

9.1 INTRODUCTION

The administration of supply chain (SC) is becoming increasingly vital in today's extremely competitive hospitality business. Hotels can better serve their guests' individual needs by utilizing supply chains, which also boost efficiency and facilitate collaboration among the establishments that make up the hotel chain as a whole (Blue Ocean, 2023). A reliable SC system is crucial to the smooth operation of any manufacturing facility, from the acquisition of raw materials to the shipment of finished goods to customers. Phases in the supply chain, characteristics of the supply chains, and individual parts of SCM are only some of the many categories into which SCM can be broken down. The four parts of the supply chain—integration, activities, buying goods, and distribution—collaborate to create a low-cost, high-volume route to market (Garber, 2021). Strategic choices in the SC are influenced by a number of factors, as stated by Simchi-Levi (2010). These include the following: (a) increased lead times as a result of globalization, (b) increased logistic costs as a result of transportation and inventory shifts, (c) risks associated with lean production, outsourcing, and unexpected events, increases in (d) labor costs, (e) pressure from stakeholders to lessen their impact on the environment, and (f) commodity price volatility. Therefore, it is crucial that all links in the SC factor these considerations into their long-term planning. Participants can reap enormous rewards from constructively interacting with the chain. Product and process quality, SC logistics, price and cost, innovation and design, and management are the five pillars on which all SC participants should concentrate in order to fortify the partnership in the supply chain, as outlined by Simamora et al. (2016). It is the responsibility of everyone in the SC to ensure that quality standards are always met. Marginally profitable pricing ensures that your items may compete in the market and inspire new ideas within your company (Simamora et al., 2016). The entire process, beginning with the acquisition of raw materials and ending with the consumption of the finished product, along with all the information flows that occur along the way. Therefore, SCM refers to a wide range of interconnected processes such as warehousing/storage, transportation, distribution, planning, demand prediction, etc. (Travelnews, 2022). This study looks at the specific components of SCM and the benefits and challenges of SCM in the hospitality industry.

9.2 LITERATURE REVIEW

9.2.1 SCM

The production of a product with the potential for high-volume sales requires coordination, cooperation, forethought, and planning. The initial stages in increasing production are organization and learning the fundamentals of a functional supply chain. Management of the processes involved in sourcing inputs, transforming them into outputs, and delivering them to customers is what is meant by "SC management" (SCM). Managing the flow of raw materials and the various processes that turn them into a finished good is what SCM is all about. Raw material suppliers, manufacturers, wholesalers, retailers, and end consumers are all part of the SC process. Hence, a SC oversight plan is a coordinated set of actions made by businesses to improve efficiency and smooth out product flow across all parties involved in the distribution process (Madhani, 2016). You must prepare ahead of time to fulfill the requirements of the distributor or the consumer. In order to keep ahead of consumer demand, preparedness is essential, even if your company is just a small cog in the supply chain. This is where forethought comes in.

9.2.2 SCM IN THE HOSPITALITY SECTOR

Supply and demand determine the prices of supplies, quasimanufactured items, materials, major services, and other products in the tourism industry. Efforts at compromise and cooperation are required for each of these factors. Inefficient use of scarce resources is possible if these factors are not coordinated properly. This has the potential to significantly impact the bottom line (or the scope) of hospitality businesses. Supplier managers must maintain a fine equilibrium between staff, procedures, and technology across all phases of the business, from studies and development to marketing and operations to strategic leadership, to guarantee that their products and services meet the needs of their clientele (Blue Ocean, 2023). Administration of the hospitality sector's SC and logistical issues is crucial. SCM, or SC management, is widely recognized as an essential component of the hospitality sector. The hotel sector relies heavily on effective SCM to maintain its edge over competitors. In the hotel business, a thriving SC is difficult to implement because guest demographics vary greatly from one site to the next (Malik, 2023). The success or failure of a hotel depends in large part on how well its supply network is managed, but this is complicated by the fact that different regions have different habits, patterns, environmental rules and regulations, infrastructure availability of goods, and so on. As the backbone of the hospitality sector, SCM is responsible for ensuring that every aspect of the business has what it needs to function smoothly (Malik, 2023). With such a wide variety of products and suppliers needed to run a successful hospitality business (including, but not limited to, food and drink, nonfood items, furnishings and other supplies, and more), it can be difficult to ensure a constant flow of high-quality goods at competitive prices.

9.2.3 ELEMENTS OF SCM

9.2.3.1 INTEGRATION

Errors can be avoided, and costs can be reduced through proper corporate communication and collaboration. When departments work together, they share knowledge and form stronger teams. By incorporating teams into the process flow, managers can more easily keep tabs on the whole and pinpoint where they can make improvements (Garber, 2021).

9.2.3.2 OPERATIONS

Maintaining steady employment for your staff is made possible by strong operations within the supply chain. Managers keep a close eye on the details of the SC to make sure everything runs smoothly (Garber, 2021). The lean manufacturing approach is widely used today and requires constant process evaluation to identify areas for improvement. The operations team may significantly enhance the SC by monitoring equipment to guarantee efficiency or by understanding when to reduce staff. Material requirements and manufacturing volume are determined by the demand market, so planning and forecasting for demand is typically necessary prior to making any purchases. In order to avoid having too much or too little inventory, which would result in revenue losses, this function is crucial in SC management. To avoid this kind of error, it is necessary to integrate demand planning and forecasting with inventory management, production, and shipping (Planet-together, 2021).

9.2.3.3 PROCUREMENT

It is important to have a clear picture of how your company's SC will function before you get started. Whether it is materials, supplies, tools, or equipment, knowing exactly what your organization needs is crucial. The success of any SC relies heavily on the hiring of capable buyers and the dissemination of inventory management knowledge amongst staff. This prevents the business from experiencing the devastating effects of a material shortage on its manufacturing schedule (Garber, 2021). The improper person in this role could end up overbuying raw materials and putting a burden on the company's finances. Raw materials are essential in the production of finished goods. The production schedule relies on the timely acquisition and delivery of these components. To accomplish this, it will be necessary to coordinate with suppliers and delivery firms to avoid any delays (Planettogether, 2021).

9.2.3.4 TRANSPORTATION

For getting resources to the factory and finished goods out to customers, transportation is a must. Shipping products on schedule is essential to the continuity of any business activity. Businesses that prioritize and maintain this factor typically have less trouble meeting delivery deadlines for their products (Christopher, 2016). It is crucial for a business to prioritize the safety and security of its transportation system. The transportation management system, whether built in-house or contracted out, has to guarantee safe delivery with no losses or damages. The foundations of safe transportation are a well-managed logistics system and accurate billing.

9.2.3.5 DISTRIBUTION

When clients buy a company's wares from a store shelf or have them shipped directly to them, which is the last link in the supply chain. After production and sales are complete, the final step is to deliver the goods to the buyers. Since the customer has not used the goods until this point, the distribution method is generally credited with enhancing the brand's reputation. Successful SCM systems allow a company to ship products quickly, securely, and affordably (Fernando, 2022). Having many distribution channels is important in case one becomes temporarily unavailable. Distribution along the SC must be well-planned to ensure that products reach their final destination. Distributors want their items to get to clients as soon as possible; thus, they may want to train personnel on logistics software or hire a third-party logistics (3PL) firm (Garber, 2021). Management of the SC is inconceivable without logistics. Important tasks include order coordinating, packing and shipping, arranging delivery times, billing, shipping, contacting customers, and collecting money. Even with third-party courier services, each handoff must be watched closely to prevent missteps or delays.

9.2.3.6 PLANNING

Planning to align supply with customer and manufacturing expectations is typically the first step in SCM processes that yields the best outcomes. Businesses need to anticipate their future requirements and plan accordingly (Fernando, 2022). This pertains to the availability of raw materials, the capabilities and constraints of manufacturing equipment, and the number of workers required at various points in the SCM process. ERP system modules are commonly used by large organizations to collect data and create plans.

9.2.3.7 SOURCING

Partnerships with suppliers are crucial to an effective SCM approach. Sourcing requires coordinating with suppliers to get all the necessary components for production. It is possible for a business to work ahead of time with a supplier to secure the supplies they need. However, there will be variations in sourcing needs between industries. One of the main goals of SCM sourcing is to guarantee that (1) all materials procured are suitable for use in the manufacturing process; (2) the costs incurred to acquire the products are consistent with market expectations; (3) the supplier has the leeway to rush products in the event of an emergency; and (4) the provider has an established track record of on-time and high-quality product delivery. There is no denying that the next crucial phase of the SC is sourcing. As we learn in our administration of SC classes, sourcing entails more than just the acquisition of raw materials (Talentedge, 2022). The sourcing manager's responsibilities go across several different areas. The value and popularity of a company's output in a given market can be profoundly affected by the caliber and cost of its input materials. Because of this, a thorough familiarity with the process is required. This process depends on a wide variety of external organizations and circumstances. When producing perishable items, SCM becomes even more important. When looking for a supplier, businesses need to consider the length of time it takes for the vendor to fulfill an order.

9.2.3.8 RETURNING

Managing product returns and exchanges is the last step in the SC process. It is bad enough when a customer has to return a product; it is even worse when the return is the result of an error on the part of the business. The corporation must make sure it can accept returned products and properly allocate refunds for such returns, a process known as reverse logistics. The interaction with the client must be rectified, whether the company is undertaking a product recall or the customer is merely dissatisfied with the product. In the eyes of many, consumer returns are just another form of communication between the company and the customer. However, communication between businesses to determine which products are flawed, out of date, or otherwise nonconforming is a crucial aspect of the customer return process. If the SCM process fails to address the reason for a customer return, the problem will likely continue (Fernando, 2022). Product return systems are another important aspect of SC management. This involves thinking of other uses for the product, such as making more of them, recycling them, or putting them back on store shelves. SCM is more than just adjusting to fluctuations in the market.

9.2.3.9 LOGISTICS

Logistics refers to the branch of SCM that ensures commodities are delivered to customers without any delays due to poor planning, buying goods, manufacturing, storing, or delivery. To get items to clients swiftly and cheaply, it helps to have excellent interaction among various divisions (Planettogether, 2021).

9.2.3.10 CONTROLLING RESOURCES

Manufacturing requires a substantial investment of resources. The goal of effective resource management is to guarantee that all available resources are put to their highest and best use. The SCM concept is a management strategy used by company executives to improve the efficiency of product procurement, manufacturing, and transportation (Ellram and Cooper, 2014; Maloni et al., 2015). The theory of SCM states that with proper process synchronization and resource planning, company leaders may significantly reduce disruptions to the SC (Madhani, 2016). This will guarantee that the most efficient manufacturing schedule is made possible. Each resource's capabilities and whether or not it can complete the tasks assigned for it must be taken into account when determining its available capacities (Planettogether, 2021). This can help you keep your manufacturing timeline realistic and prevent businesses from exaggerating expectations on orders.

9.2.3.11 PREDICTING NEEDS/DEMAND

A business's every move will be determined by how much interest is there in its goods on the market. Organizations can better plan production, raw material purchasing, and inventory storage if they have an accurate understanding of demand. In other words, all other forms of planning stem from demand planning. The company's own data can be a goldmine for demand forecasting. New technologies, such as predictive analytics, are assisting businesses in accurately forecasting annual product demand. Material demand from customers is the driving force behind SC planning. However, it is not as simple as it sounds. There needs to be meticulous preparation for the entire supply chain. The process begins with demand planning and continues through sourcing, production, storage, and distribution. Due to the critical nature of each of these, they must be examined independently. Business-wise, one must always begin where the demand originates, i.e., with the client. Once the need is established, determining how many products should be manufactured becomes straightforward. After settling on a target amount, the next stage is to map out the acquisition of primary components. A supply strategy describes this scenario. A corporation needs more than just a stockpile of raw resources. To ensure the most efficient delivery of goods, one must also ensure that necessary supplies, such as appropriate packing and labeling, are on hand. The production schedule relies on the buying department having all of the necessary materials on hand. With this strategy, we hope to coordinate the efforts of everyone involved in getting products to the consumer (Talentedge, 2022). The sales force must bring with them forecasts of future market demand. The production team needs the sales team's forecasts to plan the manufacturing. By working together, the two groups can cut down on wasteful output. It also guarantees timely delivery of products bought by clients. The production staff must arrange for the necessary items to be manufactured. They have to make sure that getting the products to the buyers by the promised dates is feasible. The unit is responsible for ensuring there is adequate manufacturing capacity to meet the customer's delivery needs. To avoid wasting resources, businesses cannot make products until they have orders for them. This is made easier with the aid of SC management, which provides clear insight across all stages of the supply chain.

9.2.3.12 INFORMATION

Distribution and exchange of information is the glue that holds the other parts of SCM together. A flood of knowledge is what drives modern life. In order to succeed, a company must always be aware of the most recent developments in all areas of manufacturing. Proper and timely dissemination of information through the different levels of a firm is crucial for understanding market trends of supply and demand for a given product. In today's information-based global market, not knowing anything might be disastrous for a company's future success. The entire process could fall apart due to ineffective information flow and communication. SC disruptions can often be avoided if the parties involved have better information and communication. To avoid misunderstandings and wasted time spent keeping everyone up-to-date on changes, it is important to have a unified system that is used throughout all departments (Planettogether, 2021). Due to the many internal and external parties involved, information plays a crucial role in supply chains. There can be no progress without an orderly exchange of data. Since the activities throughout the SC never stop, the flow of information about them continues. While most of the materials move downstream, money will move upstream, from the buyer to the seller. However, data in this system can move in any direction. This needs to go off without a hitch and on schedule. That is why most businesses rely on systems that instantly notify everyone who needs to know about any given development (Talentedge, 2022). Purchasing managers should not cut off communication with their suppliers. This will give them a better idea of where they stand in terms of raw material availability. If there will be a shortage of a certain product, suppliers might disclose that information. The company will be able to stock up on necessities and prevent running low. Having access to price history data would also aid purchasing departments in making more informed decisions when stocking up on raw materials.

The success of every SC depends on the free flow of information. Without a reliable means of communication, a number of external factors could quickly derail this process. Production schedules cannot be made without knowing the status of key inputs like raw materials and transportation options. Managers of retail establishments are responsible for keeping track of stock levels and ensuring that customers' orders can be fulfilled. To ensure on-time delivery of consumer orders, it is crucial that retailers and distributors share accurate information regarding stock levels (Talentedge, 2022).

9.2.3.13 LOCATION

In order to succeed and grow, each company must be located in a favorable environment. Consider the case of a plant producing carbonated beverages opening up in a region with limited access to potable water. Such operations cannot function without easy access to water. Inadequate water supply may reduce output and harm the company's reputation (Christopher, 2016). If a company needs to split a scarce resource with the community, it will go out of business quickly. Therefore, it is crucial for a company's success to be situated in a well-connected area that is also accessible to the source of necessary production resources. Setting up a company unit also involves thinking about the necessary and available workforce.

9.2.3.14 INVENTORY

SC also relies heavily on inventory management. It describes everything a business actually has on hand. This could be the raw materials, the finished items, or even the packaging goods that are essential to getting the product to the clients when they need it. Equipment, supplies, and gadgets are all examples of inventory that could be used to provide a service to a client (Talentedge, 2022). Seeing how inventory, which is one of a company's primary outlays, influences operations is important. Keeping inventory levels low can be financially rewarding for a business. However, the company cannot afford to lose an order due to a lack of stock. Today's consumers have come to expect instantaneous service from businesses. This necessitates the maintenance of a supply of either the final products themselves or the raw ingredients necessary to produce them quickly. The business plans to spend money on raw materials that might not be needed for quite some time. More time spent doing nothing means more money lost for the business. The same applies to manufactured things. Businesses need to stock just enough inventory to meet customer demands without incurring unnecessary expenses. Accurate sales forecasting is a key topic in SCM courses since it aids in stocking the right amount of inventory.

9.2.3.15 MANUFACTURING/PRODUCTION

Using machinery, human labor, or other outside influences, the corporation creates something new out of raw materials; this is the core of SC management. The system's capacity for production is crucial. Only when everything else in the SC works in harmony can this be accomplished. For manufacturing to begin, it is crucial to have a well-organized production plan, a steady supply of raw materials, and a well-stocked inventory. After goods have been manufactured, they undergo quality assurance testing, packaging, and final delivery preparations. Although this is the final product, it is not the end of the SCM process (Fernando, 2022). Subtasks like assembling, testing, inspection, and packing may be added to the production process. Waste and other manageable issues might lead manufacturing to deviate from original plans, so companies need to keep that in mind. If, due to lack of employee training, a company finds itself consuming more raw materials than anticipated and sourced for, it must either address this shortcoming or return to an earlier phase of SCM (Fernando, 2022). Packaging and testing fall under this part of the SC as well. Production also includes archiving data, monitoring the state of production facilities, gauging output, and ensuring regulatory compliance. Market demand, supply, and inventory are all links in the SC that affect this step. The timely delivery of products to paying consumers relies on careful preparation of the production schedule (Talentedge, 2022).

9.2.4 BENEFITS OF SCM IN HOSPITALITY

River Systems (2023) argues that a data-driven approach to SCM is essential in today's world due to the growing complexity of global supply chains. End-to-end monitoring of the information, services, and product flow from procurement to production to delivery to the end user is made possible with data-driven SC management. The bottom line can benefit greatly from efficient SCM.

9.2.4.1 PROCUREMENT

One of the most important advantages of the management of SC is its ability to facilitate the acquisition of components, materials, and services. Instead of making random purchases, businesses can instead negotiate stable contracts with their suppliers through SC management. This has double usefulness

(Talentedge, 2022). One, there is a value-for-money ratio in the long-term contracts. Second, committing to a supplier over the long term allows business leaders to worry less about suppliers and more about other areas of operation (Talentedge, 2022). When parts or supplies are in short supply, this is an absolute must.

9.2.4.2 BETTER CUSTOMER SERVICE

When everything in the SC is working as it should, we can give our customers better service. If guests had a good time, they are more likely to return and tell others about their experience (SBS and Company LLP, 2017). It has become increasingly important in today's competitive business climate to provide customers with value while keeping expenses to a minimum (Travelnews, 2022). Since performance is not just defined by actions and decisions but also by advances in return investment performance and improved profitability, there has been a rise in the popularity of SCM and logistics approaches.

9.2.4.3 STAFF MORALE BOOSTED

When workers feel content in their roles, they are more likely to remain with the company. As a result, the hotel sees less turnover and higher morale all around.

9.2.4.4 SAVED MONEY

As was previously said, effective management of the SC can help cut down on raw material expenses. The hotel might save money with better SC management. A hotel can save a lot of money if its inbound and outgoing operations are managed well. To do this, agreements are made with participants in the supply chain. This saves money since no more time is spent hunting down suppliers, haggling over prices, or placing impromptu orders (Talentedge, 2022). Logistics and SC activities are often overlooked when hotels look for ways to save money. Hotels and other service providers might benefit from implementing logistics and SC strategies because they are part of operations management. The hospitality and food service industries rely heavily on their supply chain (SBS and Company LLP, 2017). In addition, businesses can receive significant discounts from SC partners when they are awarded long-term contracts. Additionally, the contract rate is locked in for the duration of the agreement, protecting the business from the risk of price increases. Companies can save money on storage costs for low-moving inventory thanks to more precise demand forecasts, allowing them to create room for faster-moving, revenue-generating goods (Oracle, 2010). Overhead is largely driven by the price of warehousing and shipping orders. You can lessen these outlays by improving inventory management, automating mundane tasks, and rearranging your warehouse's physical space (Oracle, 2010). Hotels of all sizes need to think creatively about how to provide guests with amenities without breaking the bank. The hospitality industry is notoriously labor-intensive; thus, many hotels are taking drastic measures to save costs. It is no secret that companies have been trying to save money by freezing new hires, slashing benefits, eliminating bonuses, and lowering base salaries, among other measures.

9.2.4.5 ENHANCED RISK REDUCTION

Both high-level and detailed analyses of SC data can help identify threats, allowing businesses to better prepare for and respond to disruptions. Companies can avoid negative effects by being proactive rather than reactive to SC disruptions, quality control challenges, and other concerns. One way in which businesses can save money is by better understanding the risks they face. If businesses knew more about the dangers lurking in their supply chains, 87% of them would reduce their stock by 22% according to research from Oracle (2010).

9.2.4.6 ADVANTAGES IN THE MARKET

The hotel business can gain a sustainable competitive advantage for individual hotel companies through the implementation of a well-established logistics and SCM system. The hotel can save money and provide better service by employing effective logistics and SC techniques. In order to provide better service to customers, it is essential for workers in this business to establish reliable relationships with their suppliers and use an efficient ordering system. Logistics and SC management, when fully implemented, may help the hospitality business provide consistently reliable and high-quality service at the best costs (SBS and Company LLP, 2017).

9.2.4.7 *QUALITY CONTROL*

Companies that have more say over their supply chain, both upstream and downstream, tend to have better quality control. For instance, having standardized minimum quality criteria in place helps direct providers find and work with reliable secondary suppliers who can deliver on those standards (River Systems, 2023). Suppliers might also benefit from process guidelines in terms of meeting your company's quality standards. In order to ensure that suppliers are following the guidelines they set out, some businesses go above and beyond just establishing criteria, performing frequent audits, or requiring proof (River Systems, 2023). The best vendors and suppliers can be partnered with to ensure consistent quality if the data is analyzed.

9.2.4.8 *INCREASED PRODUCTIVITY*

Companies can avoid further delays by implementing backup plans, such as acquiring materials from a backup supplier, based on real-time information about the availability of raw materials and manufacturing delays. When businesses lack access to timely information, problems like low stock levels and late deliveries to customers might arise. Smart automation solutions not only increase productivity but also improve quality (River Systems, 2023).

9.2.4.9 *MEETING CUSTOMER NEEDS*

A store might order 7% extra inventory the following week if they see a 5% spike in demand and predict that it will last (River Systems, 2023). After seeing what looks to be a 7% uptick in demand, the next link in the chain demands an even greater increase from its supplier. It is possible that the manufacturer will see a bloated 20% rise in orders. The bullwhip effect occurs when there is a lag between when supply and demand change and when people hear about such changes (River Systems, 2023). Leaders in the SC who have access to timely, accurate information and unified data can more accurately anticipate demand and quickly adapt to shifting market conditions, thereby mitigating risks like the "bullwhip" impact.

9.2.4.10 *OPTIMIZATION OF SHIPPING/TRANSPORTATION*

The cost of shipping freight climbed by 7% between 2016 and 2017, while the cost of hiring a private or dedicated truck driver rose by 9.5% (Logistics Management, 2018). Costs for both LTL shipping and FTL shipping went up, by 6.6% for LTL and 6.4% for FTL. SC managers place a premium on delivery efficiency because of the ever-increasing prices. Companies may better serve their customers' needs and save money by determining the best delivery options for various order sizes and quantities (River Systems, 2023). The company's bottom line benefits, and customer satisfaction rises, when costs are reduced and those savings are passed on to customers.

9.2.4.11 COMMUNICATION

Members of the SC are in continual contact with one another. The firm is responsible for keeping in touch with its vendors at all times to update them on the newest quality, quantity, and material specifications it requires (Talentedge, 2022). The lead firm maintains the demand schedule and is responsible for communicating it to the suppliers in a timely manner so that sufficient materials may be obtained at the correct time.

9.2.4.12 AUTOMATION

Oracle (2010) suggests many ways in which investing in the automated processing of data flows can pay off. It facilitates management by exception, releasing resources for other areas of the organization. Managers in the SC now have more time for strategic planning and the introduction of novel ideas. It fixes the rift between marketing and the rest of the company by allowing for more immediate responses to promotional activities and shifts in demand. Because of the improved coordination with marketing, advertising is now more lucrative than ever. It promotes expansion by satisfying the needs of current clients to a greater extent and bringing in new ones.

9.2.4.13 INCREASED INCOME

All of the aforementioned improvements to decision-making, partner selection, market and demand forecasting, and the smooth running of the supply chain, as well as a decrease in SC disruptions, directly contribute to a company's bottom line (River Systems, 2023). Working with dependable suppliers, for instance, boosts cash flow since you can issue invoices for items and services and be paid for them faster. Cash flow can be improved by implementing more efficient solutions to cut down on unnecessary spending and by decreasing operating expenses. Effective SCM has direct and secondary effects that support the efficient, seamless flow of information, goods, and services from procurement to final delivery, just as SC disruptions have a domino effect, affecting every juncture along the supply chain (Oracle, 2010).

9.2.4.14 COLLABORATION

The company and its suppliers are able to work closely together, which is a major advantage of a supply chain (Talentedge, 2022). This allows for better design and innovation as well as cost savings. For businesses, managing the flow of information is a major obstacle. Seventy-six percent of organizations, per Oracle (2010), do not have an automatic flow of information across the supply chain, and fifty percent of businesses report that information fragmentation leads to missed sales opportunities. A comprehensive, end-to-end perspective of the SC is made possible by integrated software solutions that eliminate bottlenecks and facilitate the smooth exchange of information at every stage (River Systems, 2023). With SCM, SC managers have better access to data, allowing them to make better, more contextualized decisions.

9.2.4.15 VISIBILITY

Oracle (2010) claims that a more complete picture of the SC allows for a more accurate assessment of supplier risk, which in turn allows for smaller stockpiles. This reduces the likelihood of bottlenecks and improves transparency to coworkers and management by ensuring that essential information is not held by a single person. It helps with making long-term, company-wide decisions by giving business planners a bird's-eye view of different SCs based on accurate, up-to-date data. It enables the instant access to information and self-service that users (SC personnel and end users alike) have come to expect. This makes it possible to stop putting out the same flames over and over again and adopt a more methodical approach to managing the supply chain. It improves client satisfaction in a tangible way by ensuring orders are fulfilled promptly and accurately.

9.3 CHALLENGES OF SCM IN THE HOSPITALITY SECTOR

9.3.1 COST OF MATERIALS

A hotel's gift shop can provide deep discounts because of the high volume of sales they handle. These components take up the majority of the direct material budget. Since most hotel supplies are quickly spoiled, bulk purchasing discounts are not available. Because of this, there will be a greater total cost of transactions. The expense of doing business rises as a result.

9.3.2 ORDERING COST

Manual indents and purchase requisitions are typically used by each department separately. Many hotels still do not use electronic systems for indenting and purchasing. Consolidating such requests and orders is a time-consuming process. Due to difficulties in reorganization, the department of purchasing is seen to place multiple orders for the same commodities. Due to the aforementioned factors, many hotels, even those belonging to chains with multiple properties in the same city, choose not to participate in bulk purchasing. It is possible that hotels are overstocking on a variety of brands and package sizes. This has a depressing effect on economies of scale, the number of available suppliers, and prices. Hotels in the same chain may pay varying amounts to various vendors for the exact same goods. The price of transportation and other direct expenses rises dramatically as a result (Sethu, n.d.). Significant savings are possible through properly managing the supply chain.

9.3.3 INVENTORY COST

The purchasing division hoards supplies out of concern that they will not be able to get the proper products to the many departments that need them in a timely manner. This takes up a lot of room, which drives up the price.

9.3.4 EMERGENCY COST

On-the-fly requests from user departments trigger immediate purchases, which are thereafter formalized through the completion of the necessary paperwork. Unexpected spending is the rule rather than the exception when proper planning is lacking.

9.4 CONCLUSIONS

The aims of this chapter are to look at the specific components of SCM and the benefits and challenges of SCM in the hospitality industry. The hotel sector places a premium on efficient logistics and SCM. SCM plays a crucial role in the hospitality business. Effective SCM allows hotels to save a ton of money by negotiating favorable terms with their food and beverage, housekeeping, and maintenance providers, as well as other vendors. Professional SCM ensures all suppliers stick to agreed-upon criteria, including those for on-time delivery, competitive pricing, and high-quality goods and services. The ultimate goal of SCM is to provide the greatest items at the best time at the best rates, and they do just that by offering a wide range of products and services, which are the most pressing issues in hotel SC management. One of the biggest obstacles is the hospitality industry's unpredictable demand, which makes standardizing SCM procedures challenging. Cancellations and other uncontrollable events just compound the problem. One of the biggest obstacles that causes extra waste is keeping track of products throughout their lives. The established SC may be shaken up by new competitors and developing markets. Automation's positive effects and negative side effects are both contributing to the dynamic nature of the logistics and SC ecosystem. Constraints in accessibility and other areas of logistics are a constant threat to the hotel business. Invention and shifting service norms give rise to novel client requirements. The hospitality business has a severe lack of logistics and SC training.

KEYWORDS

- **supply chain**
- **SCM**
- **hospitality**
- **logistics**
- **hotels**
- **guest**

REFERENCES

Blue Ocean. SCM in Hospitality industry [Online]. 2023. https://www.blueoceanacademy.com/supply-chain-management-in-hospitality-industry/

Christopher, M. *Logistics & SC Management*; Pearson: UK, 2016.

Fernando, J. SCM (SCM): How It Works and Why It Is Important [Online]. 2022. https://www.investopedia.com/terms/s/scm.asp

Garber, R. 4 Elements of SC Management [Online]. 2021. https://www.newstreaming.com/4-elements-of-supply-chain-management/

Logistics Management. 29th Annual State of Logistics Report: Carriers Take the Wheel [Online]. 2018. https://www.logisticsmgmt.com/article/29th_annual_state_of_logistics_report_carriers_take_the_wheel

Malik, U. A. SCM Hotel Industry Challenges & Best Practices [Online]. 2023. https://pk.linkedin.com/in/usman-ahmed-malik-53730713?trk=article-ssr-frontend-pulse_publisher-author-card

Maloni, M.; Carter, C.; Kaufmann, L.; Rogers, Z. Publication Productivity in the SCM Discipline: 2011–13. *Transportat. J.* **2015,** *54* (3), 291–231. doi 10.5325/transportationj.54.3.0291:

Madhani, P. M. Application of Six Sigma in SC Management: Evaluation and Measurement Approach. *IUP J. SC Manag.* **2016,** *13,* 34–53. Retrieved from http://vbn.aau.dk/en/journals/the-i-u-pjournal-of-supply-chain-management(7eab36f3-aac9-4cdd-b684-08d3eb7949a4)/publications.html

Oracle. The Fragmented SC A Discussion on the Latest Research Findings into Information Flow in Supply Chains [Online]. 2010. https://www.themanufacturer.com/mdc2011/pdf/ChainReaction-The-Fragmented-Supply-Chain.pdf

Planettogether. The 5 Functions of SC Management [Online]. 2021. https://www.planettogether.com/blog/the-five-functions-of-supply-chain-management

River Systems. 8 Key Benefits of Effective SC Management [Online]. 2023. https://6river.com/8-key-benefits-of-effective-supply-chain-management/

SBS and Company LLP. Significance of SCM in Hospitality Industry [Online]. 2017. https://www.sbsandco.com/blog/significance-of-supply-chain-management-in-hospitality-industry

Sethu, H. S. SCM in Hospitality Industry: An Overview. *J. Hosp. Appl. & Res.* **n.d,** *2* (2), 33–44.

Simamora, M.; Aiman, S.; Subiyanto, B. How SCM Enhances SMEs' Competitiveness: A Case Study. *IUP J. SC Manag.* **2016,** *13,* 33–47. doi:10.2139/ssrn.2731524

Simchi-Levi, D. The Six Forces Driving SC Design. *MIT Sloan Manag. Rev. Winter* **2010,** 18–21. Retrieved from http://sloanreview.mit.edu/

Talentedge. What Are The Important Components Of SCM in 2022? [Online] 2022. https://talentedge.com/articles/important-components-supply-chain-management-covered-supply-chain-courses/

Talentedge. How SCM helps in Business? [Online] 2022. https://talentedge.com/articles/supply-chain-management-helps-business/

Travelnews. Significance of SCM in Hospitality Industry. [Online] 2022. https://www.chinatravelnews.com/article/167906

CHAPTER 10

Overview of Logistics Functions

MUKUL PANDEY

Arka Jain University, Jharkhand, India

ABSTRACT

Logistics is a strategic function for any organization. It is related to many vital functions of any organization and plays a significant role in modern organizations. The logistics function deals with practical and detailed arrangements and management of different functions in any organization for streamlined operations in the organization. The focus of the logistics function is transportation, arrangement, supply, and delivery of desired goods in time of requirement in operating the organization functions of production and marketing efficiently keeping total costs at the minimum level. This chapter discusses the different aspects of logistics as a key function of any organization.

10.1 LOGISTICS FUNCTION

To understand the logistics functions, let us review the definition of logistics. Logistics is a subset of supply chain management. In the supply chain, we find that the manufacturing unit is fed with input materials like maintenance, repair, and operative supplies by the supplier or a series of suppliers ending at the manufacturer of that product.

You will appreciate that to reduce the delivery time to the manufacturing unit, the supplier(s) have to maintain inventory of stocks. On-demand, these inventories are moved to the next supplier and subsequently to the last supplier to supply the product to the manufacturing unit.

Essentials of Supply Chain Management: Strategy, Planning and Operations.
Mohammed Majeed, Abdul-Rasheed Akeji Alhassan Alolo, Seidu Alhassan, and S. Sekar (Eds.)

As such what we find that the suppliers had to perform two distinct activities, namely,

1. Inventory management.
2. Movement or transportation of the product to the next supplier or manufacturer.

Logistics thus consists of the above two activities.

The logistics functions may be classified as below:

1. Customer service.
2. Demand forecasting.
3. Distribution communication.
4. Inventory management.
5. Material handling.
6. Order processing.
7. Parts and service support.
8. Plant and warehouse management.
9. Procurement of ancillary materials like packaging, crates, boxes, etc.
10. Packaging.
11. Return goods handling/reverse logistics.
12. Salvage and scrap disposal.
13. Traffic and transportation.
14. Support to marketing.
15. Provide long-term profitability.
16. Creating value for money.

10.1.1 CUSTOMER SERVICE

Customer service in any business is a very important factor. The customer "as king" has to be satisfied at any cost. The right service, at right time, at right place, in right form is of paramount importance for customer service. This requires good forecasting techniques, inventory management, and planning for proper packaging and transport of products to the customer's place. Right customer service will keep the customer happy and will fetch better a long-term business relationship.

10.1.2 DEMAND FORECASTING

The logistics service provider must have a good knowledge of the requirements of the customers in appropriate time. This will facilitate the logistics service provider to equip them in advance with product, packaging, material handling, and transportation requirement to fulfill the customer's need. This requires a good demand forecasting technique that will help the logistics service provider to better satisfy the customer needs. Today with the help of modern forecasting techniques it is possible to forecast the demand more accurately. This will reduce inventory burden on suppliers and will be able to cater to the need of the customers in time.

10.1.3 DISTRIBUTION COMMUNICATION

Today we all are in a rate race. We all want that things must be done within the shortest possible time. Also minute-to-minute tracking of the deliverables is going to help the customers to plan their own activities in a better way. Therefore, distribution communication is an important function of logistics. With the help of modern IT facilities such as Global Positioning System and other tracking tools, communicating with transporter and customers through intranet, internet, WhatsApp, or even messaging may be used for minute-to-minute situation of the distribution progress for better control of distribution and for providing satisfaction to the customers.

10.1.4 INVENTORY MANAGEMENT

Keeping low or nil inventory of the demanded product may cause enormous delay in supply to the customers, thereby creating a dissatisfied customer. This may result in poor orders or no orders in the future. This will adversely affect the business. On the other hand, keeping more than optimum inventory will cause an increase in inventory carrying cost reducing the profit. Therefore, proper and optimum inventory management of products to be supplied is an important function of logistics.

10.1.5 MATERIAL HANDLING

Material handling is very important function of logistics. Maximum number of accidents happen due to poor material handling facilities or improper method of handling. To optimize the benefits of logistics, proper materials handling equipment are important. The use of right material handling equipment will reduce the cost of handling as well as the loss incurred due to accidents. With the development of material handling technology, specific handling methods and equipment are available, which may be used to harness the benefits of logistics function.

10.1.6 ORDER PROCESSING

Fast and error-free order processing will reduce the total cycle time. This may be possible with the help of appropriate IT tools which automates the order processing at minimum time. This will enhance the efficiency of logistics and will add to the bottom line (profit).

10.1.7 PARTS AND SERVICE SUPPORT

The products require the support of logistics in supply of desired spare parts for the replacement of defective parts. Adequate servicing facilities at desired locations or at the warehouses will be able to provide necessary services to the customers in the shortest possible time. This will enhance the efficiency of logistics and will provide satisfied customers.

10.1.8 PLANT AND WAREHOUSE MANAGEMENT

The manufacturing plant and warehouse both require logistics activities. The warehouse is basically a part of the logistics. The proper management of these is important for inventory keeping, inventory management, material handling, safety of men, machines, and materials and overall functioning of plant and warehouse.

10.1.9 PROCUREMENT OF ANCILLARY MATERIALS LIKE PACKAGING, CRATES, BOXES, ETC

Logistics has to perform the procurement and proper storage of packaging materials, crates, pallets, marking materials, labels, and re-enforcement materials for the smooth flow of activities. Procurement action at right time for right materials in right form and conditions is important for the success of logistics. The general procurement department may not be able to procure the right type of material. Therefore, the procurement function has to be carried out by logistics.

10.1.10 PACKAGING

The packaging is basically an art. The logistic personnel understand the need and the type of packaging required for a particular material. Special skill and traits are required for packaging of the different materials differently.

10.1.11 RETURN GOODS HANDLING/REVERSE LOGISTICS

Return goods consists of goods that are defective and the packaging materials. This is important that the packaging materials are collected from the consumers and disposed of as per the *law of the land*. In many countries, for example, cans of cold drinks can be left here and there. Also these are having material value being made of metals. The responsibility for the collection and recycling or properly disposal rests with logistics. The process of taking back the defective materials/goods and packaging materials are termed as "reverse logistics." The reverse logistic cost is almost 10 times more than the forward logistics because of the reduction in weight, numbers, and size. This has to be taken care of in the most efficient way to contain the cost of reverse logistics.

10.1.12 SALVAGE AND SCRAP DISPOSAL

All those materials which are rejected and scrapped due to any reason and packaging materials are to be first considered for salvaging them. Salvaging is a process of making these types of materials usable. If salvaging is not possible, then these are to be disposed of in a manner that will fetch maximum value to the organization. To decide whether to salvage or dispose of is the function of logistics. Mostly, the undesired materials are disposed of by auction.

10.1.13 TRAFFIC AND TRANSPORTATION

Traffic and transportation in logistics is to find out most suitable material handling equipment, vehicle, and routing the vehicle from the right route. This will ensure the safety of materials and transportation in the minimum time. Proper selection of the above will add to the profit of the organization.

10.1.14 PROVIDE LONG-TERM PROFITABILITY

Logistics should always look to the long-term relationship with the customers. Long-term relationship may require launching programs like "customer relationship management." This will go a long way in the reputation of the organization and will fetch good business for the days to come.

Good reputation and good business will increase the profit of the logistics organization in the long run.

10.1.15 CREATING VALUE FOR MONEY

For prosperity of the organization, it is essential to create value for each rupee spent on logistics activities. The establishment of a logistics system and warehouse requires lot of capital expenditure. The return on investment should be such that it gives an extra amount to the bottom line of the balance sheet. For this, one has to think in the most logical and practical way of creating value for the money by effective logistics functions.

Thus, we find that the logistics functions are very many and each one of them is important for the organization. A company can develop and flourish only when the logistics functions are performed in the most desired form to fetch better returns in the long run.

10.2 LOGISTICS PLANNING

Planning is the first and foremost activity in any operation. Also, it is said that "well planned is half done." Logistics is not an exception to it. Performing the logistics functions, the first activity is to plan.

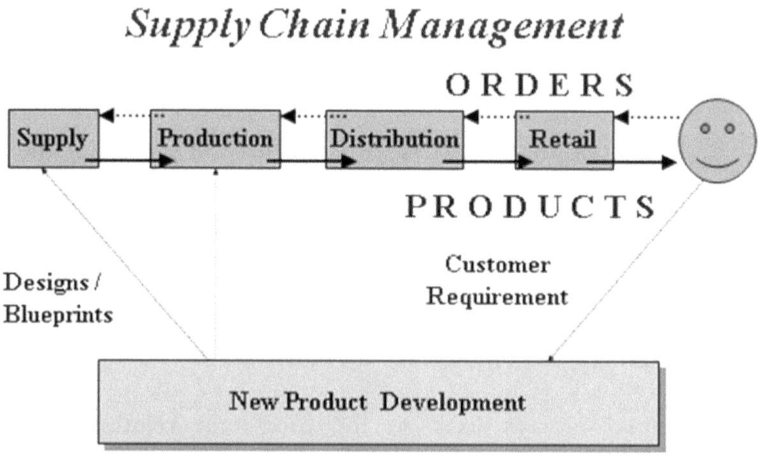

FIGURE 10.1 Supply chain management.

KEYWORDS

- **logistics**
- **functions**
- **organization**
- **strategic**
- **management**
- **transportation**

REFERENCES

Christopher, M. In *Logistics and Supply Chain Management, Financial Times Series.*
Miscellaneous articles in Supply Chain Management on internet
Reesearchgate.com
Supply-Chain-Logistics-Management, Bowersox/
Wikipedia.com

CHAPTER 11

The Green SCM Practices and Its Impact on Indian Business Environment

MRIDUL DHARWAL[1], VEENA PRASAD[2], K. D. V. PRASAD[3,4], SATHI JYOTHIRMAYE REDDY[5], and KIRTI AGARWAL[6]

[1]*School of Business Studies, Sharda University, Greater Noida, Uttar Pradesh, India*

[2]*NKES College of Arts Commerce and Science, Mumbai, Maharashtra, India*

[3]*Symbiosis Institute of Business Management, Hyderabad, India*

[4]*Symbiosis International (Deemed University), Pune, India*

[5]*Faculty of Management Studies, Marwadi University, Rajkot, Gujarat, India*

[6]*ITERC College, Institutional Duhai Road, Delhi, India*

ABSTRACT

The objective of green_supply chain management (G_SCM) is to optimize financial gains while concurrently ensuring the availability of appropriate products at the correct time and place. The performance of a business as a whole is influenced by the efficiency and efficacy of its G_SCM. The effectiveness and efficacy of a production process and its management are contingent upon various factors. These factors include the selection of suppliers for materials procurement, the strategies employed for inventory stocking in terms of location and method, the efficient and timely distribution of goods and/or services, and the mode and timing of payments. The primary objective

Essentials of Supply Chain Management: Strategy, Planning and Operations.
Mohammed Majeed, Abdul-Rasheed Akeji Alhassan Alolo, Seidu Alhassan, and S. Sekar (Eds.)

of this chapter is to examine the methods and practices of G_SCM and their impact on the profitability, turnover, and sustainability of a business.

11.1 INTRODUCION

Green_supply chain management (G_SCM) has been examined by numerous scholars. Ganes and Harris (2022) define G_SCM as a system of facilities and choices pertaining to the distribution of goods or services. This system encompasses the procurement of materials, their transformation into both unfinished as well as the finished products, and the subsequent distribution of the finished products to end consumers, while the unfinished products are sent to final producers as intermediaries. According to Lee and Corey (2021), G_SCM encompasses the comprehensive integrating of the various activities within the supply chain (SC) network. These activities include the acquisition of raw materials and transforming these materials into goods and/or services, and the subsequent delivery of these products and/or services to end customers through a formal distribution channel. According to Christofer (2008), an SC encompasses multiple organizations that are connected to a central organization, either upstream or downstream, and are engaged in diverse activities or processes that ultimately generate value in the form of a product or service, which is then made accessible to the end user. Therefore, G_SCM refers to the methodical and strategic management of conventional business operations and associated strategies within an organization. Its purpose is to facilitate effective planning and coordination among various internal and external stakeholders, with the ultimate goal of ensuring seamless SC operations and enhancing the long-term-based performance of the company in question.

The contemporary world is characterized by ongoing and simultaneous development, which has a profound impact on the manner in which firms perform their operations. The success of a company is heavily reliant on the inventive expansion of SC strategies. This expansion not only facilitates ongoing improvements in the firm's operations and positions it for success in future scenarios but also enables the generation of revenue from the acquired knowledge. The implementation of G_SCM practices has been noted as a means for leading global companies to restructure their SCs in accordance with the principles of a globalized and interconnected world. These practices encompass various solutions pertaining to the operational aspects of a company, such as demand forecasting, supply planning, sourcing and procurement, execution of SC execution as well as asset management. Therefore, it has become imperative for firms to effectively managing their SCs. This practice not only enhances the client experience but also ensures a harmonious equilibrium between costs and benefits, so granting the company a competitive advantage. In general, the concept of G_SCM aims to integrate various stakeholders, including manufacturers, all suppliers, retailers, transporters, distributors, customers, and warehouses, into a cohesive and dynamic process that facilitates the continuous flowing of products, finances, and information.

11.2 LITERATURE REVIEW

Traditionally, the available drivers of this chain were thought to be the manufacturers. They were in charge of controlling the rate at which the goods were manufactured and distributed further. The numerous elements were melted down into one pot, or G_SCM, with the help of marketing and distribution management, buy and material management, haulage and logistics management, and operations and information technology (IT) management. Each of these business facets is harmoniously included in the all-encompassing G_SCM concept in order to create an SC strategy that eventually improves an enterprise's performance. The specialization inside the chain started in the 2010s with the introduction of warehouses, nonasset-based carriers, and its administration because these were outside the purview of transportation and logistics, but rather within the realm of supply chain management (SCM).

These days, companies are scrambling to meet client expectations for alternatives, features, and styles, as well as for quick order execution and delivery. Manufacturing quality used to be viewed as the key distinction between businesses. When this component approaches parity today, meeting customer needs for product delivery becomes the next crucial element for maintaining a competitive edge in the market. Businesses that are working to advance G_SCM will one day tell their success stories. Between 2010 and 2020, the number of multinational corporations more than doubled. The SCs have not only expanded geographically, but they have also engulfed more and more businesses. For a variety of operations to be outsourced, the majority of these organizations foresee a growth in reciprocal relationships with other third parties and suppliers (Corsten and Kumar, 2020). The SCs must, however, also keep up with the rapidly expanding as well as tightening product portfolios in order to function properly. Contrarily, SCs are unable to cope with cost volatility; thus, businesses now view cost minimization as their top priority in relation to them, in addition to business expansion and product/service innovation.

As the SC progresses toward the end consumer, each intermediate member in the chain fulfills certain value-added functions in the relation to the products or services it is associated with. According to Mowat and Collis (2021), the concept of G_SCM primarily revolves around the careful consideration and fulfillment of the ultimate consumers' requirements. This is done in a manner that maximizes the value provided to customers and enhances the returns for all stakeholders involved in the SC. While many studies have argued that it is the duty of G_SCM practitioners to maintain and promote a customer-centric culture, others have posited that the fundamental objective of G_SCM is to align with customer demands. According to Taylor (2020), a crucial part of G_SCM is directing attention toward customers during the final stages of the whole SC. The phenomenon of outsourcing has become increasingly prominent, leading to the continuous development of G_SCM during the 2010s. Given that G_SCM is driven by consumer demands, it is crucial to ensure that its requirements are delivered promptly and accurately while minimizing waste and faults. In essence, G_SCM entails the harmonization and integration of many operations, encompassing both upstream and downstream activities within the SC.

The primary objective of G_SCM, as it pertains to transportation and logistics management, is to reduce inventory levels inside and across enterprises, while simultaneously enhancing service quality. SC managers are consistently confronted with dynamic and competitive situations as a result of the emergence of new global markets. This evolution necessitates the need for these managers to operate under stressful conditions. The typical and customary tradeoffs were no longer seen viable, prompting corporations to seek methods and strategies to optimize their SCs. Due to the distinct objectives and priorities of individual companies, the configuration of SCs exhibited variability between enterprises. In addition to this, there were additional problems that arose due to the availability of electronic links for enhancing supply chain (SC) performance. Consequently, companies faced increased difficulty in monitoring the actions of other companies, which led to a heightened emphasis on efficiency and cost reduction. According to Mehra and Iman (2021), the implementation of quality management efforts offers potential solutions for addressing these difficulties. Moreover, the use of traditional G_SCM practices, which primarily focused on supplier selection based solely on price considerations, yielded outcomes that deterred enterprises from engaging in global market competition.

11.3 RESEARCH METHODOLOGY

In light of intensifying competition among Indian enterprises, it is evident that every market participant is driven to improve their operational performance in order to get a competitive advantage over their rivals. In the context of sustainable supply chain management (S_SCM), the implementation of G_SCM practices has a crucial significance. These practices enable organizations to reduce costs, enhance value, provide customer satisfaction, and ultimately increase their profits.

a. **Hypothesis of the study**—The profitability (PR), turnover (TO), and sustenance (SUS) of revenue in firms of all sizes, including small, medium, and large, are positively connected with the implementation of G_SCM practices.

The relationship between the variables can be denoted by the equation $y = f(x)$, where y represents the dependent variable representing PR (%), TO (crores), and SUS (years) of revenue, and x represents the independent variable indicating the competence of G_SCM practices stated in terms of a score.

The following is the conceptual framework of the G_SCM process, wherein the variables considered for research are identified as the factors that impact the level of maturity of the G_SCM processes.

I. The company enters into cooperative agreements regarding the forecasting of their products and services as well as their replenishment needs "(Collaborative, Planning, Forecasting, and Replenishment, GREEN_SCM.01)."
II. The organization of first models optimizes these models, and finally converts the models into plans that can actually be implemented "(Supply_Chain Simulation and Optimization, GREEN_SCM.02)."
III. The organization keeps in touch with all of the relevant stakeholders and related parties, and communicates with them as well as maintains a monitoring system for information based on orders "(Integrated Based Fulfillment, GREEN_SCM.03)."
IV. Following the transformation of planning outcomes into production as well as service orders, the organization works to satisfy those productions as well as orders of service "(Manufacturing—Service Execution, GREEN_SCM.04)."
V. An organization will respond to predictable variation in an SC by either administering the supply (through inventory management,

capacity planning, etc.) or administering the demand. Both of these types of administration are related to supply and demand management "(Monitor and Control_Supply Chain Variation, GREEN_SCM.05)."

b. **Data Collection Method**—In this study, data were obtained using the questionnaire approach. The questionnaire was designed to capture the impact of G_SCM practices as well as procedures on PR, TO, and SUS in the food and grocery retail sector in India.

c. **Data Analysis Techniques**

   i. The analysis of G_SCM examines the impact of data using statistical approaches such as calculating the average and mode. As per the research technique, the variable "x" represents the mean value of the ratings obtained from continuous data, which is categorized based on frequency intervals such as 1–10 crores, 11–100 crores, and so on. The mode value of a rating is determined for discrete data and represents the rating of a certain variable that has been occurred the greatest number of times. The purpose of this study is to assess G_SCM practice capability and process maturity of different organizations based on their ratings of PR, TO, and SUS. Furthermore, the weighted "average ($\bar{x}$ (w))" has been computed to determine the sample mean of the complete population. This measure is employed to analyze the effectiveness and development of G_SCM practices and procedures in terms of PR, TO, and sustainability, as well as their corresponding ranges. Additionally, the standard deviation (σx) was calculated for the average and mode intervals to evaluate data dispersion and prediction confidence. It has been proposed that a lower standard deviation between the average and the mode indicates a higher level of accuracy in the findings.

   ii. In the analysis of the facts pertaining to process maturity, the absolute count of the rating for each of the five criteria or elements is assessed and evaluated in relation to the specific variables of PR, TO, and SUS. The examination of count data can provide insights into the "skewness and kurtosis" of the underlying distribution. Skewness is confirmed by the higher rating percentage, while Kurtosis is confirmed by the dispersion of percentage values over rating value. The study of these findings is supported by the absolute count approach, which is further validated by the examination of average and mode values. The accuracy of the analysis is confirmed by considering the standard deviation. It is proposed that a smaller value of standard deviation corresponds to a better degree of confidence in the forecast.

11.4 RESULTS

The findings of the data analysis unveiled the impact of the Capability of G_SCM practices and the maturity of the G_SCM processes on PR, TO, and SUS. The scope of this survey is limited to the variables associated with the maturity of the G_SCM process—("Collaborative, Planning, Forecasting, and Replenishment [Green_SCM.01], Supply Chain Simulation and Optimization [Green_SCM.02], Integrated-Fulfillment [Green_SCM.03], Manufacturing—Service Execution [Green_SCM.04], Monitor-Control Supply Chain Variation [Green_SCM.05]").

11.4.1 INFLUENCE OF G_SCM PRACTICES CAPABILITY ON PROFITABILITY

TABLE 11.1 Green SCM Capability Impact Analysis.

Profit (%)	Average (x)	Mode
0–(−10)	4.2	4.0
0–10	3.6	3.0
11–20	3.7	3.0
21–30	3.8	5.0
31–40+	4.1	4.0
x(*w*)	3.8	3.6
Sigma-*x*	0.2	0.8

TABLE 11.2 Green SCM Capability Rating Count and % Score.

Rating	Impact	Count	% Score
1	Limited	5	4
2	Fair	6	6
3	Good	30	28
4	Very good	37	34
5	Excellent	31	28

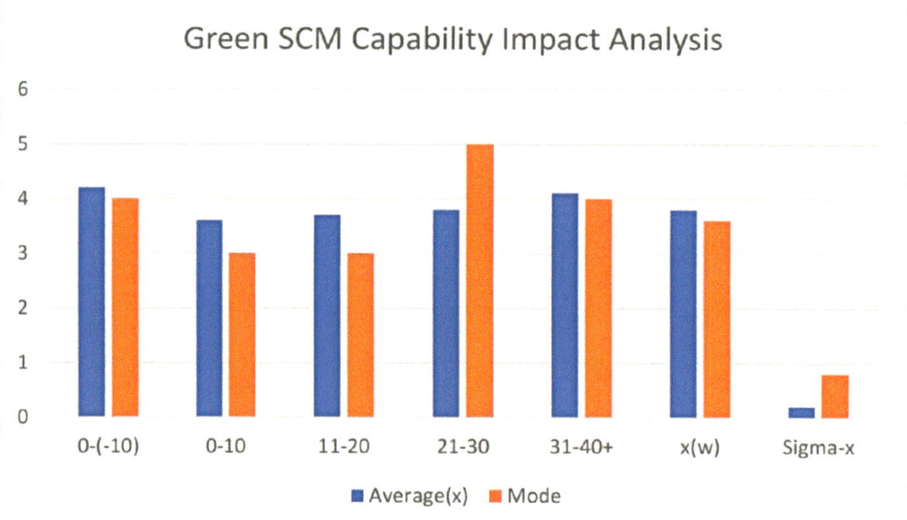

FIGURE 11.1 Green SCM capability impact analysis.

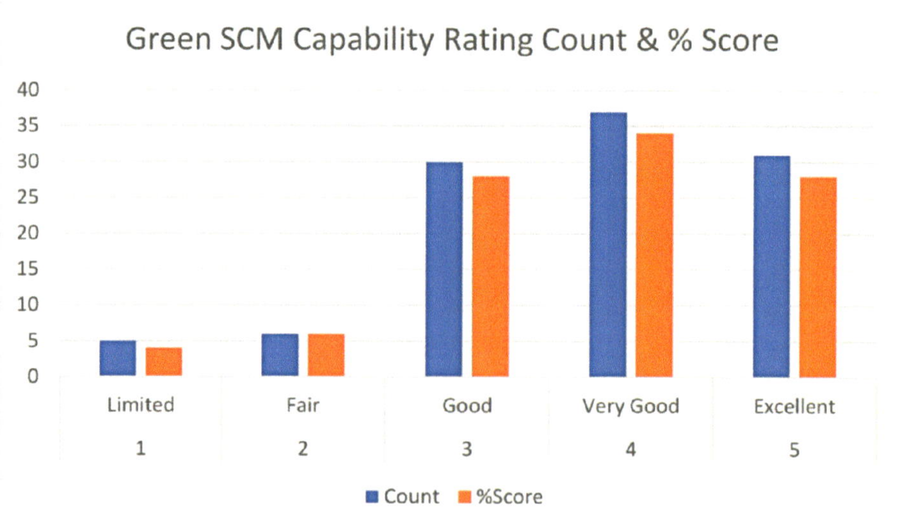

FIGURE 11.2 Green_SCM capability rating count and % score.

The following information has been provided by statistics in Tables 11.1 and 11.2:

- In Indian companies, G_SCM practice has noticeably rating 4 influence [average: = 3.8, $\sigma x = 0.2$, and mode: = 3.6, $\sigma x = 0.8$] on PR.
- Organizations with 0–20% PR show that G_SCM practice capacity only improves PR, whereas 20–30% organizations focused on PR and say G_SCM practice capacity has a great impact on their PR. In fact, 30–40% organizations have this much PR having a great impact.
- While 62% of organizations revealed that G_SCM practice capability has on PR, rating 4 to rating 5 influences, 28% companies have rating 3 control of G_SCM practice capabilities on the same.
- Only 6% of the companies have G_SCM practice with rating 2 influence and 4% companies have rating 1 influence.
- As per Table 11.2 ("PR_Green_SCM Capability Rating Count and % Score"), organizations revealed that overall G_SCM practice capabilities has rating 4 influence on PR of companies.

11.4.2 IMPACT OF G_SCM PRACTICE CAPABILITY ON TO

TABLE 11.3 Green_SCM Capability Impact Analysis.

Turnover (Cr)	Average (x)	Mode
1–10	3.8	3.0
11–100	3.5	3.0
101–1000	3.5	4.0
1001–10,000	3.6	4.0
10,001+	3.8	3.0
x(w)	3.6	3.0
Sigma-*x*	0.1	0.5

TABLE 11.4 Green_SCM Capability Rating Count and % Score.

Rating	Impact	Count	% Score
1	Limited	6	19
2	Fair	5	38
3	Good	36	33
4	Very good	41	5
5	Excellent	21	5

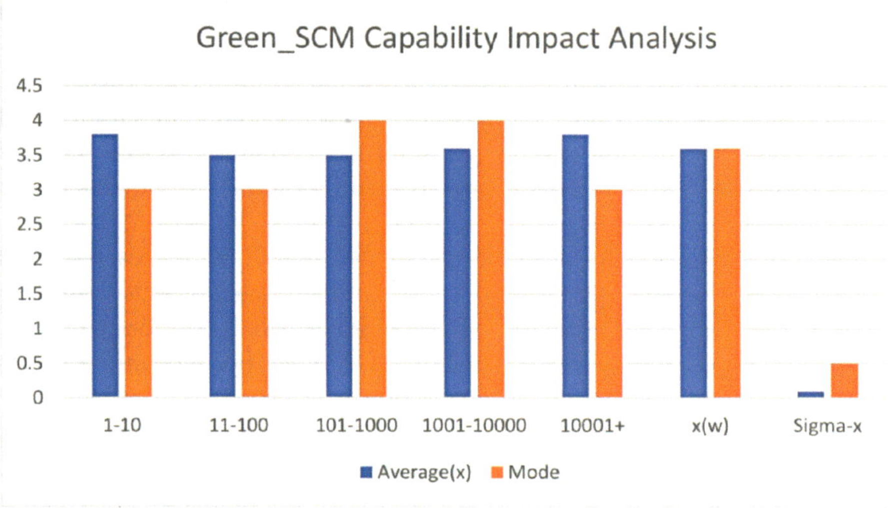

FIGURE 11.3 Green_SCM capability impact analysis.

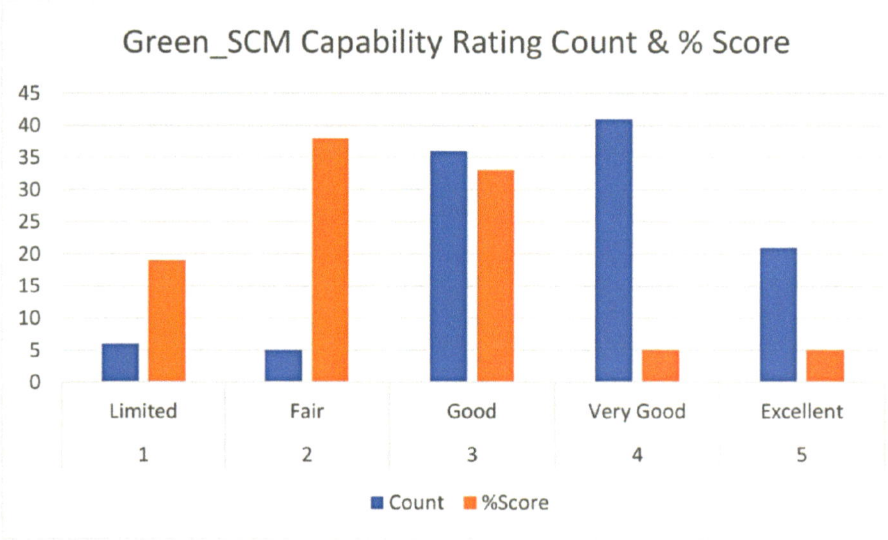

FIGURE 11.4 Green_SCM capability rating count and % score.

The following information has been provided by the statistics in Tables 11.3 and 11.4:

- The implementation of environmentally S_SCM practices has been found to has a significant positive effects on the financial performance of firms with a TO ranging from 100 to 10,000+ crores. However, for organizations with a TO between 11 and 100 crores, the influence of their SC practice capabilities on financial performance is only deemed as good.

- The average value of 3.6, with a "standard deviation of 0.1," and the mode value of 3.6, with a "standard deviation of 0.5," indicate that the competence of the G_SCM practice has a rating of 4 in terms of its influence on the TO of enterprises.
- According to a survey, 57% of firms report that their implementation of G_SCM practices has a significant impact, with ratings ranging from 4 to 5. In contrast, 33% of organizations indicate a moderate impact, with a rating of 3.
- A mere 5% of firms possess a grade of 2 in terms of their influence on G_SCM practice capabilities, while an additional 5% hold a rating of 1 in this regard, impacting the company's TO.
- In general, the research indicates that the implementation of G_SCM practices has a significant impact on firms' TO, with ratings of either 4 or 3.

11.4.3 IMPACT OF G_SCM PRACTICE CAPABILITY ON SUS

TABLE 11.5 Green_SCM Capability Impact Analysis.

Sus. (years)	Average (x)	Mode
0–10	3.4	3.0
11–20	3.4	3.0
21–30	3.8	4.0
31–40	3.9	4.0
41–50+	3.9	4.0
$x(w)$	3.6	3.5
Sigma-x	0.2	0.5

TABLE 11.6 Green_SCM Capability Rating Count and % Score.

Rating	Impact	Count	%Score
1	Limited	5	4
2	Fair	10	9
3	Good	30	28
4	Very good	38	35
5	Excellent	26	24

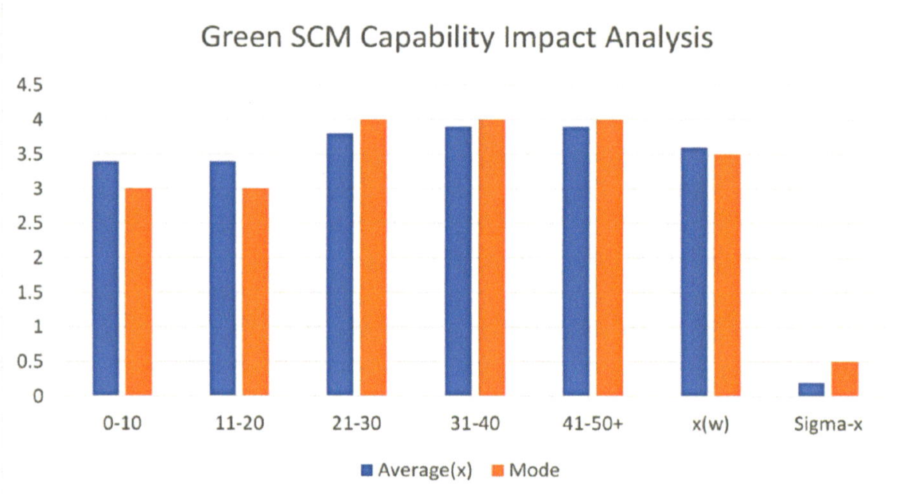

FIGURE 11.5 Green_SCM capability impact analysis.

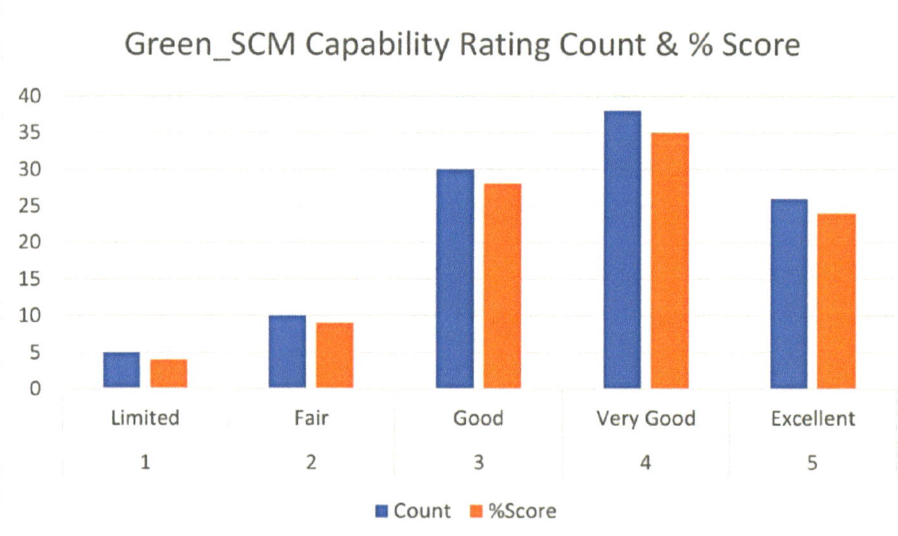

FIGURE 11.6 Green_SCM capability rating count and % score.

The following information has been provided by the statistics in Tables 11.5 and 11.6:

- In this instance, the average demonstrates a significantly reduced standard deviation, resulting in enhanced predictability about the impact of G_SCM practice capability on SUS, in comparison to the mode.
- In the context of the Indian corporate environment, the implementation of G_SCM practices has been observed to have a significant impact on the sustainability factor, with a notable grade of 4.
- In the case of organizations with a tenure of 1–20 years, the capability of implementing G_SCM practices demonstrates a positive influence on sustainability, with a rating of 3. However, for companies with a tenure of 21–50+ years, this influence is even stronger, with a rating of 4.
- According to a survey conducted, it was found that 59% of firms reported that the capability of implementing G_SCM practices has a significant influence on their sustainability, with a rating ranging from 4 to 5. On the other hand, 28% of companies stated that the influence of G_SCM practices has a rating of 3.
- Only 9% of organizations possess a rating of 2 in terms of their influence on the capabilities of implementing G_SCM practices, while a mere 4% of companies have a grade of 1 influence.
- According to the findings presented in Table 11.6 (SUS-G_SCM capability rating count and % score), it has been determined that the practice capability of G_SCM has a rating of 4, which significantly impacts the sustainability of businesses.

11.4.4 IMPACT OF THE MATURITY OF GREEN_SCM'S PROCESSES ON TO, PR, AND SUS

TABLE 11.7 Green_SCM Leading Managerial Processes Analysis.

Statistics	**Average (x)**					**Mode**				
	G_SCM 0.1	**G_SCM 0.2**	**G_SCM 0.3**	**G_SCM 0.4**	**G_SCM 0.5**	**G_SCM 0.1**	**G_SCM 0.2**	**G_SCM 0.3**	**G_SCM 0.4**	**G_SCM 0.5**
$x(w)$	**3.6**	**3.7**	**3.6**	**3.7**	**3.6**	3.7	4.3	3.5	3.2	3.7
Sigma-x	**0.2**	**0.1**	**0.1**	**0.1**	**0.1**	0.4	0.4	0.5	0.5	0.5

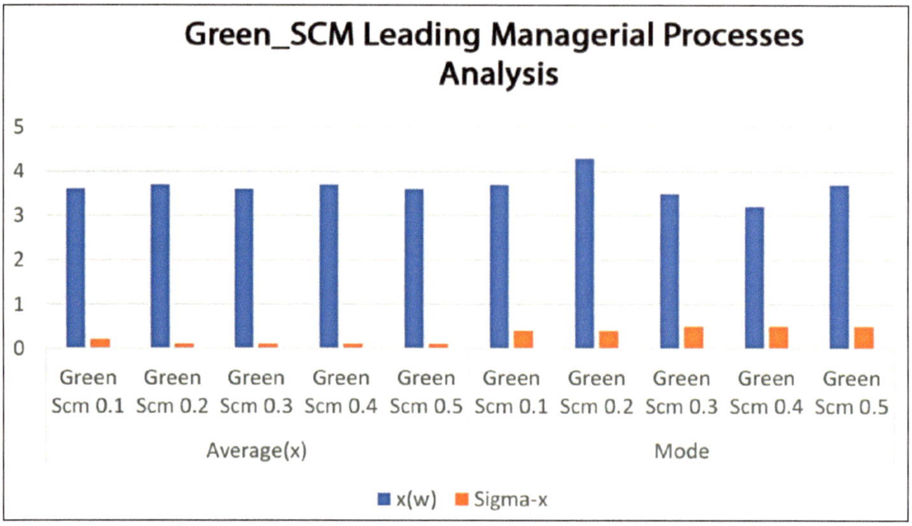

FIGURE 11.7 Green_SCM leading managerial processes analysis.

- According to the concept of G_SCM, organizations with a budget of up to 10,001 crores demonstrate a high level of process maturity. Approximately 44–65% of the population concurs with the aforementioned assertion.
- Organizations with a TO ranging from 1001 to 10,000 crores exhibit a high level of maturity in their collaborative-planning, forecasting, and replenishment processes. The given data, with average = 3.6, $x = 0.2$, and mean = 3.7, $x = 0.4$, indicates that Indian enterprises generating annual revenues of $1,000,000 or higher exhibit a high level of maturity in their collaborative planning, forecasting, and replenishment processes.
- The average score of 3.7 suggests that the SC execution planning process demonstrates a high level of process maturity and a strong ability to predict outcomes ($x = 0.1$). On the other hand, the mode score of 4.3 indicates that the SC execution and planning process exhibits a high level of process maturity but has a lower level of predictability ($x = 0.4$). The data provided, with an average value of 3.7 and a "standard deviation of 0.1" for the category "average," and an average value of 4.3 and a "standard deviation of 0.4" for the category "moderate," indicates that enterprises with annual revenues ranging from 1 crore to 10,001+ crores exhibit a high level of process maturity in their SC execution and planning process. This

level of maturity is consistently maintained by a significant portion, specifically 55–75%, of the population.

- The data suggest that the integrated fulfillment process, as measured by the average score of 3.6, exhibits a high level of process maturity and a strong capacity to anticipate outcomes ($x = 0.1$). However, the mode score of 3.5 indicates that while the process still demonstrates a high level of process maturity, its ability to predict outcomes is somewhat lower ($x = 0.5$). The data provided indicates that the average value is 3.6, with a corresponding "value of x equal to 0.1." Additionally, the mean value is reported as 3.5, with a corresponding "value of x equal to 0.5." These findings suggest that enterprises with annual revenue of $1 billion or more possess an integrated fulfillment process that is supported by a substantial portion of the public, ranging from 44 to 68%.
- According to the findings, businesses with revenues of 10,001+ crores demonstrate a very advanced level of development in the manufacturing and service execution process, as per the G_SCM.04 framework. The data presented indicates that firms with an average annual revenue of $1,000,000 or more demonstrate a high level of maturity in their manufacturing and service execution processes. This is evidenced by the mean value of 3.2 and the average value of 3.7, with corresponding values of x being 0.5 and 0.1, respectively. Furthermore, it is observed that between 49 and 60% of the population supports these processes.
- The average score of 3.6 indicates that the process of monitoring and controlling SC variation, also known as G_SCM.05, demonstrates a high level of process maturity and predictability, with a standard deviation of 0.1. On the other hand, the mode score of 3.7 suggests that the same process exhibits lower predictability but still maintains a good level of maturity, with a standard deviation of 0.5. The statistical measures of the average, mode, and standard deviation for the variables indicated that enterprises with TOs ranging from 1 to 10,001+ crores exhibit a high level of process maturity in their monitor and control_SC variation processes. This level of maturity is consistently maintained by around 50–56% of the population.

11.5 DISCUSSION

- Overall influence of G_SCM practice capability on the PR—very good—while 62% companies reveal that G_SCM practice capability has rating 4 to rating 5 influence on PR, 28% companies have rating 3 influence of G_SCM practice capability.

- Overall influence of G_SCM Practice Capability on TO—very good—while 57% companies reveal that G_SCM practice has rating 4 to rating 5 influence on TO, 33% companies have rating 3 influence.
- Overall influence of G_SCM practice capability on SUS—very good—while 59% companies reveal that G_SCM practice capability has rating 4 to rating 5 influence on the SUS factor, 28% companies reveal that G_SCM practice capability has rating 3 influence on the same.

11.6 CONCLUSION

In conclusion, it can be asserted that the efficacy of SCM methods has a significant impact on the financial performance, operational efficiency, and long-term viability of an organization. According to industry-based estimates in India, the expenditure on G_SCM and logistics accounts for approximately 15–16% of the country's gross domestic product (GDP). In contrast, global estimates indicate that China's expenditure in this area is around 14–15% of its GDP, while the United States spends approximately 9–10% of its GDP on G_SCM and logistics. Moreover, within the context of India, the expenditure associated with transportation constitutes approximately 45% of the overall production costs. It is worth noting that over 50% of the commodities are transported by road networks. In the realm of road transportation, the trucking industry holds a significant share, amounting to over 70% of the total. Notably, a substantial portion of this sector, approximately 67%, comprises tiny, unorganized entities. Moreover, trucking operations contribute to approximately 60% of the overall logistics expenditure. The road transportation is afterward succeeded by rail transportation, which is subsequently followed by coastal shipping as a means of transportation. However, it is ironic that rail transit has been experiencing a decline in influence as a result of biased governmental regulations and policies, as well as inherent deficiencies. In spite of the cost-effectiveness of water transportation and the existence of extensive marine routes, its utilization remains limited due to inadequate government regulations and a lack of innovation within the private sector. Air transportation, albeit a notable mode, is limited to a relatively tiny percentage of cargo and messengers. There exist various expenditure indicators within the realm of G_SCM, including inventory costs, inbound transportation expenses, distribution costs, and others. These indicators may differ among businesses; nevertheless, data from CMIE suggests that they have been declining over a specific period. These organizations allocate approximately 16–18% of their net sales toward various logistical activities, while the global average stands at approximately 10–12%. Therefore, there exists significant potential to reduce logistical expenses, thereby enabling enterprises to improve their operating margins and achieve above-average PR.

KEYWORDS

- **green_SCM practices**
- **grocery retail**
- **food retail**
- **sustainability of a business**

REFERENCES

Christofer N. Strategies for Reducing Costs and Improving Services in Logistics & Green SCM. *Qual. Manag. J.* **2008,** *9* (2), 59–72.

Corsten, D.; Kumar, N. Do Suppliers Gain from Collaborative Relationships with Outsized Retailers? *Qual. Manag. J.* **2020,** *9* (1), 80–90.

Ganes, R.; Harris, T. P. Supply Chain Management. *Eur. J. Purch. Supply Manag.* **2022,** *6* ([illegible]), [illegible].

Lee, H. L.; Corey, B. Supply-Chain-Management Models - Evolution and Practice. *J. Operat. Manag.* **2021,** *25*, 42–63.

Mehra, S.; Iman, R. A. *Purchase Management and Business Competitiveness in the Coming Time. J. Bus. Logist.* **2021,** *22* (7), 711–720.

Mowat, A.; Collis, R. Supply Chain Management in an Emerging Industry. Supply Chain Management: An Insight Story, 2021; vol *7* (1), pp 45–57.

Taylor, D. Logistics and Supply Chain Management - Global Cases. *Int. J. Operat. Prod. Manag.* **2020,** *10* (2), 21–34.

CHAPTER 12

Demand Planning in Supply Chain Management Process

ABDUL GANIW HUSSEIN

Tamale Technical University (TaTU), Tamale, Ghana

ABSTRACT

Demand planning (DP) is a major component of supply chain management in any organization. DP is crucial to the operation of an organization and a supply chain because it provides input information for other key planning areas, including manufacturing scheduling, resource management, and budgetary considerations. Hence, the purpose of this chapter is to provide our understanding of DP areas and processes with respect to supply chain. Companies can better anticipate their customers' needs with the help of demand forecasting. In addition, a company's production, inventory, pricing, and marketing and sales efforts can all benefit from DP planning. The accuracy of forecasts can be checked through regular monitoring once they have been developed. This can be done by comparing the actual results to the predicted results. Adjustments to the forecasting methods utilized should be made if the predictions are inaccurate. Economic conditions, rivalry, consumer fads, pricing, availability, and marketing are only a few of the documented influences on DP. That is why it is crucial for firms to coordinate their supply and demand strategies for maximum financial gain. The success of a company can be directly impacted by accurate DP. The majority of an organization's preparations rely on DP, including demand, inventory, production, and procurement preparations. The ability to accurately predict future demand is crucial for every company, as it affects nearly every aspect of operations. In order to prevent revenue loss from late deliveries and stockpiling of unsold

Essentials of Supply Chain Management: Strategy, Planning and Operations.
Mohammed Majeed, Abdul-Rasheed Akeji Alhassan Alolo, Seidu Alhassan, and S. Sekar (Eds.)

goods caused by overproduction, it is important to understand the elements that impact DP and planning.

12.1 INTRODUCTION

Due to rising levels of competition and growing supply chain (SC) complexity, organizations are focusing more on improving the effectiveness of their SCs (Prasad and Shankhar, 2011). Companies have begun to recognize that high SC expenses are a motivating factor in focusing on SC performance. Managing the SC in a way that takes into account the varying demands of customers is crucial to the success of any SC. Companies that try to market their products universally are more likely to fail (Lee, 2002). A company cannot afford to lose consumers if it does not adequately cover and plan for fluctuations in demand (Gupta and Costas, 2013). Efficient management of stock requires pinpointing the factors contributing to a gap between sales and purchases. Inventories efficiency analysis is one method for accomplishing this. Service quality, logistical expenses, and stalled capital will all be more than necessary if productivity is not maximized (Relph and Milner, 2015).

The sales prediction, together with additional inputs and insights contributions from various departments, all go into the SC activity known as demand planning (DP) (Raza and Kilbourn, 2017). In other words, DP provides a one-of-a-kind chance to make projections that help businesses change and grow (Armstrong et al., 2017). In particular, DP helps businesses comprehend the dynamics of consumer demand and tailor their responses accordingly. Ability to quickly assess the circumstances and make adjustments is crucial for demand-chain management in today's global business climate. DP also benefits greatly from the insights provided by dynamic capability theory. For the purposes of this research, we define "DP" as "a dynamic everyday including an established and determined set of procedures, including setting objectives, collecting information, anticipating demand, relating the demand predictions, and coordinating supply with demand" (Cassettari et al., 2017).

Profitability for a given sales channel or product line can be increased by better DP due to more precise revenue projections and stock levels that correspond with demand spikes and dips (Anaplan, 2023). The goal of DP is to find and keep a state of "lean supply equilibrium," in which stores have only as much of a given product on hand as customers need. Finding the sweet spot between having too much and not enough can be challenging. Even as this equilibrium is a primary focus of DP, so is the ongoing work to influence demand via strategic advertising. Accurately anticipating future demand trends is a key component of effective DP, which also brings other benefits like higher firm efficiency and happier customers.

However, many decision-makers fail to appreciate DP's actual or potential benefits. As a result, research into DP is warranted because of its role in helping to reliably forecast future demand. Few studies have looked into how DP might help lessen operational risk-induced interruptions. In parallel, a few of the most recent research suggests that DP could be quite useful for managers in dealing with the repercussions of DP and control (Swierczek, 2019). Some DP strategies have been shown in other research to either reduce or exacerbate operational risk-driven disruptions (Swierczek and Szozda, 2019). The primary goal of this chapter is to provide our understanding of DP areas and processes with respect to SC.

12.2 CONTRIBUTION

Our chapter's primary objective is to furnish general knowledge concerning the value of DP to SCs. The following are the most significant gains from this research. We begin by advancing the concept of DP, which, in accordance with the theory, is a key component of supply chain management (SCM) strategy. As an added bonus, to the best of our knowledge, this is one of the first literature-based studies to seek to analyze desktop data that contributes to DP in SCs. Finally, our review evaluates the importance of contextual aspects that may impact DP's efficacy in SCs.

12.3 LITERATURE REVIEW

12.3.1 DP

Management's first and most essential duty is planning, which is determining in advance "what" will be done, "when" it will be done, "how" it will be done, and "who" will do it. It is a mental procedure that defines the goals of an organization and brainstorms potential strategies for getting there. It lays out, step-by-step, the best way to complete a certain task. The goal of DP in the management of SCs is to help businesses accurately predict consumer demand and successfully adapt their products and services to meet that need. For consistent product delivery and happy consumers, SC managers must engage in a process known as "DP." Profitability for a given sales channel or product line can be increased by better DP due to more precise revenue projections and stock levels that correspond with demand spikes and dips (Anaplan, 2023). DP's ultimate goal is to maintain equilibrium between supply and demand in an SC (Raza and Kilbourn, 2017). If businesses have a firm grasp of client needs and expectations, they will have an easier time preparing for fluctuations in demand. According to Kotler (2003), the marketing department is in charge of demand management; hence, an organization's demand prediction is the product of a deliberate marketing strategy. In order for businesses to succeed, planning should not just replicate demand; it should also have an impact on customer preferences (Crum, 2003). Materials and resources are two primary factors that must be taken into account while assessing DP.

12.3.2 ELEMENTS OF DP

12.3.2.1 MANAGING A VARIETY OF PRODUCTS AT ONCE

Considering commodities and their lifespans in depth is crucial for effective DP. Portfolio management for products does this by cataloging a product's history from inception to retirement. Product portfolio management also helps a business see how one change in demand can impact other, "neighboring," product lines (IBM, 2023).

12.3.2.2 PREDICTIONS BASED ON STATISTICS

The statistical forecasting technique is a method of developing SC forecasts by analyzing historical data using complex algorithms, based on the idea that previous performance typically serves as the best indicator of future accomplishments. Accurate data (free of outliers, exclusions, or assumptions) is essential for the precise process entailed in forecasting using statistical techniques (IBM, 2023).

12.3.2.3 SENSING THE NEEDS OF THE MARKET

In order to detect disruptions and demand effects in immediate terms, demand monitoring integrates an assortment of novel types of data (such as weather, healthcare patterns, government information, and more) with past trend data and applies artificial intelligence (AI) (IBM, 2023).

12.3.2.4 CONTROL OF MARKETING FOR EXPORTS

Getting people interested is crucial to making it in the retail industry. Special events (such as reduced pricing or freebies) are used in trade promotions and other forms of marketing to increase sales. Management of promotional activities in international trade ensures that such chances are taken advantage of effectively and yield the desired results (IBM, 2023).

12.3.3 BENEFITS OF DP

12.3.3.1 MAINTAINING A HEALTHY INVENTORY

The primary goal of DP is to find a happy medium between supply and demand. This is crucial in ensuring client happiness and expanding the company's sales pipeline. DP serves an important purpose, but precise outcomes are notoriously difficult to attain (IBM, 2023). DP is notoriously difficult since it necessitates cooperation from every department in a business. Having too much stock on hand prevents a company from investing in new products and cutting-edge research, and it also increases overhead expenditures in the form of inventory carrying costs. Backorders, the unwise purchase of more expensive raw materials, and, perhaps most crucially, the company's reputation can all suffer from a lack of stock. Customer dissatisfaction, which can have a negative impact on the company's reputation, is a common result of insufficient stock (IBM, 2023).

12.3.3.2 ACCURACY OF PREDICTIONS

The task of developing a reliable demand prediction might be daunting. DP relies heavily on this, and it is a process that may be refined over time. Not only can forecasting help determine the quantity of goods needed, it can also provide light on the potential income. Over time, the accuracy of demand projections will increase as manufacturing groups develop forecasts and compare them to actual demand (Planet Together, 2021). If the corporation overestimates demand for a product, for instance, it can learn from past mistakes and improve its forecasting techniques in the future.

12.3.3.3 CONTROLLING STOCK LEVELS

The ability to adjust stock in response to fluctuations in demand is facilitated by DP. Manufacturers will be able to stock just the correct amount of products thanks to the integration of DP methodologies with real demand signals (Planet Together, 2021). This safeguards adequate supplies during times of high demand and prevents storing surplus inventory during periods of low demand. Optimization of manufacturing timetables—manufacturing companies may optimize their production schedules, stock levels, and delivery routes by anticipating when purchases will occur. The ability to schedule manufacturing in advance is a cost-cutting measure. By avoiding times when there are a lot of orders on the books, the capacity plan can help you figure out when is the optimum time to do required maintenance on machines. As a result, the production schedule can be modified to avoid unscheduled machine malfunctions and save money during the planned downtime.

12.3.3.4 IMPROVE WORKLOAD SCHEDULING

Knowing how many employees you will need to finish orders on schedule is crucial, as labor expenses are among the highest in production. Your company's fulfillment time and daily order completion rate will fall when there are not enough staff to meet demand (Planet Together, 2021). Having too many employees might be expensive, but it is crucial to keeping client satisfaction at a high level and meeting their expectations. With better inventory control, forecasting, and production scheduling, you will have a better idea of how many employees to hire to meet your production deadlines (Planet Together, 2021).

12.3.4 DP PROCESS

Since consumers are now the ones who set the pace for demand, it is crucial for businesses to track their customers as they adapt to new fashions and ways of living (Gharde, 2016). DP continues to be difficult areas of focus. The garment industry faces a number of issues, including competitors and the rapidly shifting economic landscape that affect its SC operations. Technology, globalization, political upheaval, socio-economic difficulties, commitment to the environment, and ecological uncertainty are all elements that affect the forecasting and planning of demand in the sector (Matsoma and Ambe, 2016). The following are the processes that Bajwa (2022) outlined for DP in enterprises to achieve successful SCM. Setting objectives, collecting data, making forecasts, sharing those forecasts, and coordinating supply and demand are all steps in the DP process (Croxton et al., 2002).

12.3.4.1 DATA DEFINITION AND COLLECTION

The first and most crucial stage is to gather the information that will be useful in making a demand forecast. The data are open to interpretation because it depends on the specifics of each organization and its activities. Planners do this by consulting with in-house sales and marketing teams about when to implement price increases, decreases, and other promotions that may affect demand.

12.3.4.2 USING THIRD-PARTY INFORMATION

After finishing your internal database, you can move on to gathering the necessary external information. Measurements of producers' and dealers' recent efficiency and completion times, as well as the most up-to-date purchase patterns of your most valuable clients, are examples of external data. The economic climate is another element that may affect your product's popularity and sales.

12.3.4.3 REVIEW EXPECTED INCOMING DEMAND

Professionals will collect and analyze both internal and external data to determine the best forecasting model for your company. Once a model has been selected, the quantity of stock required to meet expected demand can be calculated.

12.3.4.4 TRACK PERFORMANCE

The final stage is to compare the actual demand to the predicted one. This is a crucial stage in the forecasting process, since it will determine how well you can predict the future. Key performance indicators (KPI) are defined by experts in DP and used to gauge the success of a plan (Matsoma and Ambe, 2017).

12.3.5 ASPECTS OF DP

12.3.5.1 MANAGING PRODUCT LINE-UP

The introduction of a new product all the way until its retirement is managed under the umbrella of product portfolio management. There is often a need to consider the impact of a new product on the demand for an existing product line in order to arrive at the optimal product mix for increasing market share (Michigan State University, 2023).

12.3.5.2 PREDICTIONS BASED ON STATISTICS

Using complex statistical algorithms, statistical forecasting may generate SC forecasts based on past data. It is crucial to evaluate the precision of each model, note exceptions and omissions, and comprehend the underlying assumptions in this field (Michigan State University, 2023).

12.3.5.3 ADMINISTRATION OF TRADE PROMOTION

Particularly in the retail sector, demand can be affected by trade promotion or marketing events. Trade promotions are events that aim to increase product demand by connecting brands with consumers through in-store giveaways, discounts, and promotions (Michigan State University, 2023).

12.3.6 FACTORS INFLUENCING DP

12.3.6.1 THE STATE OF THE ECONOMY

The degree of demand for a product or service is heavily influenced by macro-economic indicators including gross domestic product growth, unemployment rate, inflation rate, and consumer confidence (Deskera, 2023). Predicting future product demand can be difficult even the best of economic circumstances. Because fewer individuals will be able to afford high-priced luxury items if the economy enters a downturn or recession, the demand for low-priced generic items is likely to rise (The Fulfillment Lab, 2023). Since globalization has eliminated national barriers, businesses must now take into account a wider range of factors before entering a foreign market. Among these are variations in governmental or legal frameworks, the environment, currencies, and exchange rates (Ayers and Odegaard, 2018). An increase in fuel costs, fluctuations in currencies, as well as fluctuations in lending rates and inflation are all examples of unforeseen economic shifts that could raise product pricing or cause a sudden shift in consumer demand (Xiao and Jin, 2011).

12.3.6.2 COMPETITION

The demand for a service or good can be affected by the level of competition in the market. Greater availability of a product or service may result in lower demand (Deskera, 2023). Demand might fall or rise dramatically depending on whether or not there is new competition. Existing businesses may feel the effects of competition when a new entrant enters the market and begins vying for its share of the pie; on the other hand, demand for other businesses may increase if an existing competitor folds or begins losing ground due to bad product, service, or PR (The Fulfillment Lab, 2023). Product demand is affected by the quantity of rivals in a market. In addition, new competitors always pose a threat in a mature sector (Mathur, 2022). In this setting, projection of demand is extremely challenging.

12.3.6.3 SEASONALITY

The term "seasonality" refers to the fact that the demand for a good or service is typically stronger at some times of the year than to others. The only way for a business to avoid inventory shortages and lost revenue is to anticipate these shifts. In contrast to nonseasonal goods, periodic demand for goods is notoriously difficult to forecast (Quantics, 2023). Demand can fluctuate with the seasons. A very seasonality brand, often known as a cyclical firm, may experience a period of high sales volume subsequently followed by a period of low sales activity (The Fulfillment Lab, 2023). Products utilized at certain times of the year (boating equipment in the summer), festivities (costumes and candy on Halloween), and occasions can all be used as instances of seasonality in DP (e.g., wedding).

12.3.6.4 DATA

The process of forecasting relies heavily on data. However, reliable information is not always easy to obtain. In the absence of sufficient data, businesses frequently must rely on estimates and assumptions (Quantics, 2023). DP based on poor information will produce inaccurate results and poor choices.

12.3.6.5 PRODUCT CATEGORIES

The planning of demand for various goods and services varies greatly. If the prognosis is off, a lot of money could be lost on perishable commodities with a limited shelf life. The product's target market is established by the nature of the good, its characteristics, and its practicality. Existing product demand can be easily approximated by looking at historical sales trends, analyzing the market for similar products, and considering any alternatives that may exist. However, it is not easy to gauge how much of a hit a new product will be (Anjali, 2018). However, for a monthly subscription business that sends out boxes to the same people every month, demand can be forecasted with some degree of accuracy (given stable customer retention and churn rates) (The Fulfillment Lab, 2023).

12.3.6.6 LEAD-TIME

Since it is far more difficult to predict what will happen in a year from now than in the next week, long-term demand forecasts have a higher risk of being incorrect. When looking far into the future, demand estimates can become less reliable (Quantics, 2023).

12.3.6.7 PRICE

The level of demand is strongly influenced by the price. When the price of something goes up, people may buy less of it (Deskera, 2023). When trying to predict future demand, price is a crucial aspect. Alterations in pricing strategies have a considerable impact on DP inside an organization. DP becomes problematic under these conditions (Mathur, 2022). The estimated demand for a product or service is very sensitive to the estimated price. Indicators of future demand for a commodity can be gleaned from pricing strategies and price swings in the present market.

12.3.6.8 GLOBALIZATION

Globalization is a factor that affects the accuracy of demand forecasts and plans in the retail clothing sector (Janggaa et al., 2015; Matsoma and Ambe, 2016). Predicting and planning have become more difficult in South Africa and around the world as a result of the decline in domestic garment production and the increase in imports (Matsoma and Ambe, 2016). Increased rivalry among businesses is a direct result of the ease with which people, goods, and services can be transported throughout the world and the production of goods may be offshored to countries with lower labor costs (Babai et al., 2013).

12.3.6.9 TECHNOLOGY

It is essential for generating accurate predictions of future demand. Rapid technological advancement has the potential to render some products and technologies obsolete (Jacobs and Chase 2018). There has been a dramatic drop in the market for floppy discs, for instance, since the introduction of CDs and pen drives for data storage in computers. Future demand for current products is hard to predict under these conditions (Mathur, 2022). Supply chains work to ensure that firms can quickly get supplies, begin production, and begin distributing finished goods. Apparel merchants are feeling the effects of demand variations as customers are readily swayed by the opinions they read online and the convenience with which things may be shipped to them (Nagurney and Yu, 2012). Retailers of clothing would be wise to reconsider their SC strategy in light of recent developments that could make it easier for them to meet customer needs or increase their bottom line. In order to maximize earnings, stores should reorganize their operations in light of the impact of social media (Shen et al., 2017).

12.3.6.10 THE ENVIRONMENT

Environmental responsibility in the SC is essential. Governments have been under pressure from citizens to reduce SC irresponsibility, and businesses have responded by developing more environmentally friendly industrial processes and safer working conditions (Du et al., 2017). This has resulted in an increased emphasis on the selection of sustainable local and global SC partners by businesses. Further, businesses have discovered that "going green" not only entails purchasing environmentally friendly technologies or using recyclable materials but also provides the benefits of waste reduction during production and lowered resource usage, thereby reducing costs within the SC (Jacobs and Chase, 2018). The ability of SC partners to adapt to shifting conditions and respond quickly is crucial to the success of SCM

(Sukati et al., 2012). The fashion industry is a fast-paced and unpredictable arena. Organizations' capacity to accurately predict how external environment shifts would affect SC performance is hampered by the inherent uncertainty of the environment itself (Janggaa et al., 2015). Supply networks need to be able to adapt quickly to new circumstances; therefore, flexibility and responsiveness have become crucial management tactics. Investing in cutting-edge technology that facilitates fast communication and the sharing of reliable data across the SC is recommended by Heizer et al. (2017) to lessen the impact of unforeseen changes within the environment.

12.3.6.11 CONSUMER DEVELOPMENT AND TRENDS

For sustainable success, accurate forecasting of future consumer volume is crucial. DP from new consumers is far more difficult than from established ones (Quantics, 2023). The demand for a good or service can be significantly affected by consumer trends. Demand for other goods and services may be affected by consumers' preferences for one set of goods and services over another (Deskera, 2023).

12.3.6.12 AVAILABILITY

The degree to which a product or service is readily available may also influence demand. When supplies of a product or service are limited, their demand tends to rise (Deskera, 2023) if they are in low supply.

12.3.6.13 GEOGRAPHY AND LOCATION

The manufacturing plant's location and the demographics of the intended market both play a role in demand forecasting. The SC, production, and distribution can all be affected by the location of a manufacturer; therefore, it is crucial to make an informed decision (Anjali, 2018). In addition, the convenience of storage and shipping options for clients might have a constructive effect on demand estimates (Deskera, 2023).

12.3.7 FUTURE OF DP IN SCM

SC and DP are two more company processes that are increasingly digital. Recent developments in the SC's use of machine learning have made it possible to instantly adjust and revise demand projections, allowing for leaner inventory management without sacrificing responsiveness to customers. SC brain refers to digital demand management, which Anaplan (2023) says is the next generation of demand management. Structures, frameworks, and digital business models that are driven by demand are the focus. Consumers' omnichannel purchasing patterns are met by the coordinated efforts of multiple groups through the free flow of information, ideas, and solutions. Customers' individual purchasing behaviors are just one example of how the marketplace demand environment has shifted in recent years. Any business that does not make adjustments in response to quickly developing digital marketplaces, new competitors, and swifter market shifts runs the risk of going out of business. By providing a synchronized knowledge base in real time, DDM enables a sharper focus on the needs of each individual consumer. DDM's inception comes from questioning the status quo of linear SC thinking. Professionals in the SC can find new ways to reduce operational costs, increase revenue, and provide a greater competitive edge by learning how to use digital enterprise architectures and implementing AI and machine learning programs that can help optimize a lean, agile, and data-driven approach. With a more efficient SC, DP may be done in the moment. DP has the potential to be a game-changing procedure in increasing SC profitability if done correctly (Matsoma and Ambe, 2017).

Decisions made in a linear fashion take longer to implement and can lead to an exaggeration of erroneous demand signals. The fundamental shift is from conventional functional measurements to DDM, which promotes coordinated activity throughout the SC. The resulting demand management structure facilitates full digital collaboration by permitting simultaneous, dynamic, real-time horizontal, and vertical planning inside an enterprise. DDM necessitates a process-control approach to smart digital network management, as well as a novel planning model that permits causal and external factor analysis. DDM's strength lies in its capacity to function within a bound of tolerable variation that has already been established. Real-time DDM forecasts allow participants to agree on performance bands, commitment horizons (periods of risk), and outlier scenarios based on standard deviations and the range of probable consumer actions. This productive digital partnership facilitates advanced DP.

The future of DP lies, fundamentally, combining AI and machine learning inside a framework that allows for the gathering and input of a broad array of data and one that can be adjusted as needed. Predictive analytics can be used to examine hundreds of factors, both internal and external, that influence demand in the context of DP. Predictive analytics is just one tool that can be used in conjunction with the others discussed below to create a comprehensive demand strategy. Those businesses who have access to the most data will be the most well-informed and thus the most effective at making decisions swiftly. Being adaptable and quick to react to market conditions will help you save money and get better results. In times of significant uncertainty, a company's bottom line and morale benefit from having as much knowledge as possible and being able to communicate that information properly both inside and outside the company. Boosting customer satisfaction and earnings is possible with careful DP. Big data and advanced analytics, along with automation and continual optimization, will shape the future of DP. New tools can help e-commerce business owners quickly and accurately plan for demand utilizing a broader range of complex data.

12.4 CONCLUSION

The primary goal of this chapter is to provide our understanding of DP areas and processes with respect to SC. Businesses need to be able to anticipate how unexpected adjustments to demand will affect their business activities and financial matters, therefore, being able to plan for that impact is a crucial asset. Businesses can better prepare for disruptions if they have a good idea of how their operations as well as their finances can be impacted. In addition, a company's ability to foresee the effects of a rapid shift in demand can help it prepare for the consequences of any external circumstances that could affect its operations. With this information in hand, firms will be better able to adapt to the ever-changing market and maintain their competitive advantage.

Economic conditions, rivalry, consumer fads, pricing, availability, and marketing are only few of the documented influences on DP. That is why it is crucial for firms to coordinate their supply and demand strategies for maximum financial gain. The success of a company can be directly impacted by accurate demand forecasting. The majority of an organization's preparations rely on demand forecasting, including demand, inventory, production, and procurement preparations. The ability to accurately predict future demand is crucial for every company, as it affects nearly every aspect of operations. In order to prevent revenue loss from late deliveries and stockpiling of unsold goods caused by overproduction, it is important to understand the elements that impact DP.

KEYWORDS

- **SCM**
- **demand planning**
- **processes**
- **supply chain**
- **companies**
- **customers**

REFERENCES

Anaplan. The Fundamentals of DP. [Online] 2023. https://www.anaplan.com/blog/demand-planning-fundamentals-and-futures/

Anjali, L. Demand Forecasting. [Online] Nov 3, 2018. https://theinvestorsbook.com/demand-forecasting.html

Armstrong, J. S.; Green, K. C.; Graefe, A. Golden Rule of Forecasting: Be Conservative. *J. Bus. Res.* **2015,** *68* (8), 1717–1731.

Ayers, J. B.; Odegaard, M. A. In *Retail Supply Chain Management*, Second Edition; CRC Press: Boca Raton, Florida, 2018.

Babai, M. Z.; Ali, M. M.; Boylan, J. E.; Syntetos, A. A. Forecasting and Inventory Performance in a Two-Stage Supply Chain with ARIMA Demand: Theory and Empirical Analysis. *Int. J. Prod. Eco.* **2013,** *143* (2), 463–471.

Bajwa, R. DP: What It Is and Why It's Important. [Online] Jan 4, 2022. https://www.globaltrademag.com/demand-planning-what-it-is-and-why-its-important/

Cassettari, L.; Bendato, I.; Mosca, M.; Mosca, R. A New Stochastic Multi Source Approach to Improve the Accuracy of the Sales Forecasts. *Foresight* **2017,** *19* (1), 48–64.

Christopher, M. In *Logistics and SCM*, 5th Ed.; Pearson Education: Harlow, 2016.

Croxton, K. L.; Lambert, D. M.; Garcıa-Dastugue, S. J.; Rogers, D.S. The Demand Management Process. *Int. J. Logist. Manag.* **2002,** *13* (2), 51–66.

Deskera. Demand Forecasting: Definition, Factors, and Techniques! 2023. https://www.deskera.com/blog/demand-forecasting/

Du, S.; Hu, L.; Wang, L. Low-Carbon Supply Policies and Supply Chain Performance with Carbon Concerned Demand. *Ann. Oper. Res.* **2017,** *255* (1), 569–590.

Gharde, A. Influence of Factors on Clothing Sales and its Future Trend: Regression Analysis and Time Series Forecast of Clothing Sales. *J. Text. Appar. Technol. Manag.* **2016,** *10* (2), 1–11.

Gupta, A.; Costas D. M. Managing Demand Uncertainty in SC Planning. *Comput. Chem. Eng.* **2003,** *27* (8), 1219–1227.

Heizer, J.; Render, B.; Munson, C. In *Principles of Operations Management: Sustainability and Supply Chain Management*, Tenth Edition; Pearson: Boston, 2017.

IBM. What is DP? [Online] 2023. https://www.ibm.com/topics/demand-planning#:~:text=Demand%20planning%20is%20a%20supply,services%20—%20according%20to%20those%20projections

Jacobs, F.; Chase, R. In *Operations and Supply Chain Management*, Fifteenth Edition; McGraw-Hill Education: New York, 2018.

Janggaa, R.; Ali, N. M.; Ismail, M.; Sahari, N. Effect of Environmental Uncertainty and Supply Chain Flexibility Towards Supply Chain Innovation: An Exploratory Study. *Procedia Eco. Fin.* **2015,** *31*, 262–268.

Mathur, V. Demand Forecasting: Steps, Benefits and Influencing Factors. [Online] 2022. https://www.analyticssteps.com/blogs/demand-forecasting-steps-benefits-and-influencing-factors

Matsoma, N. J.; Ambe, I. M. Factors Affecting DP in the South African Clothing Industry. *J. Econ. Behav. Stud.* **2016,** *8* (5), 194–210.

Matsoma, N. J.; Ambe, I. M. DP Approaches Employed by Clothing Industry Stakeholders in Gauteng, South Africa. *J. Transp. Supply Chain Manag.* **2017,** *11*, 1–9.

Michigan State University. How DP Can Improve the SC. [Online] Jan 18, 2023. https://www.michiganstateuniversityonline.com/resources/supply-chain/how-demand-planning-improves-supply-chain/

Nagurney, A.; Yu, M. Sustainable Fashion Supply Chain Management under Oligopolistic Competition and Brand Differentiation. *Int. J. Prod. Eco.* **2012,** *135* (2), 532–540.

Planet Together. 4 Advantages of DP. [Online] May 4, 2021. https://www.planettogether.com/blog/4-advantages-of-demand-planning

Prasad P. S. S.; Shankhar, C.; Cost Optimisation of SC Networks using Ant Colony Optimisation. *Int. J. Logist. Syst. Manag.* **2011,** *9* (2).

Quantics. Demand Forecasting: 10 Key Complexity Drivers. [Online] 2023. https://quantics.io/resource/demand-forecasting-10-key-complexity-drivers

Raza, D. N.; Kilbourn, P. J. The Impact of Point-of-Sale Data in DP in the South African Clothing Retail Industry. *J. Transp. SCM* **2017,** *11*, 1–8.

Relph, G.; Milner, C. Inventory Management: Advanced Methods for Managing Inventory within Business Sytesms, 2015.

The Fulfillment Lab. 6 Types of Demand Forecasting and Projection Benefits. [Online] 2023. https://www.thefulfillmentlab.com/blog/demand-forecasting#benefits

Shen, B.; Qian, R.; Choi, T. M. Selling Luxury Fashion Online with Social Influences Considerations: Demand Changes and Supply Chain Coordination. *Int. J. Prod. Eco.* **2017,** *185*, 89–99.

Sukati, I.; Hamid, A. B.; Baharum, R.; Yussoff, R. The Study of Supply Chain Management Strategy and Practices on Supply Chain Performance. *Procedia Soc. Behav. Sci.* **2012,** *40*, 225–233.

Xiao, T.; Jin, J. Coordination of a Fashion Apparel Supply Chain under Lead-Time-Dependent Demand Uncertainty. *Prod. Plan. Control* **2011,** *22* (3), 257–268.

Index

A

Agri-food industry, 170
Arise situations, 30–31
Aspects
  demand planning (DP)
    product line-up, 238
    statistical forecasting, 238
    trade promotion, 238
Automation, 199
Average variance (AVE), 21

B

Benefits
  demand planning (DP)
    demand prediction, 235
    healthy inventory, 235
    stock levels, 235–236
    workload scheduling, 236
Better customer service, 196
Break-even charts
  break-even point, 36, 37
  chart, 37
  fixed costs, 36
  plots, 36
  revenue line, 36
  unit price, 36
  variable costs, 36
Break-even cost analysis, 31–32

C

Chi-Square analysis
  hypothesis 1, 57
  hypothesis 2, 58
  hypothesis 3, 58–59
  hypothesis 4, 59
Cloud computing, 50–51
Competition, 239
Conceptual model, 44
Consumer development, 242
Cost methods
  break-even cost analysis, 31–32
  economic cost analysis, 31
  simple cost analysis, 31
Create value, 210
Crucial procurement, 32–34
Customer satisfaction, 139
Customer service, 206

D

Data analysis
  challenges, 136–139
  customer satisfaction, 139
  descriptive statistics, 134–136
  respondents information, 134
Data migration, 167
Demand forecasting, 206–207
Demand planning (DP), 231
  aspects
    product line-up, 238
    statistical forecasting, 238
    trade promotion, 238
  benefits
    demand prediction, 235
    healthy inventory, 235
    stock levels, 235–236
    workload scheduling, 236
  contribution, 233
  elements
    exports marketing, 235
    market needs, 234
    predictions, 234
    products, variety, 234
  factors influencing
    availability, 242
    competition, 239
    consumer development, 242
    data, 239
    economy, 238–239
    environmental responsibility, 241–242
    geography and location, 242
    globalization, 240–241

lead-time, 240
price, 240
product categories, 240
seasonality, 239
technology, 241
and trends, 242
literature review, 233–234
process, 236
data definition and collection, 237
expected demand, 237
third-party information, 237
track performance, 237

E

Efficient inventory management, 177
Electronic data capture, 178

F

Food supply chain management (FSCM), 166
challenges, 167
inventory management, 168
logistics, 168
quality control, 168
sustainability, 168, 173
warehouse management system (WMS), 172
efficient inventory management, 177
electronic data capture, 178
factors, 176–177
frameworks
agri-food industry, 170
interpretive structural modeling (ISM), 169
radio frequency identification (RFID), 169
leveraging technology, 179
models
advanced technologies, 171–172
optimal inventory levels, 178
purpose and scope, 176
research methodology, 176
research problem, 173
studies
issues, 174
significance, 175
supply chain participants, 178–179
system implementation
data migration, 167
go-live, 167
needs assessment, 166
system configuration, 167
system selection, 167
system testing, 167
user training, 167
transportation management, 178
uncertainty, 177–178
warehouse management, 178
Fourth Industrial Revolution, 49

G

Game theory, 118–120
Ghana Nuts Company Limited (GNCL), 113, 120
data analysis
challenges, 136–139
customer satisfaction, 139
descriptive statistics, 134–136
respondents information, 134
research methodology
designs, 128–129
population, 130
strategy, 129–130
sampling and sample size
approach, 131
data analysis, 134
data collection procedures, 132–133
instruments, 132
method and technique, 131
non-probability sampling, 131
probability sampling, 131
theoretical review
game theory, 118–120
transport management, 121–122
challenges, 124–125
distribution channels, 123–124
firm's performance, 127–128
organizational performance, 126–127
transportation, 114
challenges, 115–116
importance of, 122–123
product distribution, 115
studies and objectives, 116–118
Green supply chain management (G_SCM), 214

capability on to
impact, 221–223
literature review, 215
research methodology
conceptual framework, 217–218
data analysis techniques, 218–219
data collection method, 218
results
influence of, 219–221
supply chain (SC) performance, 216
sustenance (SUS)
impact, 223–225
maturity of, 225–227
value-added functions, 216

H

Hospitality industry
factors, 186
supply chain (SC), 186
supply chain management (SCM), 185
automation, 199
better customer service, 196
collaboration, 200
communication, 199
controlling resources, 191–192
cost of materials, 200–201
distribution, 189–190
emergency cost, 201
enhanced risk reduction, 197
increased income, 199–200
increased productivity, 198
information, 193–194
integration, 188
inventory, 194
inventory cost, 201
literature review, 187–188
location, 194
logistics, 191
manufacturing/production, 195
market, 197
meeting customer needs, 198
operations, 188
ordering cost, 201
planning, 190
predicting needs/demand, 192–193
procurement, 188–189, 195–196
quality control, 198
returning, 191
saved money, 196–197
shipping/transportation, 198–199
sourcing, 190
staff morale, 196
transportation, 189
visibility, 200

I

Industry 4.0
Chi-Square analysis
hypothesis 1, 57
hypothesis 2, 58
hypothesis 3, 58–59
hypothesis 4, 59
cloud computing, 50–51
conceptual model, 44
correlation analysis, 56–57
decision making
gathering data and information, 51–53
distribution function, 53–54
frequency analysis, 55
implications, 59–60
literature review
big data, defined, 49
Fourth Industrial Revolution, 49
internet, 48
Internet of Things (IoT), 49
processing techniques, 49
Made in India
programs, 47
regulations, 46
reliability analysis, 55
robots
horizontal integration, 50
vertical integration, 50
smart factories, 47
supply chain management, 48
unmanned aerial delivery, 47
Interpretive structural modeling (ISM), 169
Inventory management, 168, 207

K

Knowledge management (KM), 93, 96

L

Leveraging technology, 179
Logistics, 168, 205

create value, 210
customer service, 206
defined, 2
demand forecasting, 206–207
distribution communication, 207
functions, 206
inventory management, 207
literature review
outsourcing, 6–7
retail industry in Ghana, 5–6
long-term relationship, 209–210
material handling, 207
order processing, 208
outsourcing
customer order processing, 9–10
information technology (IT), 8–9
inventory management, 10–11
retail firms' performance, 11–12
supplier relationships, 7–8
third-party logistics (3PL), 12–13
packaging, 208
parts and service support, 208
planning, 210
plant and warehouse management, 208
problem statement, 4
third-party logistics (3PL), 3
procurement and proper storage, 208
research
objectives, 4
research methodology
data analysis, 16
data collection, 16
design, 14–15
sample size, 15–16
strategy, 15
studies, population, 15
results and data analysis
demographic data, 17–19
discriminant distinctiveness, 20–21
hypothesis testing, 21–23
reliability and loadings, 19–20
return goods, 209
salvage and scrap disposal, 209
suppliers, 206
theoretical review
Transaction Cost Theory (TCT), 13–14
traffic and transportation, 209
Long-term relationship, 209–210

M

Make-or-buy decision strategy
arise situations, 30–31
break-even charts in
break-even point, 36, 37
chart, 37
fixed costs, 36
plots, 36
revenue line, 36
unit price, 36
variable costs, 36
choice, 30
cost methods
break-even cost analysis, 31–32
economic cost analysis, 31
simple cost analysis, 31
crucial procurement, 32–34
factors affecting
capacity, 34
cost, 34
economic conditions, 35
expertise, 34
flexibility, 35
lead time, 34
legal and regulatory requirements, 35
quality, 34
strategic importance, 35
supply chain management strategy, 32–34
technology, impact
automation, 35
data analytics tools, 35–36
e-commerce, 35
globalization, 35
supply chain management (SCM), 36
Manufacturing industries
customer focus, 93
dimensions
continuous improvement, 98
customer service, 98
logistics, 98
organizational performance, 100–101
performance measurement, 98
planning, 97
production, 97–98
sourcing, 97
strategic supplier alliances, 99
opinion toward (SCM) practices, 104–105
organizational performance, 94

paradigm analysis, 97
risk management strategies, 93
strategy, 102
studies
research approach, 104
supply chain, 94
knowledge management (KM), 96
marketing professionals, 95
operationalizing customer value, 95
valuation practitioners, 95
supply chain collaboration, 93
supply chain management (SCM), 94
supply chain management performance (SCMP), 102
competitive advantage, 103–104
cost reduction, 103
dimensions, 106–107
improved customer satisfaction, 103
increased efficiency, 103
risk management, 104
technology adoption, 93

N

National Health Insurance Scheme (NHIS), 75

O

Operationalizing customer value, 95
Outsourcing
customer order processing, 9–10
information technology (IT), 8–9
inventory management, 10–11
retail firms' performance, 11–12
supplier relationships, 7–8
third-party logistics (3PL), 12–13

P

Performance systems
demand, 156
factors affecting, 154–155
information technology, 155–156
inventory management, 155
lead time, 155
transportation, 155

Q

Quality control (QC), 168, 198

R

Radio frequency identification (RFID), 169
Resource-Based View (RBV), 67
Retail industry in Ghana, 5–6
Robots
horizontal integration, 50
vertical integration, 50

S

Salvage and scrap disposal, 209
Sampling and sample size
approach, 131
data analysis, 134
data collection procedures, 132–133
instruments, 132
method and technique, 131
non-probability sampling, 131
probability sampling, 131
Smart factories, 47
Supply chain integration (SCI), 63
dimensions
customer integration, 70
internal integration, 70
supplier integration, 69
financial performance, 71, 72
customer integration, 72
internal integration, 73
literature review
in heath sector, 66–67
problem statement, 64
dwindling lifespan, 65
studies, 65
research methodology
data analysis, 79
data collection, 78–79
demographic data, 79
design, 75–76
educational background, 81–84
gender, 79–80
Ghana, health care situation, 74–75
initial hypothesis (H1), 84–85
measures and questionnaire, 77–78
National Health Insurance Scheme (NHIS), 75
population and sampling, 77
respondents' age, 80–81
strategy, 76–77
work experience, 81

research objectives, 66
underpinning theory, 68
Resource-Based View (RBV), 67
Supply chain management (SCM), 2
automation, 199
better customer service, 196
collaboration, 200
communication, 199
conceptual framework, 156–157
controlling resources, 191–192
cost of materials, 200–201
distribution, 189–190
emergency cost, 201
enhanced risk reduction, 197
hypothesis development, 156–157
implementation, 147
increased income, 199–200
increased productivity, 198
information, 193–194
integration, 188
inventory, 194
inventory cost, 201
literature review, 187–188
location, 194
logistics, 191
manufacturing/production, 195
market, 197
meeting customer needs, 198
operations, 188
opportunistic behavior, 152–153
ordering cost, 201
performance systems
demand, 156
factors affecting, 154–155
information technology, 155–156
inventory management, 155
lead time, 155
transportation, 155
planning, 190
practical consequences, 161–162
predicting needs/demand, 192–193
procurement, 188–189, 195–196
quality control, 198
research methodology, 157
elements' influencing, 159–160
factors affecting, 158
returning, 191
saved money, 196–197
shipping/transportation, 198–199
SMEs
challenges, 150
goals, 149
strategies, 151–152
success factors, 148
sourcing, 190
staff morale, 196
transportation, 189
visibility, 200
Supply chain management performance (SCMP), 102
competitive advantage, 103–104
cost reduction, 103
dimensions, 106–107
improved customer satisfaction, 103
increased efficiency, 103
risk management, 104
Supply chain participants, 178–179
Sustenance (SUS)
impact, 223–225
maturity of, 225–227

T

Third-party information, 237
Third-party logistics (3PL), 12–13
Track performance, 237
Traffic and transportation, 209
Transaction Cost Theory (TCT), 13–14
Transport management, 121–122
challenges, 124–125
distribution channels, 123–124
firm's performance, 127–128
organizational performance, 126–127
Transportation, 114
challenges, 115–116
importance of, 122–123
product distribution, 115
studies and objectives, 116–118
Transportation management, 178

U

Uncertainty, 177–178
Underpinning theory, 68
Resource-Based View (RBV), 67
Unmanned aerial delivery, 47
User training, 167

V

Valuation practitioners, 95
Value-added functions, 216
Vertical integration, 50

W

Warehouse management, 178
Warehouse management system (WMS), 172